Dedication

For my beloved parents:
Mzee Andindilile Silisyene Mwalonde and Bibi Maria Nyala Jengela
And my beloved family:
My wife, Frida Mwakyambiki, daughters, Nelusigwe and Maria,
and son, Bryan Andindilile

About the Series

The African Humanities Series is a partnership between the African Humanities Program (AHP) of the American Council of Learned Societies and academic publishers NISC (Pty) Ltd. The Series covers topics in African histories, languages, literatures, philosophies, politics and cultures. Submissions are solicited from Fellows of the AHP, which is administered by the American Council of Learned Societies and financially supported by the Carnegie Corporation of New York.

The purpose of the AHP is to encourage and enable the production of new knowledge by Africans in the five countries designated by the Carnegie Corporation: Ghana, Nigeria, South Africa, Tanzania, and Uganda. AHP fellowships support one year's work free from teaching and other responsibilities to allow the Fellow to complete the project proposed. Eligibility for the fellowship in the five countries is by domicile, not nationality.

Book proposals are submitted to the AHP editorial board which manages the peer review process and selects manuscripts for publication by NISC. In some cases, the AHP board will commission a manuscript mentor to undertake substantive editing and to work with the author on refining the final manuscript.

The African Humanities Series aims to publish works of the highest quality that will foreground the best research being done by emerging scholars in the five Carnegie designated countries. The rigorous selection process before the fellowship award, as well as AHP editorial vetting of manuscripts, assures attention to quality. Books in the series are intended to speak to scholars in Africa as well as in other areas of the world.

The AHP is also committed to providing a copy of each publication in the series to university libraries in Africa.

AHP Editorial Board Members as at July 2017

AHP Series Editors:
Professor Adigun Agbaje, University of Ibadan, Nigeria
Professor Emeritus Fred Hendricks, Rhodes University, South Africa

Consultant:
Professor Emeritus Sandra Barnes, University of Pennsylvania, USA (Anthropology)

Board Members:
1. Professor Akosua Adomako Ampofo, Institute of African Studies, Ghana (Gender Studies & Advocacy) (Vice President, African Studies Association of Africa)
2. Professor Kofi Anyidoho, University of Ghana, Ghana (African Studies & Literature) (Director, Codesria African Humanities Institute Program)
3. Professor Ibrahim Bello-Kano, Bayero University, Nigeria (Dept of English and French Studies)
4. Professor Sati Fwatshak, University of Jos, Nigeria (Dept of History & International Studies)
5. Professor Patricia Hayes, University of the Western Cape, South Africa (African History, Gender Studies and Visuality) (SARChI Chair in Visual History and Theory)
6. Associate Professor Wilfred Lajul, College of Humanities & Social Sciences, Makerere University, Uganda (Dept of Philosophy)
7. Professor Yusufu Lawi, University of Dar-es-Salaam, Tanzania (Dept of History)
8. Professor Bertram Mapunda, University of Dar es Salaam, Tanzania (Dept of Archaeology & Heritage Studies)
9. Professor Innocent Pikirayi, University of Pretoria, South Africa (Chair & Head, Dept of Anthropology & Archaeology)
10. Professor Josephat Rugemalira, University of Dar-es-Salaam, Tanzania (Dept of Foreign Languages & Linguistics)
11. Professor Idayat Bola Udegbe, University of Ibadan, Nigeria (Dept of Psychology)

Published in this series

Dominica Dipio, *Gender terrains in African cinema*, 2014

Ayo Adeduntan, *What the forest told me: Yoruba hunter, culture and narrative performance*, 2014

Sule E. Egya, *Nation, power and dissidence in third-generation Nigerian poetry in English*, 2014

Irikidzayi Manase, *White narratives: The depiction of post-2000 land invasions in Zimbabwe*, 2016

Sylvia Bruinders, *Parading Respectability: The Cultural and Moral Aesthetics of the Christmas Bands Movement in the Western Cape, South Africa*, 2017

THE ANGLOPHONE LITERARY-LINGUISTIC CONTINUUM:
English and Indigenous Languages in African Literary Discourse

MICHAEL ANDINDILILE

Published in South Africa on behalf of the African Humanities Program by NISC (Pty) Ltd, PO Box 377, Grahamstown, 6140, South Africa
www.nisc.co.za

First edition, first impression 2018

Publication © African Humanities Program 2018
Text © Michael Andindilile 2018

All rights reserved. No part of this publication may be reproduced or transmitted in any form or by any means, electronic or mechanical, including photocopying, recording, or any information storage or retrieval system, without prior permission in writing from the publisher.

ISBN: 978-1-920033-23-1 (print)
ISBN: 978-1-920033-24-8 (PDF)
ISBN: 978-1 920033-25-5 (ePub)

Manuscript mentor: Leonie Viljoen
Project manager: Peter Lague
Cover design: Advanced Design Group
Cover photographs: Chinua Achebe (top left) ©ZUMA Press, Inc. / Alamy Stock Photo; Nadine Gordimer (top right) ©Motlhalefi Mahlabe / South Photographs / Africa Media Online; Nuruddin Farah (bottom left) © dpa picture alliance archive / Alamy Stock Photo; Ngũgĩ wa Thiong'o (bottom right) ©Agence Opale / Alamy Stock Photo

Printed in South Africa by Digital Action

The author and the publisher have made every effort to obtain permission for and acknowledge the use of copyright material. Should an inadvertent infringement of copyright have occurred, please contact the publisher and we will rectify omissions or errors in any subsequent reprint or edition.

Contents

Acknowledgements	ix
Foreword	xi
Preface	xiii

Chapter 1 The case for an Anglophone African literary-linguistic continuum — 1

Introduction	1
Historical roots of the African novel in Anglophone Africa	5
The Tower of Babel and the intricate African linguistic landscape	8
Africa and the compound, complex literary-linguistic situation	12
English as a vehicular language	14
Plurality in modern African literatures	17
Conclusion	23

Chapter 2 Achebe and Anglophone African literary discourse — 25

Introduction	25
Traditional literary elements and Achebe's aesthetics	28
Duality of purpose in Achebe's literary-linguistic project	31
Beyond stereotyping: The implication of Achebe's aesthetics	38
Conclusion	44
Notes	45

Chapter 3 Ngũgĩ, nativism, English and translingualism — 47

Introduction	47
The original Anglophone project	52
Novels in transition: On the threshold to nativism	56
The Gikuyu project and translation	61
Conclusion	66
Note	67

Chapter 4 Gordimer, English, race and cross-cultural translation — 68

Introduction — 68
They 'Spoke and Shouted in a Language [She] Didn't Understand' — 71
'In the Safety of Their Own Language' — 76
'Speaking an African Language was Simply a Qualification' — 80
Conclusion — 88
Note — 89

Chapter 5 Farah, English and cosmopolitanism — 90

Introduction — 90
Farah's literary-linguistic project — 96
Intricacies of re-imagining the nation in a former colonial language — 98
Cultural identification beyond linguistic expression — 100
National mosaic — 102
Language of violence and nationalistic discourse — 104
Conclusion — 108
Note — 109

Chapter 6 Anglophonism, the novel and the African literary-linguistic continuum — 110

Introduction — 110
The African novel and the English 'home' in Africa — 113
Bickerton's theory and the African literary-linguistic continuum — 117
Literary-linguistic continuum as a trajectory in modern African literatures — 120
Conclusion — 131

Bibliography — 133

Index — 146

Acknowledgements

The manuscript for this publication was prepared with the support of the African Humanities Fellowship Program established by the American Council of Learned Societies with a generous grant from the Carnegie Corporation of New York.

This work is a culmination of the many efforts and contributions of numerous people and institutions.

As an African Humanities Program (AHP) postdoctoral fellow, I took up residence at the Makerere Institute of Social Research (MISR), Makerere University, Uganda, which enabled me to carry out additional research to update my readings for my monograph project that prepared ground for the development of this book. In this regard, I thank MISR for accommodating me at the Institute under the leadership of Mahmood Mamdani, its Executive Director. While there, I had access to resources and a stimulating intellectual environment that enriched my study. Furthermore, I am forever thankful to Leonie Viljoen, my manuscript mentor, who worked tirelessly with me to bring various strands of materials into a coherent book. She ensured that I remained on track whenever I was side-tracked. I also sincerely thank the AHP publication team for their invaluable support in the manuscript development process.

However, although developed with the support of the African Humanities Fellowship Program, this book is a spin-off of my dissertation entitled 'Reimagining African Communities: Achebe, Ngũgĩ, Gordimer, Farah and the Anglophone African Novel' and has a history that obliges me to mention and thank the people who contributed in one way or another from genesis to its final realisation. I thank Christopher GoGwilt, my supervisor at Fordham University, who alerted me to the idea of a continuum that became the fulcrum of further inquiry. I acknowledge my readers, Fawzia Mustafa and Nicola Pitchford, both of Fordham University, although Nicola is now at Dominican University of California. I appreciate their support. I also acknowledge the support of my teacher, mentor and friend, Leonard Cassuto, of Fordham University, who has been a pillar of strength at various stages of my academic and professional journey.

My thanks would be incomplete without a mention of my friend, Arvind Thomas, with whom I spent many memorable hours reading and revising initial drafts of articles in the making at various Starbucks dotting the New York City landscape during the post-doctoral phase of my career at Fordham. Arvind is now a member of faculty at the University of California, Los Angeles (UCLA).

Back in Dar es Salaam, I wish to acknowledge my friend and colleague, Eliah Mwaifuge, who encouraged me to soldier on till the fruition of this work.

Last but not least, I acknowledge the support from my dear family: My wife, Frida Mwakyambiki, my daughters, Nelusigwe and Maria, and my son, Bryan. I know, at times, they missed quality time with me as I worked on this project. Yet, they were always supportive and so understanding that I was able to carry on to its logical conclusion.

Foreword

> The English language facilitates…creativity impelled by the phantasmagoria of…native idiom. As an African, I endeavour to tame the English language and put it in my pocket; and use it when I must…. Obu Udeozo[1]

Rather than engage in the important longstanding debate about the language of African literature as embodied by Chinua Achebe and Ngũgĩ wa Thiong'o on two sides of the divide, this book explores the relationship between English and African indigenous languages in the discourse of that literature. In his exploration of African literature in English, Michael Andindilile shares the concern of both these writers with individual, cultural and national responsibility and, ultimately, the preservation of African ideals among sustained multilingual diversity.

The project draws on Derek Bickerton's (1973) pioneering theory of a linguistic continuum that exists in the English Creole used in Guyana, ranging from socially prestigious forms at the one extreme to language variations that are considered of low status on the other, with a whole intermediate zone of variants in-between. It argues that African literary works in English, a former colonial language that has found its home in Africa, are part of a continuum of Anglophone African literatures that embodies the twists and turns of linguistic variation, cultures and unique socio-political contexts of diverse African communities. It traces the existence of such a continuum across the fiction of four prominent Anglophone novelists, Chinua Achebe of Nigeria in West Africa, Ngũgĩ wa Thiong'o of Kenya in East Africa, Nadine Gordimer of South Africa, and Nuruddin Farah of Somalia in the Horn of Africa.

The book illustrates how these African writers mould the former colonial language to represent the peculiarities of local African languages by the infusion of, among others, local idioms, proverbs and sometimes untranslated words into literary English. In this way, English both influences and is influenced by the indigenous languages and the local cultures and contexts they represent. Ultimately, whether an African work is written in English or in an African language, it creates a unique literature that embodies the life, language and culture of unique African communities in their plurality. The study of the four chosen authors further reveals that the continuum represents not only linguistic and literary variation but also embodies an inherently committed engagement with current societal concerns, thus echoing Azuike's insistence that writers in Africa have a duty to society to address issues instead of indulging in the luxury of the aesthetics alone (2008).[2]

This important book will be of interest to students of English literature and Anglophone African literature, academics and scholars working in the field of African literature in English, and the general public interested in translingualism, translation studies, colonial, postcolonial and neocolonial influence of the English language on African literature and the continuing debate on what constitutes Anglophone (and, by extension, also Lusophone and Francophone) African literature.

At a juncture where, according to Alain Mabanckou,[3] the celebrated Congolese writer, 'a damaging literary divide' still exists in global French-language literature, and the work of important French-language writers are to be found on 'foreign literature' shelves, regarded as 'authors who write with an accent', Michael Andindilile has laid a solid foundation for further exploration of how English-language literature in its global diversity embraces the work of an array of important African writers such as Mariama Bâ (in translation), Buchi Emecheta, Bessie Head, Ayi Kwei Armah, Yvonne Vera and Chimamanda Ngozi Adichie in an Anglophone African literary-linguistic continuum.

Leonie Viljoen PhD (UCT)
Formerly Associate Professor and Research Fellow
Department of English Studies, University of South Africa
Somerset West, 25 February 2018

Notes

1. Udeozo, Obu. 2008, 21, cited in Su'eddie Agema, Commitment and the Language of African Literature, 2010. https://sueddie.wordpress.com/2010/12/08/commitment-and-the-language-of-african-literature/
2. Azuike, McPherson. Unpublished interview with Su'eddie Agema. University of Jos, Plateau State: 20 November 2008.
3. Quoted in "Macron's French Language Crusade Bolsters Imperialism – Congo Novelist", *The Guardian*, Monday 19 February 2018. https://www.theguardian.com/world/2018/feb/19/emmanuel-macron-challenged-over-attitude-to-frances-former-colonies

Preface

The idea of an Anglophone African literary-linguistic continuum first emerged during my doctoral studies in the United States (US) when I was doing a dissertation entitled 'Re-imagining African communities: Achebe, Ngũgĩ, Gordimer, Farah and the Anglophone African novel'. The thrust of this original project was to look at the various manifestations of the African novel in re-imagining national communities along the lines of Benedict Anderson's conception of the 'imagined communities' (Anderson, 1991). The original project had looked at national particularities that appear in the novels by these diverse authors to account for their differences and similarities. However, contact with Derek Bickerton's article 'Creole continuum' (Bickerton, 1973) opened the door to examining the application of the English language in these novels to establish the kind of continuum that emerges. Indeed, the English language binds them together regardless of individual styles, national influences and varied linguistic impacts. In fact, when I met Simon Gikandi at Princeton University in the US during a presentation on Ngũgĩ, he was insistent that instead of bothering about the polarising debate on the language question, it would be better to focus on what the writers do with the language to produce their literary works. This occurred during a campus visit job talk where I was one of the finalists for a job placement at Princeton. Notable in the audience were Anthony Appiah of Princeton and Aldin Mtembei of the University of Dar es Salaam, then teaching Kiswahili at the institution. Although I did not get the job, Gikandi's intervention started a long period of experimentation and examination of various manifestations of the English language in Anglophone African literature.

This book, therefore, is a culmination of ideas that have been developed over the years. It sets out to answer two basic but related questions. First: Does an Anglophone African literary-linguistic continuum exist? And second: If so, in what form does it exist in the varied works of Anglophone African writers? To answer these questions, the genre of the novel is primarily a matter of preference. Specifically, I examine the novels of purposively selected Anglophone writers who add something different to the issue of writing in English. I hesitate to use the word 'debate' because the primary purpose of this book is not to venture into the seemingly intractable debate on the language of African literature (which appears to have petered out of late) as doing so would undermine the thrust of this work. The selected African writers wrote or have been writing over a sustained period and hence provide an opportunity to learn about the various manifestations of English in their works. The first is Chinua Achebe, a West African writer, who is not only considered in some circles as the 'father' of modern African literature but is also comfortable with writing in English. More significantly, he has been dubbed a proverb-based writer because of his seamless fusion of African orality in Anglophone literary expressions. Achebe died on 21 March 2013, in Boston, Massachusetts, in the US and was buried in his home land of Nigeria. The second is Ngũgĩ wa Thiong'o, an East African writer whose contribution to Anglophone African literary discourse belies the 'pro-nativist' tag he has come to be identified with. The third is Nadine Gordimer, because she raises a question pertaining to the place of the white African settler community in Anglophone literary discourse. In fact, she could also represent other Africans, white or black, including Creole intellectuals in West Africa, who see the English language as their first language. Gordimer died on 13 July 2014, in Johannesburg, South Africa. The fourth and final writer is Nuruddin Farah, from Somalia on the Horn of Africa, who comes from a nation that speaks a single language, Somali, and yet writes in English. These four writers provide a test case for interrogating the various manifestations of Anglophonism in African literature.

1
The case for an Anglophone African literary-linguistic continuum

Introduction

Even though the seemingly endless debates surrounding the use of English in African literatures (in plural as Michael Chapman [2003] alternatively calls them) may have ebbed of late, what has remained indisputable is that English has not only helped to raise the profile of literatures from Africa within Africa and abroad but also to provide what can be regarded as continuity in Anglophone African discourse. Obi Wali's (1963) prophecy that continued use of former colonial languages in the production of African literature could only lead to 'sterility', as African literatures can only be written in indigenous African languages, has not materialised. Instead of an imminent 'death', such African literatures have continued to flourish not only in English but also in other former colonial languages such as French and Portuguese in Francophone and Lusophone Africa respectively, which are outside the scope of this work. I focus on Anglophone African writings primarily because they belong to a tradition I have been exposed to and because of what English has come to represent globally.

In fact, an Anglophone African literary-linguistic continuum appears to exist based on the sustained use of the English language in African literatures to represent diverse ethnicities, languages, cultures, beliefs and experiences. This Anglophone African literary-linguistic continuum can be defined as variations in the literary usage of English in African literary discourse, with the language serving as the base to which writers add variations inspired by indigenous languages, beliefs, cultures and, sometimes, nation-specific experiences. Moreover, the variations witnessed in the use of English in a traditionally non-native literary universe of discourse affirm what happens when a language operates in different sociocultural and linguistic situations. After Gérard (1981), this can be called the 'cultural substratum', something that remains when there has been contact between the conquered peoples and the conquerors. Though Gérard uses the term 'substratum' to refer to indigenous languages and cultural expressions, they are by no means subordinate to the Western or modern influences, as influences cut both ways and the indigenous cultures have never been passive. Instead, they have shown resilience, resulting in their sustainability.

The definition of the Anglophone African literary-linguistic continuum deployed in this work has been informed by Bickerton's pioneering study on the Creole continuum. In the 1970s, Bickerton applied the term 'Creole continuum' to the form of English Creole used in Guyana (Bickerton, 1973). This Creole continuum constitutes a continuous range of variations found in Creole-speaking communities between the forms used at the lowest social levels and those used at the highest. Because of the diverse contexts in which English is used in Africa, there is also a range of manifestations in the English language that is used. Moreover, Bickerton's example hints at the relationship between the English language and variations in the application of the language in Anglophone African literatures written by different authors in different countries.

Though Bickerton focused on the 'language continuum', which primarily deals with the relationship between basilects, or socially-stigmatised language varieties, and the acrolect, or the prestigious variety in each speech community, there is room for combining the linguistic and literary, resulting in the linguistic-literary dimensions as applied in this work. A 'literary continuum' refers to continuity in a literary tradition. Thus, the term 'linguistic-literary continuum' imputes the fusion of the linguistic and the literary, focusing on how the language is used in literature. To emphasise the literary focus of this work, this combination has been reversed to read 'literary-linguistic'. Normally, the language is the locus of a linguistic study; however, this study uses the literary approach to understand the linguistic elements embodied by the literary language. In fact, this combination helps to situate the multiplicities of Anglophone literary productions in Africa and other traditionally non-English contexts dubbed Anglophone literatures. In this case, African writers variously deploy the English language and hence the multiplicities of styles, uses and influences. The term 'literary-linguistic' therefore suits this work, as it is based on the use of the English language in African literature. Furthermore, the term facilitates the examination of how the varied applications of English in African literary discourse affect both the literary and – to a certain extent – the linguistic aspects of the works of art in a bid to interrogate the existence of a 'literary-linguistic continuum' as it relates to Anglophone African literary discourse.

This Anglophone African literary-linguistic continuum is explored through the novels of Achebe of Nigeria, Ngũgĩ of Kenya, Gordimer of South Africa and Farah of Somalia. These four authors re-imagine their communities within what Richard Bjornson calls a nation-specific 'universe of discourse' (Bjornson1991, xi), and how their backgrounds and sociocultural contexts influence their contribution to the Anglophone African literary-linguistic continuum. Simply put, these writers loosely represent the four 'axes' of sub-Saharan Anglophone Africa and their diverse cultural, ethnic, geographical, linguistic, racial, and religious backgrounds, issues that complicate the analysis of African literary discourse. Inevitably, they represent the plurality of Anglophone African writings that continues to defy a unified literary-linguistic theory, mainly because of the linguistic and cultural circumstances surrounding the authors and their respective nations. Moreover, the impact of the Anglophone African literary-linguistic continuum remains much greater than we acknowledge. It is against this backdrop that this continuum is examined, looking at convergences and divergences in the works of these authors and how they variously deploy or engage with the English language. This continuum could serve as a trajectory for understanding the various manifestations of English in Anglophone African writings that could also apply to other areas where English is not traditionally a 'home' language.

Furthermore, the continued use of standard English as the base (acrolect) from which variants of Anglophone African literary expressions (basilects) spring suggests that this trend will persist, mainly because of the language's role in facilitating communication in multilingual, multi-ethnic and multicultural African societies as either a national or official language, especially amongst the educated African elites. The African linguistic situation, which allows the English language to enjoy an unprecedented prestigious status in relation to other languages, just like the acrolect-basilects linguistic relationship in a Creole community in Guyana that Bickerton (1973) talks about, creates an environment for sustaining such a continuum. African writers who primarily write in English often subordinate indigenous languages and other cultural expressions to the primary base, English discourse. This reality appears to influence the extent to which African writers engage with the English language and its literary tradition. Inevitably, this situation leads to a plurality in the literary Anglophone tradition shaped by different socioeconomic, political, cultural and linguistic factors, but united by a common language. Thus, these diverse manifestations of African literary discourse are linked in a continuum by the English literary tradition and language that African writers engage with.

The variations in the Anglophone literary tradition witnessed in Africa and elsewhere in traditionally non-English contexts emerge because meaning in language depends on many sociological and historical factors. Thus, when English is subjected to a set of diverse sociocultural and linguistic values as in Africa, variations that are not evident in a native English setting appear. Mikhail Bakhtin (1987) calls this linguistic phenomenon 'social heteroglossia', which privileges context over text as social, historical, meteorological and physiological conditions tend to influence semantics; that is, the way people assign meaning to language. Languages, Bakhtin (1987, 291) notes, 'do not *exclude* each other, but rather intersect with each other in many different ways'. Hence, the confluence of English and indigenous African languages – and indeed other languages – has led to a condition that allows for the development of new varieties and new meanings. Achebe, for example, uses in his novels a multiplicity of language varieties, including Pidgin English, an offshoot of such an intersection, in depicting cultural and nation-specific speech communities. After all, the novel form, as Bakhtin further asserts, is unique in its capacity to portray heteroglossic contexts. And so, the different language varieties in Achebe's novels – both standard and non-standard – help not only to generate meaning but also to situate his writings in realistic fictional local contexts, the Igbo and Nigerian universe. The same argument can be extended to Ngũgĩ, Gordimer and Farah.

Although in principle Achebe, Ngũgĩ, Gordimer and Farah belong to the same Anglophone linguistic community in Africa, and their texts therefore reflect similarities, they also, inevitably, reveal dissimilarities. Differences emerge partly because these writers come from different nations with different sets of problems and partly because of their divergent ideological and political inclinations. On the surface, Achebe and Ngũgĩ appear diametrically opposed because of their different stands on the question of the language of African literatures. This difference of opinion, however, neither invalidates, nor undermines their respective contributions to the development of the literatures of their nations and of Africa in general. In fact, these differences affirm the diverse, but complementary, ways of approaching Africa's national imaginings in the English language.

For these writers, their national contexts situate their contribution to the Anglophone African literary-linguistic continuum. Though of late trans-national discourse appears to have upstaged national discourse under globalisation, nation-specific discourses in Africa and elsewhere can benefit our understanding of the problematical position within the national discourse of literatures written by Africans in former colonial languages. In fact, Christopher Miller (1993) in his essay 'Nationalism as resistance and resistance to nationalism in the literature of Francophone Africa' suggested that a close examination of African publications can help us determine how they contribute to national cultures. Miller (1993) made this point because, despite critiques of postcolonial nation-states as having the potential of 'supporting and creating a national culture', this area of investigation has in 'a curious way [...] not attracted a great deal of attention' (Miller 1993, 95). By criticising particular regimes, he explained, African publications help evolve a nation-specific universe of discourse. In this context, what African authors write about the nation 'matters less' than the fact that they directly or indirectly 'address [...] the question of the nation and thereby contribut[e] to a national discourse' (Miller 1993, 95). Miller identifies this as one way through which nationalism legitimates and makes itself inevitable. Although Miller based his premise on Francophone literatures, we can extend the same argument to Anglophone and Lusophone African literatures, since they all use a language that largely came with colonial intervention.

Historical roots of the African novel in Anglophone Africa

Former colonial languages are so established in their post-colonies that in the case of English one might even argue for the existence of Anglophonism defined as a tradition of actively or passively using English as a medium of literary discourse in traditionally non-English cultures because of socioeconomic and colonial (and neocolonial) encounters. This definition also alludes to historical and practical factors that have helped to entrench the Anglophone tradition in Africa. The historical factors are both colonial and postcolonial, and are well documented. Colonialism ushered in European languages, but post-colonies retained the privileged position these languages enjoy, mostly as mediums of national unity. In the case of Liberia and Sierra Leone, the descendants of freed African slaves introduced English in areas where they settled. The practical factors favouring English include globalisation, publishing prospects, and authorial linguistic convenience, not to mention the diverse Anglophone audiences the African writers tend to target within and outside their national boundaries.

Moreover, the common form – the novel – the four authors use remains pivotal in defining Africa's national consciousness among Africa's educated elite. Anderson (1991) in his seminal work *Imagined communities* appears to legitimise the attention that fiction gets when it comes to national re-imagining. Anderson sees the nation as a fiction or 'imagined community' that emerged with the birth of print capitalism, with the novel and newspaper playing a significant role in its formation. This perspective arises from his definition of a nation as 'an imagined political community – and imagined as both inherently limited and sovereign' (Anderson 1991, 15). His insights on the novel and its role in national narrations help situate the African novels in relation to the nations they tend to represent. He asserts that the novel depicts,

> The movement of a solitary hero through a sociological landscape of a fixity that fuses the world inside the novel with the world outside. The picturesque tour d'horizon – hospitals, prisons, remote villages, monasteries, Indians, Negroes – is nonetheless not a tour du monde. The horizon is clearly bounded. (1991, 35)

Chapter 1

Protagonists in the novels of these writers negotiate through fictional sociological landscapes representative of the real world in a 'limited' space. Timothy Brennan supports this idea when he says the novel in its genesis 'objectif[ied] the "one, yet many" of national life, and by mimicking the structure of the nation, a clearly bordered jumble of languages and styles' (Brennan 1990, 49). In all these novelistic portrayals, the nations upon which the authors base their fictional universes allow us to place the characters and their actions in a particular locale, and socioeconomic and political context.

Anderson was also aware of the limitations of his conception of the nation and hence avoided making 'global pretensions' regarding his seminal work. In his revision to his first edition, Anderson (1991, xiv, 176) introduced three colonial institutions – the census, the map and the museum – which helped to 'shape the way in which the colonial state imagined its dominion – the nature of human beings it ruled, the geography of its domain, and the legitimacy of its ancestry'. For Africa, the first two – 'census' (demographic constitution of African nations) and 'maps' (the arbitrariness of African national borders) – are key to understanding the dynamics of an African nation. The third, 'museum', can represent what in *The Africans* Mazrui (1986) calls African triple cultural heritage – indigenous, Islamic and Western influences, which continue to mould African national imaginings. Even after revising the section on 'Third World' nationalisms, Anderson left it for those with 'greater knowledge' of other parts of Asia (other than Southeast Asia, his area of specialty) and Africa to consider whether his argument on how ex-colonial nations evolved applies on a 'wider historical and geographical stage' (Anderson1991, 64). However, the very conception and composition of African nation-states and their failure to function effectively because of both internal and external factors make it difficult to fully explain the concept of the African nation using Anderson's model alone. Although Anderson's model may not apply to all aspects of the complex nature of the multi-ethnic, multicultural African nation-states, he still sheds light on some aspects of the African nation. In addition, the mass radio broadcasts in many African nations tend to shape nationalism more than the entire print media industry combined, since these electronic media can reach large swathes of territories in the rural areas in the post-colonies where most of the citizens live, far removed from the print world.

Some African writers such as Ngũgĩ see the continued use of English and other former colonial languages in African discourse as a way of legitimising imperial control over the post-colonies under the aegis of neocolonialism, since the language, he contends, helps *colonise* their minds. In other words, his call for the abolition of English departments in Africa and his theory on the language of African literature that insists on ceasing the use of English as a primary vehicle of literary expression in African national discourse amounts to an organised attempt to wrest power from neocolonialism. And yet, modern African literatures, especially fiction, also implicitly entail considering the role of the former colonial languages, and the European novel.

After all, the emergence of modern African literature – or to use Janheinz Jahn's phrase, 'Neo-African literature' (1968, 15) – coincided with increased use of the novel form as a literary tool for articulating African discourse coupled with the application of foreign languages in African literatures, both largely by-products of the colonial encounter. On the one hand, these two factors helped many African writers to develop a counter-discourse against denigrating colonial writings, especially in the imperial adventure fiction, and contributed to the rapid growth of modern African literatures from the mid-twentieth century into the form we know today. On the other hand, because of how these literatures evolved in Africa, some consider these factors, especially the language component, as a maladroit consequence of colonialism that should be dispensed with altogether, particularly as primary vehicles of African literary expression.

In reality, some 'good' – as Achebe (1975) would call it – in African literary discourse came out of this colonial experience. Education under both the missionaries and colonial educators enabled African writers to write in both indigenous and colonial languages, thus turning the largely oral literary tradition of sub-Saharan Africa into the written one that many can access. Before the advent of missionary and colonial education, many African linguistic communities lacked orthography, and hence relied on the oral tradition for their literary output and its preservation for posterity. Missionaries changed all that and introduced orthography in these languages, primarily to disseminate the gospel. Though African writers initially appropriated the novel form from Europe, they have over time Africanised the form, adding some uniquely African features, mostly from orature. Of course, neo-African literatures have oral antecedents, which the so-called 'bolekaja' ('come down let's fight') scholars, Chinweizu and Madubuike (1983), insisted upon as preceding colonial intervention; however, the mid-twentieth century writing phenomenon in sub-Saharan Africa generated literatures, including Anglophone African literatures, that can stand on their own as a *genre*.

Consequently, African literary scholarship suffers from the effects of contradictions resulting from the Christianisation and Westernisation processes under colonial rule when written discourse in African and colonial languages emerged to join the already established orature. As a result, African 'authored texts' assumed a primary position in literary discourse, and eventually subordinated other modes of expression, especially orature – the main form of expression for most African peoples. Even then the written literary discourse, as V. Y. Mudimbe (1994, 177, 179) – who sees 'neo-African literature' as nothing other than 'a commodity' and a 'recent invention' – aptly notes, 'do[es] not constitute a hiatus in terms of African experience'. Most local communities in the rural areas still rely on the oral traditions to express their cultural experience. Mudimbe insists that, although the notion of modern African literature signals 'an internal historical and sociological dimension', it 'does not and cannot mean that the possibility could be elsewhere than on the exteriority of the very literature' (Mudimbe 1994, 180). In fact, Mudimbe argues against considering these literatures as anything other than a discourse. More importantly, Mudimbe alludes to the varied literary interpretations on the African literary stage that arise because of the nature of this discourse and how it emerged:

> Depending on our state of mind, these norms allow us all the liberties we wish. From them we can today decide that Chinua Achebe's and E. Mphahlele's works are an internal part of English literature, Senghor's, Rabemananjara's, or Camara Laye's of the French. And, tomorrow, with the same conviction we could demonstrate exactly the contrary and celebrate our authors as mirrors of African authenticity. (Mudimbe 1994, 180–81)

Therefore, Ngũgĩ's earlier and often contentious argument – which he has since revised to embrace a more accommodative position – towards the exclusion of African literatures in former colonial languages from the continent's literary discourse has only limited validity, since we can find justification for embracing Anglophone African literatures as an integral part of authentic African literary discourse.

The Tower of Babel and the intricate African linguistic landscape

Opponents of English as a medium of African literary expression such as Obi Wali and subsequently Ngũgĩ, who have dismissed African literatures written in English, have often tended to oversimplify the African literary-linguistic realities. They have also overlooked the fact that English has, arguably, also become an African language, if not an established language in Africa, not only for Africans who are descendants of white settlers but also for black Africans whose first language is English, and those whom Ali Mazrui calls 'Afro-Saxons' (Mazrui 1975). In South Africa and Zimbabwe and other pockets of Africa, descendants of white colonials use English as their first language. Then in Sierra Leone (to a certain extent) and Liberia, there are Africans – the first native English-speaking black Africans – who are descendants of freed African slaves. Finally, there are black Africans in inter-racial and inter-ethnic marriages who speak English as their first language. Since all these remain part of African communities, excluding them from African discourse because their first language is English misses the point. This anomaly appears to arise from a tendency to view former colonial languages as perpetually European modes of expression that have no home in Africa, despite a significant presence of native speakers of such languages in Africa. Excluding all these literary contributions when they write in English would discredit any argument of the authenticity of African writing, since it amounts to excluding linguistic groups of bona fide Africans.

The descendants of African-Americans in Africa acquired English after being robbed of whatever original African languages they spoke before being forced into slavery. In the case of Sierra Leone, George Padmore observes:

> The Creoles of Sierra Leone rapidly became the first Westernized community in Africa. Drawn as they were from heterogeneous elements, cut adrift from their ancestral cultures, traditions and customs, the repatriates intermarried and adopted the English way of life. The Queen's language became their normal medium of communication. (as cited in Mazrui 1975, 38)

Intermingling between the Creoles and the indigenous ethnic groups in and around Freetown enabled English to become Africanised into *Krio*. Later, Creoles and Europeans tried to eradicate Krio in favour of promoting English as part of the educational policy of the country (Mazrui 1975, 41). Conversely, Liberia remains the only African country to owe its Anglophonism to the United States rather than directly to British colonial rule. It is the only black African country in which English serves as a native and first language for the country's descendants of freed African-American slaves. Indeed, these Liberians, alongside minority white South Africans and Zimbabweans, justify the existence of English as an established African language.

In fact, the antecedents of English usage in African liberation rhetoric can be traced to liberated Africans who settled on the West African Coast. Mazrui goes as far as tracing African nationalism to the Pan-African political thoughts of WEB Du Bois, Padmore and Marcus Garvey, whose language of expression was English. Mazrui (1975, 38) notes:

> Many of the things which one can say about the significance of the English language for the development of African ideas one can also say about the French language. But there are certain areas of thought where one language has been more important than the other. Among areas where English has been particularly significant is the development of certain notions of self-determination.

His emphasis on the significance of English as a medium through which the story of African liberation unfolds, highlights the linkage between the language and African national determinism. Before assuming the form of opposition to colonial (and eventually neocolonial) domination, English had a place in the anti-slavery liberation rhetoric. Anti-slavery movements in Britain and the United States used the language to push for the emancipation of enslaved Africans, and these efforts culminated in the settlement of former slaves from Britain and America in Sierra Leone and Liberia respectively. These former slaves served as pioneers, not only in the use of English as their first language among black Africans, but also in sowing the seeds of liberation rhetoric that would later develop into colonial and postcolonial Anglophone African resistance.

Colonial intervention further spread the European languages to other parts of Africa through an arbitrary process. Moreover, Africa's arbitrary boundaries following the Berlin Conference of 1884/5, which hastily demarcated borders without any due regard to who and which linguistic group ended up in the demarcated areas also helped to distort the linguistic picture of present-day African nation-states. The conference lumped together what Ngũgĩ calls 'nations within a nation' (or people from different linguistic and ethnic groups), regardless of whether members from a myriad of ethnic groups (who were not consulted on the make-up of the nation in the first place) would get along. When Anglophone African states gained their political independence, the colonial languages automatically became languages of national unity, mostly in the absence of a common language amongst these disparate groups. In fact, Ngũgĩ (1990) appears to quarrel with English partly because of this unequal co-existence between English and African languages. He notes that the relationship between English and most 'so-called Third World languages did not occur under conditions of independence and equality' (Ngũgĩ 1990, 284). The effects of this unequal meeting of the colonial and indigenous languages – one as a language of power and the others without power – continue to be felt in Africa today. Yet Ngũgĩ's explanation does not account for the intricate linguistic environment within Africa that has left many African nations preferring – for political, economic, linguistic, or simply colonial hangover concerns – to retain the privileged position of English in African discourse rather than elevate African languages to that *sanctified* position.

Furthermore, the presence of more than one thousand languages in Africa, the total for each nation varying from case to case, has complicated the process of choosing languages for national literary discourse. Sub-Saharan Africa is one of the most linguistically complex areas in the world, particularly in terms of population-language ratios. Except for a few countries, such as Somalia, Swaziland and Lesotho, most African countries have a labyrinth of language choices. Even then, as Somalia demonstrates (as discussed in Chapter 5), a single national language does not guarantee unity. Despite claims for Somali exceptionalism, the most well-known author writes in English, his fourth language, and not in Somali. Of course, the factors behind this inclination are diverse, as I will illustrate. On the one hand, Africa has too many languages that can potentially serve as media for pan-national – as opposed to ethnic – literary expression. On the other, the sheer number of languages makes choosing one language over scores of others a daunting task, forcing many African countries to opt for *neutral* former colonial languages.

Correspondingly, African leaders – eager to establish hegemony over disparate ethnic groups in the post-colony – merely kept colonial languages in the name of safeguarding national unity after inheriting the arbitrary boundaries, then picked local languages to serve at provincial or regional levels and relegated the rest of the local languages to the bottom of the pile. English, French or Portuguese often served as the language of higher education, business, government and the law. The provincial languages were often 'national' languages catering to particular national needs, including serving as languages of primary education and local government. The remaining languages were mainly used in the domestic sphere of everyday social interaction. The political will of African leaders helped to entrench the use of English as the official or national language. As Kahombo Mateene (1985) explains (as cited in Pütz 1995, 1):

> African countries use European languages [...] in nearly all their official business, and almost to the exclusion and to the detriment of their national languages [...]. In this way, African countries obligatorily use foreign colonial languages in almost all the important fields where national languages should have full vent, or even the exclusive right of use.

The dominant role assigned to former colonial languages as a colonial inheritance in Africa has led to linguistic inequality and serious language conflict situations in sub-Saharan nation states. For a large part, in the postcolonial period such use of English was politically motivated. African leaders seeking to establish political hegemony over disparate ethnic groups opted to retain the use of colonial languages as 'national' and official languages. On this point Madumulla, Bertoncini and Blommaert (1999, 309) note,

> Leaders frequently referred to language in the context of larger political goals and plans. [...] [T]he introduction of the ex-colonial language was motivated by a desire to build national unity through a 'neutral' medium [...] 'not ethnically marked' [...] and to use the foreign language [...] to establish or maintain [...] contacts with the western world [...] to attain a desired level of development. Thus also, leaders often tried to 'repatriate' French, English or Portuguese and turn them into 'African' languages and symbols of Africanness.

Indeed, African leaders argued that continued use of ex-colonial languages would help them promote national unity and enhance nation building, and eventually help resolve conflicting identity politics. Even then, as Anderson notes, it is 'always a mistake to treat languages' as 'emblems of nation-ness' because the 'most important thing about language is its capacity for generating imagined communities, building in effect *particular solidarities*' (Anderson, 1991 133; my emphasis). In many Anglophone African countries, English helps to accomplish this objective. Furthermore, Ernest

Gellner observes in his analysis of Ernest Renan's 1882 Sorbonne lecture, 'What is a nation?' that his 'main purpose' was to 'deny any naturalistic determinism of the boundaries of nations' as 'these are not dictated by language, geography, race, religion, or anything else' as nations are 'made by human will' (Gellner 1987, 8). Language alone thus cannot be a determinant of nation-ness.

Africa and the compound, complex literary-linguistic situation

The literary-linguistic situation in Africa has been compounded by the failure of governments to promote literacy in indigenous languages. Overall, there are 'less [sic] attempts' in Africa, except for exceptional cases such as Tanzania, to press for 'promot[ing] indigenous languages as media for literacy' and 'less linguistic nationalism generally' (Mazrui 1984, 299). To make matters worse, these indigenous African languages are usually neglected and mostly lack the institutional and political support that English enjoys. The hierarchy of language stature – which Batibo (2005, 86) lists as 'language of national prestige', 'language of regional prestige,' 'language of local prestige' and 'language without special prestige' – exposes the problems of language placement in many African countries.

Tanzania, one of the few success stories in East Africa that managed to develop a national language other than a European one, has Kiswahili as the only language to enjoy national stature after being declared 'language of national prestige' immediately after the country's independence in 1961. Further developments also helped to fortify the position of Kiswahili. These include the 1967 Arusha Declaration that turned Tanzania into a socialist country; the creation of the National Kiswahili Council, known by its Kiswahili acronym as BAKITA; the introduction of Kiswahili as the medium of universal primary-school education; the application of Kiswahili as an official language; and the creation of a task force to prepare the employment of Kiswahili in all literary campaigns. Kiswahili thrives because it has 'all the necessary charms like prestige, modernity, lingua franca, social promotion and wider acceptance' (Batibo 2005, 93). Nevertheless, Tanzania retained English as an official language alongside Kiswahili, to be used in prime institutions such as the high court and institutions of higher learning; it also serves as the language of instruction in secondary schools.

Normally, there is a need for deliberate policies aimed at developing indigenous African languages. However, many African countries keep on expanding the sphere of English and French usage in educational institutions. Tanzania, which has done so well in developing Kiswahili, has been shy when it comes to developing ethnic languages, fearing that doing so would only fuel ethnic tensions based on language differences and ethnic affiliations. Consequently, Tanzanians can publish newspapers and broadcast in both English and Kiswahili, but not in other indigenous languages. Of course, different countries in Africa have different policies regarding indigenous languages, but they appear uniform in their stand on developing former colonial languages. The prestige attached to these languages not only in official circles but also in domestic spheres entails – ironic and contradictory as this may appear – that these languages continue serving as media for national cultural expression with very little stigma attached to them. However, the promotion of former colonial languages in Africa has not helped to bring about the envisaged national cohesion. On the contrary, Mazrui and Tidy (1984, 300) observe that

> English and French are invaluable in various ways for modern African development: they help to integrate Africa in world culture; they are politically neutral in the context of Africa's multi-ethnic societies. But they do not necessarily help overcome the crisis of national integration facing African countries. English and French as inter-ethnic languages at first sight might seem to lend themselves to the task of national integration. For the inter-ethnic communication at the grass-roots level, European languages are intrinsically and hopelessly ill-equipped to meet the challenge, and thus constitute an impediment to the process of national integration. The use of a national and regional language, however, like Kiswahili in East Africa and a regional language like Hausa in West Africa, could promote integration at two levels: horizontally among the masses of different ethnic groups and vertically to narrow the gap between the masses and the educated elite.

As weapons for national integration, foreign languages have failed to bring about the envisaged national cohesion; ironically, the same reason cited for promoting them. This has to do with the disproportional number of actual English speakers in Africa in relation to the population of speakers of other languages.

This shortcoming notwithstanding, Anglophonism has continued to thrive in Africa, much to the embarrassment of the opponents of the use of former colonial languages in the African space. Consequently, different shades of Anglophone countries have emerged within Africa's 'Tower of Babel'. There are those such as Zambia (which officially does not have an indigenous national language, and instead uses provincial languages alongside English as the official and national language) that use English as the primary national and official language; there are those such as Tanzania (whose national language is Kiswahili) that use English alongside a national language; and there are those such as the Sudan (whose national language is Arabic) that use English as a secondary language of discourse. Moreover, for some linguistic communities in Liberia, South Africa, Sierra Leone and Zimbabwe, as indicated earlier, English remains their first contact language, and has over the years developed its own characteristics. Thus, in one form or another, Anglophonism endures, and in some countries it does so as the main vehicle of literary discourse, although Africans generally associate the language with colonialism and neocolonialism. Mazrui (1976, 331) justifies this wide application of English as follows:

> The English language, the most important linguistic medium that mankind has so far, acquired this importance not only because of the role which the English-speaking powers have played in world history, but also because mankind now feels the need for shared global languages much more than it has ever before. Both English and French meet a new need in the world – and mankind is using them as tools which happen to be at hand.

Within the trans-national framework, globalisation appears to validate continued application of the English language in African discourse.

English as a vehicular language

Many factors have inevitably contributed to establishing English in Anglophone Africa as what Deleuze and Guattari (1986, 24) call the 'vehicular language'. Deleuze and Guattari relied on Henri Gobard's tetralinguistic model to explain that we can classify languages into vernacular, maternal or territorial languages used in rural areas, an attribute which most of the more than one thousand African languages found on the continent share. As the 'here' languages, the usage of many of these languages remains confined to inter-ethnic dialogue. In such a situation, another form of language – the 'vehicular' or 'everywhere' language – caters for other social functions in the public domain, particularly multilingual, multi-ethnic, multicultural and pan-national and trans-national spaces. This type of language thrives in urban, governmental and international domains. It also serves as a vehicular language of business and commerce, and as a kind of 'deterritorialisation' medium. For many African nation-states, with varying degrees of application, this language is English, or French, or Portuguese, depending on their colonial history. These former colonial languages operate in diglossic and triglossic situations, that is, in combination with national and/or regional or ethnic languages. It is in this context that English is being considered as an African vehicular, though not necessarily an everywhere, language.

This justification of the role of Anglophonism in African literary discourse is essential primarily because many of the issues raised above remain unresolved and hence contentious. However, this discussion demonstrates that when critics dismiss English as one of the African languages, they tend to overlook its history and its communication value within African national discourse. From the foregoing discussion, one can argue that English has over the years established itself as an African language, not only because some Africans use it as their first language, but also because conservatively, for more than one hundred years, Africans have worked with

English as their first or second or third language and so forth. In addition, African nation-states have established structures and policies that enable the Anglophone African literary-linguistic continuum to continue unabated. Considering how long Africans have been in contact with the English language, Achebe, who has always acknowledged that he has been given a language and he intends to use it, wondered:

> There has been an impassioned controversy about an African literature in non-African languages. But what is non-African language? English and French certainly. What about Arabic? What about [Ki]Swahili even? Is it then a question of how long the language has been present on African soil? If so, how many years should constitute effective occupation? For me it is again a pragmatic matter. A language spoken by Africans on African soil, a language in which Africans write, justifies itself. (Achebe 1975, 93)

Achebe's statement here seeks not only to justify the use of English in African letters, but also raises questions on some of the established African languages. Arabic and Kiswahili are so established in Africa that no one may associate them with foreign roots or influences. Indeed, the question of the language of African literature demands complex answers because of the complex reality of the African linguistic and literary scene.

The dilemma facing opponents of the use of English in African literary discourse lies in the role that the language continues to play in bridging the communication gap, not only *within* nations but also *across* nations within Africa and beyond. Internationally, the results of such a trend are there for all to see. As Brennan (1990, 47) notes, 'The recent interest in Third World literature reflected in special issues of many mainstream journals and new publishers' series, as well as new university programs, is itself a mark of the recognition that imperialism is, culturally speaking, a two-way flow'. In this dialogue, English plays a pivotal role. Ngũgĩ, one of the fiercest opponents of using English as the primary vehicle of African literature (one can call him a disciple of Obi Wali), has since undergone a 'transformation' with his 'sudden – and unaccounted [for] – return to the English he had loudly rejected in *Decolonising the Mind*' (Gikandi 2000, 276). Gikandi explains that Ngũgĩ's 'return' to English could be attributed to difficulties of working and living in exile as an intellectual and writer, removed from the roots of the language he wants to promote. Even more difficult, Gikandi continues,

> is how to explain this return in the contexts of Ngũgĩ's politics of language and to account for his theories and practices as they were being shaped, not by the peasants and workers of Kenya, or even African institutions of higher learning, but by the very Western institutions whose policies he had previously attacked. (Gikandi 2000, 276)

Chapter 1

Ngũgĩ's (2000, 119) own statement best summarises his dilemma: 'The more I call for the abolition of English departments, the more calls I get for lectures from departments of English!' In this statement lies the reality of Anglophonism in the world today. This reality also confirms the inextricability of literatures written in English from African literary discourse. Perhaps it is for this reason that Ngũgĩ (2000, 119) ends up declaring:

> So the study of African, Asian, or Latin American literatures must be seen as part and parcel of teaching literature and culture in the West. The really important thing is to see connections. It is only when we see real connections that we can meaningfully talk about differences, similarities, and identities. So the border, seen as a bridge, is founded on the recognition that no culture is an island unto itself. It has been influenced by other cultures and other histories with which it has come into contact. This recognition is the basis of all other bridges that we want to build across our various cultural borders. The bridges are already there, in fact. The challenge facing, say, teachers of English literature, of African or of Asian literature, is to recognize and find those bridges and build on them. That is why teaching literatures and teaching languages is a privilege that faces us all – the challenge to see connections between literature and that wholeness that we call *society*, a wholeness constituted by all that comes under economics, politics, and the environment.

As part of national and trans-national discourse, Anglophone African literatures contribute towards building such bridges. And yet this reality should not come at the expense of indigenous languages that help enrich world cultures. In this regard, Ismail Talib in *The Language of Postcolonial Literature* (2002, 17), insists that 'Postcolonial literatures can be defined as literature written by colonised and formerly colonised peoples [...] in various languages, and not only in the language of the colonisers'. It is only logical that indigenous African languages and former colonial languages be acknowledged to have a complete set of literatures created on the African continent. In this regard, Ngũgĩ cautions people in the Third World against entirely ignoring their own native languages by assuming that English constitutes the basis of defining not only 'our own identity' but also 'our own being' to the extent that they become 'captives of this language,' and develop 'certain positive identification with English' while 'distancing ourselves from our own languages [and] our own cultures' (Ngũgĩ 2000, 122). This work does not dispute the importance of indigenous languages in the production of art. But it considers how the English language co-exists with the languages and cultures it helps to promote within Africa and other parts of the world, mainly serving as a cross-cultural and linguistic bridge whose users should remember not to abandon their own languages. In fact, the broader application of the term 'Anglophone' to texts in translation from other literary-linguistic traditions also attests to the significance of English as a communication bridge.

Plurality in modern African literatures

On balance, the same 'Afro-European literatures' still constitute an integral part of African (on the continental level) and national imaginings (on the local level). Even Ngũgĩ's own early literary works written in English remain African literature (in English), just like Achebe's, Gordimer's and Farah's. The works by these writers published in English remain part of the process of national representation. The application of the plural form 'African literatures' attempts to address some of the difficulties inherent in referring to African literature in its singular form. The singular form, after all, has remained controversial since the 1962 historic Conference of African Writers of English Expression held at Makerere University College in Kampala, Uganda, when attempts to define African literature exposed the limitations of coming up with a 'neat' definition of African literatures. On this point, Michael Chapman (2003, 1) observes that 'the plural form African Literatures' reminds us 'that Africa is far from homogenous in language, culture, religion, or the processes of modernity'. The plural form embraces many aspects otherwise ignored during the de-colonisation days when the singular pan-Africanist concept remained the norm. Achebe was also wary of the simplistic approaches to African literatures by cautioning against 'cram[ming] African literature as one unit' when it should be perceived as 'a group of associated units – in fact the sum total of all the *national and ethnic* literatures of Africa' (Achebe 1975, 92; emphasis added). For Achebe, a national literature takes the whole nation for 'its province' and has 'a realised or potential audience throughout its territory'. Thus, a national literature constitutes one 'written in the *national* language' and an 'ethnic literature' one available only to 'one ethnic group within the nation' (Achebe 1975, 93; emphasis added). Achebe implicitly explains the challenge that the multiplicity of languages in most African nations pose for writers when producing 'national' as opposed to 'ethnic' literatures, both of which remain an integral part of national discourse, one from an esoteric and the other from the exoteric perspective.

Thus, an Anglophone African literary-linguistic continuum has to take cognisance of the complex issues regarding the application of English in Africa and, indeed, in other traditionally non-English contexts. However, there exists enough ground on which to account for a literary-linguistic continuum in Anglophone African writing, and the various ways in which the four authors use the language in the development of their art reinforce that idea. On a linguistic level, South Africa and to a certain extent Nigeria have developed distinct Englishes that can qualify as variants in their own right; however, the focus is primarily on the literary-linguistic rather than the linguistic per se. It is for this reason that we examine the works of the four authors and the literary-linguistic elements these writers varyingly bring to the novel form because of their different backgrounds.

Chapter 1

The publication of Achebe's *Things Fall Apart* in 1958 appears to be a turning point in modern African literature because the novel helped to expose not only the issues of the English language as it relates to African literary discourse, but also the African aesthetics in the Anglophone tradition. In the study of modern African literatures, Achebe and his first novel – which many consider an archetypical African novel – occupy a pivotal role, particularly with regard to defining Anglophone African literatures, and in this case how to approach the Anglophone African literary-linguistic continuum. *Things Fall Apart* was hailed as a milestone in 'modern' African literature when it first came out in print because it helped to highlight many linguistic and cultural aspects of neo-African literature (details appear in Chapter 2). Although many other African works, including Amos Tutuola's *The Palm-Wine Drinkard* (1952) and Gordimer's *The Lying Days* (1953), had preceded this novel, many observers controversially see Achebe's novel as a marker of the emergence of 'modern' African literature. One can, however, even go way back in terms of the first work of Anglophone African fiction. In this regard, credit goes to Joseph J Walters' *Guanya Pau: The Story of an African Prince*, published in 1891, some 20 years before JE Casely Hayford's *Ethiopia Unbound* that came out in 1911.

On the other hand, it should be stated from the outset that *Things Fall Apart* is no more authentically African than *The Lying Days* or *The Palm-Wine Drinkard*, but the novel helped us to become conscious of a particular discourse relevant to the understanding of Africa. In contrast, Gordimer's novels were initially treated as part of the European literary tradition, and few took Tutuola's novels as serious works of art (though he has been vindicated since). Achebe's novel became a standard-bearer, and – in many respects – set the framework for imagining African communities, particularly in the African Writers Series (AWS) published by Heinemann. The novel marks the acknowledgement of a discourse that helped to move Africa from the wilderness of literariness to recognition. The colonial legacy, as *Things Fall Apart* and *Arrow of God* of 1964 demonstrate, destroyed the social base that allowed African societies to function in the pre-colonial contact period. As many critics have observed, this created the problems that Achebe continued to examine in *No Longer at Ease* of 1960 and, more importantly, *A Man of the People* of 1966. This engagement also facilitated Achebe's contribution to novel African aesthetics, which has in turn enriched the Anglophone African literary tradition. Although Achebe claims to use English because he takes the whole nation as his 'province', his cultural reference remains – particularly in his early novels – mainly the Igbo community.

From Achebe's engagement with established notions and literary traditions, three aspects emerge. First, he introduces local cultural-specific literary elements into his mode of Anglophone discourse. These elements include Igbo proverbs, songs, myths, legends, non-English words and typically Nigerian idiomatic expressions. There is also his use of the vernacular style in his writing, while he uses nation-specific heteroglossic contexts to show the different speech acts. Indeed, we find different language varieties – standard and non-standard – helping not only to generate meaning in Achebe's novels but also to situate his writings in realistic fictional local contexts, the Igbo and Nigerian universe. All these aspects become a rhetorical weapon in furthering Achebe's literary-linguistic agenda.

Ngũgĩ, like Achebe, in his early works tried to find the connection between African traditions and modern trends. He represents in *The River Between*, *Weep Not, Child* and *A Grain of Wheat* the African national experience as nation-states emerged from colonial domination. In his later works, *Petals of Blood*, *Devil on the Cross* and *Matigari*, Ngũgĩ shifts his attention to the neocolonial environment, in which he sides with the dispossessed. The question Ngũgĩ poses is why citizens should remain alienated from their own nation, their land, and their production forces. Consequently, Ngũgĩ switches to writing primarily in Gikuyu as a medium for 're-imagining' not only the Gikuyu 'nation' but also of Kenya, because he realises – rather controversially so – that though he championed the cause of the common man, his rhetoric remained elitist, and did not target the English illiterate common man who spoke other languages. Paradoxically, it is his writing in English, whether in translation or not, which has brought him international standing.

Also, his aesthetics within the Anglophone tradition suggests that one can engage with the tradition directly, by writing in English or through translation. Both Gikuyu and English novels draw upon the three pillars of his people's oral traditions – songs, dance and, to a certain degree, mime. One major difference lies in the primary medium of literary expression – English or Gikuyu – which, in turn, dictates the orientation of the novelistic forms, with those originally written in English stronger in the European realistic mode and those in Gikuyu stronger in the fabulist mode modelled on traditional oral story-telling aesthetics. In his early career, Ngũgĩ subordinated Gikuyu and Kiswahili discourses to the primary literary medium of English discourse. In the latter, Ngũgĩ subordinates English and other discourses to the main Gikuyu. Even then, he carefully intercalates English expressions to demonstrate how the language of power helps to further reinforce imperialism through acculturation.

But these common people Ngũgĩ writes for in Gikuyu constitute only one segment of the Kenyan society, and hence he must rely on other languages, including English, to reach his potential readers within Kenya, Africa and beyond. In his first novel, *The River Between*, Ngũgĩ in a sense benefits from the Achebe-inspired aesthetics regarding the manipulation of English to 'reclaim' the past, using the colonial language in a manner that reflects the local context. Indeed, the way Ngũgĩ integrates Gikuyu sayings, myths, legends and traditional cultural belief systems

Chapter 1

in this novel emphasises this inherent difference. Ngũgĩ relies on the realist mode borrowed from the European novel as a platform for this novel. At this stage, Ngũgĩ appears to experiment with the English language and the European form of the realist novel to realise his artistic project. Like Achebe, Ngũgĩ introduces traditional elements such as song, folklore and the local myth of creation (Mumbi and Gikuyu). In his Gikuyu novels, which combine both the realistic and fabulist modes, the main narrative frame mostly relies on the traditional forms of storytelling borrowed from his country's rich oral tradition.

Gordimer, as a white South African, poses challenges when interpreting the question of race in national imaginings. Gordimer's fiction grasps the place of English within a continuum of African literary-linguistic and cultural traditions, and the English of her novel-writing becomes a literary-linguistic medium through which a range of African languages are imaginatively and concretely embodied. Although writing within the white settler codes, her multi-ethnic and multiracial South Africa, whose national well-being had for years been ravaged by apartheid policies, exemplifies the dilemma facing a nation seeking to promote nationhood based on racialised policies. From *The Lying Days* (1953), and *July's People* (1981) to *None to Accompany Me* (1994) and finally *The Pickup* (2001), Gordimer addressed the issues of race and nation. And the problem of racialisation politics Gordimer confronts, both in the apartheid and post-apartheid periods, has far-reaching implications for the identity of contemporary articulations of the 'African national' in Africa itself and in the diaspora. Gordimer offers a perspective on the vanity of national systems based on racialised categories. After all, part of Gordimer's engagement with South African realities was finding the place of the white minority in the African mosaic. In a 1959 essay 'Where do Whites fit in?' Gordimer wrote:

> Some of us in South Africa want to leave […] and I myself fluctuate between the desire to be gone – to find a society where my white skin will have no bearing on my place in the community – and a terrible, obstinate and fearful desire to stay. I feel the one desire with my head and the other with my guts […] If one will always have to feel white first and African second, it would be better not to stay on in Africa. (Gordimer 1959, 27, 30).

By insisting on thinking African first, white second, Gordimer attempts to elevate the common African identity, and subordinate the race issue. Elevating the question of colour has been the bane of racial harmony because such a course of action undermines the human element, and hence robs people of a common identity. As white South Africans discovered at a severe cost, racialisation ultimately benefits neither the (supposed) 'herrenvolk' ('master race') nor the non-whites they are (supposedly) 'destined' to subject. Most importantly, Gordimer demonstrates that white Africans, whose first language is English, face the challenge of how to use the language to enhance relations with other ethnic groups, not to undermine such relations. In fact, her novels attempt to demonstrate how English has been used to further racialised policies, and she drives the English language into a crisis in *July's People* to expose its limits in South African discourse, and paradoxically to confirm its position in African literary discourse.

Gordimer, whose linguistic and racial background causes some to view her work as closer to the European tradition than to the African one, allows for the examination of how she embodies other cultures, for example through cultural translation. On the surface, her literary project appears to have a closer affinity with the European than the African literary-linguistic tradition. But that is only half the story. Indeed, she does acknowledge having been influenced by European masters such as Proust, Chekhov and Dostoevsky, but almost all the African writers brought up under the colonial education have also been varyingly influenced by European writers. She relies primarily on the English language and uses other African languages as feeder languages that help her fiction reflect the reality of the linguistic community she writes about. Not surprisingly, she lacks the heavy reliance on the African oral literary forms that define the literary projects of many first-generation black African writers. For her, English also serves as the medium for inter-racial discourse for her characters in a multicultural and multilingual fictional universe. She uses the language to expose shortcomings in inter-racial and ethnic communication among social groups in the racially-divided society of the apartheid era. Although Gordimer wrote from a predominantly European novel tradition and in English, a European language, the South African socio-political and economic as well as linguistic circumstances shaped her writings towards African rather than European aesthetics. Here one has in mind Edmund Bamiro's description of 'Afrolect' and 'Eurolect' influences in African literary discourse. Bamiro (2000, 72) defines Afrolect literary influences in African literary discourse as a 'linguistic experimentation in variants of an imperial language' to mirror 'characteristics of African oral traditions', and Eurolect as 'literary productions that exhibit considerable influences from European literature in content, language, and style'. Yet, variations within the Anglophone African novel – basically hybrids of a European invention, the novel, and African oral traditions, orature – demonstrate that such a reductive taxonomy is inadequate in explaining, let alone differentiating, what constitutes African literature. It is against this backdrop that writings in both the so-called Afrolect, for example, Achebe's and Ngũgĩ's, and the so-called Eurolect, for example, Gordimer's and Farah's, are analysed to determine convergences and divergences in the use of the English language within the Anglophone African literary-linguistic continuum.

In Gordimer's case, the base languages of her fictional characters include both English and Afrikaans, the two languages whites introduced to South Africa, and indigenous African languages for black characters. All these languages, whether directly or indirectly reproduced in her writings, help shape her writing in the African literary mode. In her later novels, Gordimer attempted to integrate not only words from African languages but also African beliefs, a process of maturation that demonstrates the effects of the local context on Anglophone writing. It also shows that even native speakers of English are not immune to the linguistic and cultural influences of the nation-specific universes they write in.

Finally, Farah comes from one of the few African nations with one people, the Somali, speaking one national language, Somali, but which has suffered from cold-war spillover, dictatorships and disintegration partly due to inter-clan infighting and the colonial legacy that divided segments of the Somali people ruled by the English, French, Italians and (in the enclave of Ogaden) Ethiopians. Farah's fictional Somalia provides a fertile ground for re-examining the idea of the African nation and post-nation, its literature and culture, because the pre-'national' existence of the Somali people and Somali language does not warrant a stable national imagining. The civil war in Somalia tests the elasticity of national imaginings as well as literary-linguistic applications. Farah lives in exile and revisits his native country through his novels. Despite his alienation in both the linguistic and spatial sense, his novels constitute a part of Somali national literary discourse and culture. Farah's Anglophonism embraces various aspects of the mixed grill of today's international English – mostly a blend of British and American English. Farah's engagement with the social and political complexity of Somalia has always and increasingly been from the perspective of a seemingly disengaged, cosmopolitan and literary English point of view.

Farah's texts highlight some of the significant aspects of his literary career, and the nature of an Anglophone literary-linguistic continuum in African discourse. Farah relies on the Somali belief system and linguistic repertoire to construct a Somali novel. Like his forerunners, Achebe and Ngũgĩ, Farah uses myths, legends, traditional beliefs and proverbs to construct a Somali novel, though, as many have noted, he tries to avoid wallowing in the politics of Africanising the English language, even though there is evidence of his doing so in some of his texts. Farah admits that he cannot give a strong flavour of another language in English, the way Achebe does, because his 'writing is metaphor and leitmotiv-based, not proverb-based' (Jussawalla and Dasenbrock 1992, 51). Although Farah describes himself as a non-proverb-based writer in the mould of Achebe, his first novel makes use of these proverbs. In this case, the English language, which he adopts as his first literary language, is elastic enough to accommodate both indigenous (or localised) and imported forms of expression. The wider Anglophone African audiences, with a variety of linguistic influences, remain British because the education of many African writers even in the post-independence nations remain modelled on the British system, and American because of American cultural influences in the neocolonial situation in the form of American pop culture, literature, film and even soap operas. Farah draws upon techniques of European modernism to produce novels that rely on Somali culture. But his linguistic and literary influences remain multidimensional.

The form of the novels when written primarily in English also tends to follow traditional novel plots. However, when written in indigenous languages, the aesthetics also tilt towards the oral forms, as in the case of Ngũgĩ in his Gikuyu novels. Ngũgĩ tends to explore more traditional forms of story-telling in his Gikuyu novels than he does in those he primarily wrote in English. This inclination also appears to have been influenced, in part, by criticism that he has received over the years. Gikandi, for example, finds Ngũgĩ's attempt to reconcile competing phenomenological interpretations into one nativistic linguistic theory unrealistic. Gikandi (1997, 139) suggests that Ngũgĩ should give up the realistic European novel form, resolve his contradictory materialist and romantic theories of language, and accept the concept of nation and its cultures as a 'space inherently polyglot' and not 'harmoniously monolingual'. His efforts, in fact, also highlight the various ways in which English and indigenous African languages can co-exist. As Achebe admits, the way he tells the stories in English is 'not the only way we can tell the story' because if he were to tell 'a story in the Igbo language' it would be 'different in different ways' (Rowell 1989/1997, 176). An Igbo narrative targets primarily Igbo speakers, who share not only a language, but also traditions, culture and beliefs. For such an audience, with direct access to Igbo culture and beliefs, the story would be direct, and no linguistic bridge would be necessary. As Achebe's novels constitute a national project, he uses English in a bid to address Nigerians with varying linguistic and cultural backgrounds in a common communication medium.

Conclusion

The novels of these writers demonstrate that nation-specific events and crises inform their writings and influence the way they use the English language, and hence their contribution to the Anglophone African literary-linguistic continuum. Although primarily as a medium in the communication of ideas from Anglophone Africa, English survives alongside the feeder indigenous languages in this continuum, albeit in an unequal relationship, as well as the nation-specific contexts which inspire the writings. The resultant literatures remain attached to the place because of the primary events and indigenous linguistic influences that inspire such writing. Often, critics ignore that African languages survive because Africans sustain them though the oral tradition, and some of the elements developed in these languages help enrich the Anglophone African written tradition. The analyses in this book attempt to examine the varied literary-linguistic manifestations in the works of four African writers, with perhaps different ideological viewpoints and influences, to make a case for the existence of an Anglophone African literary-linguistic continuum. The subsequent chapters examine the literary-linguistic features found in the works of the four authors to establish the nature of the Anglophone African literary-linguistic continuum before a synthesis is provided in the final chapter.

2

Achebe and Anglophone African literary discourse[1]

Introduction

This chapter extends Derek Bickerton's (1973) pioneering study on the Creole continuum to the study of Anglophone African literature to examine how English, a former colonial language, serves as an arbiter in the re-imagining of diverse African communities. It revisits Chinua Achebe's fiction to examine the relationship between literary English and the indigenous languages and cultures it imaginatively and concretely embodies in traditionally non-native universes of discourse. The chapter further considers how Achebe's literary English embodies local culture-specific literary elements to illustrate that Anglophonism thrives in the national discourse of a non-native English environment when it has utilitarian value, an integral part of Achebe's theory on the language of African literature. Achebe's works show that English serves as a linguistic bridge in complex multi-ethnic and multicultural Nigeria and in the rest of Africa. Finally, the chapter establishes that local features introduced into literary English do not necessarily represent a break from the main Anglophone literary-linguistic tradition but are a manifestation of an Anglophone African literary-linguistic continuum with peculiar characteristics and divergences imposed by a localised context.

Though Achebe has been dubbed as a 'proverb-based' writer in some circles, for example by Nuruddin Farah (Jussawalla and Dasenbrock 1992, 51), his writing in English reveals how English continues to thrive in traditionally non-English contexts, how it has made Africa a home, and how it continues to serve as a medium for pan-national and trans-national discourse. As the chapter will demonstrate, the 'proverb' part is only a minute portion of myriad manifestations of English. In this regard, a concluding scene in *Anthills of the Savannah* (Achebe 1987) involving the child-naming ceremony, which serves as a symbol of the need for national renewal, situates Achebe's theory on the role of English in national discourse in a traditionally

Chapter 2

non-English context. During this traditional ritual, an old man – in an apparent recognition of his status as a guardian of African traditional norms and values – leads the naming ceremony of the child ironically already named by the young female character Beatrice. This passage in the post-civil-war novel based on the fictitious nation of Kangan reads in part:

> 'May these young people here when they make the plans for their world not forget her. And all other children.'
> '*Isé!*'
> 'May they also remember useless old people like myself and Elewa's mother when they are making plans.'
> '*Isé!*'
> 'We have seen too much trouble in Kangan since the white man left because those who make plans make plans for themselves only and their families.'
> Abdul was nodding energetically, his head bent gently towards his simultaneous translator, Emmanuel.
> […]
> Abdul, a relative stranger to the kolanut ritual, was carried away beyond the accustomed limits of choral support right into exuberant hand-clapping.
> 'I have never entered a house like this before. May this not be my last time.'
> '*Isé!*'
> 'You are welcome any time,' added Beatrice following Abdul's breaking of ritual bounds. (Achebe 1987, 211–12)

In this excerpt, traditional discourse has entered the main English discourse of the novel to resolve divisive national issues. Although '*Isé!*' comes from one of the linguistic communities in this fictitious nation of Kangan, which largely represents Nigeria,[2] the expression has been presented here as a word to which a representative sample of *all* the members of the nation are assenting. For Achebe, the solution, at least based on the suggestion in *Anthills of the Savannah*, appears to lie in the co-existence of formal and traditional sub-discourses for a nation to become a representation of all.

The child-naming ceremony combines modernity and traditional elements, or standard and non-standard literary English, in the same way that Achebe fuses traditional forms of storytelling with appropriated European narrative techniques. The coming together of the old couple and the young generation represents this convergence of traditionalists and modern Nigerians, Moslems and Christians. As Achebe notes, 'One of such gains [is the] awareness [of this group] of the totality of the community as opposed to an elite setting sitting up there and not even knowing the names of the people they were dealing with or where they lived' (Wilkinson 1987, 146). It is English – a former colonial language – that helps those from a different linguistic community not only to communicate but also to understand and participate in the ritual. Indeed, this passage brings together many facets of Achebe's theory on the question of African literature, and underlines his contribution to the Anglophone African literary-linguistic tradition.

Communication among the various parties participating in this ritual demonstrates the value of English as a tool for inter-ethnic communication. Achebe appears to suggest this method as one way through which the linguistic gap between literate and non-literate Anglophones can be bridged. During the ceremony, Abdul can follow the proceedings and nod 'energetically' because Emmanuel, his interpreter, translates into English from an ethnic language what Abdul does not understand (Achebe 1987, 212). Similarly, as Achebe's *A Man of the People* (1966/1989) seems to suggest, English as a literary language does not completely alienate non-English speakers, let alone illiterate segments of the population. In Achebe, national discourse appears to presuppose the existence not only of pluralistic voices uttered through ethnic varieties but also of a common linguistic choice through which esoteric and exoteric discourses become tenable. The elder's vernacular style seamlessly fuses with Beatrice's modern style. I will return to these issues later.

Generally, based on Achebe's writings on Nigeria, Anglophonism can thrive in the national discourse of a traditionally non-native English environment if it has functional value. In Achebe's representation, English serves as a linguistic bridge in the complex multi-ethnic and multicultural Nigeria. Even when he focuses on one ethnic group of the nation – the Igbo – the message presented in English targets a larger group belonging to the national community and beyond. In a multi-ethnic and multicultural society, national culture remains a conglomeration of cultures and beliefs as no single culture can exclusively claim national space. Through his fictional representation, Achebe makes the otherwise *alien* culture of one ethnic group discernible to the rest of non-Igbo readers. He uses the former colonial language, English, to address a national rather than ethnic audience, which thus becomes a vehicular language that helps to bridge linguistic gaps between disparate ethnic and social groups. Since English does not generate Igbo values, the language in this case serves primarily as a communication tool that facilitates cross-cultural exchange and discourse. Accordingly, English's capacity to accommodate various cultural and ethnic beliefs and indigenous idiomatic expressions helps Anglophonism to thrive in Nigeria's national discourse mostly amongst the educated African elite.

This chapter, therefore, examines Achebe's contribution to the Anglophone African literary-linguistic tradition by focusing on three elements inherent in his fiction: traditional Igbo literary values introduced into English, the sociolinguistic context, and Nigeria's national socioeconomic and political realities. These factors, I argue, shape the orientation of Achebe's fiction and his contribution to the Anglophone African literary-linguistic tradition. The local culture-specific literary elements Achebe introduces into his mode of Anglophone literary discourse include

Igbo proverbs, songs, myths, legends, non-English words and Nigerian idiomatic expressions. These literary-linguistic aspects represent the sociocultural elements of the formerly colonised people, which in the intermingling of cultures and cultural expressions embody the nature of Achebe's contribution to Anglophone African literary discourse.

Traditional literary elements and Achebe's aesthetics

The fusion of traditional literary elements in Achebe's novels orientate his fiction towards African rather than English aesthetics, even when he uses English as the medium for his novels. It follows that the English language as employed in his works is not static but dynamic, as one would expect from this fusion with particularities found in Igbo and Nigerian society. In fact, Achebe's writing largely has what Bamiro (2000, 72) calls 'Afrolect' literary influences as opposed to 'Eurolect' influences. Useful as this distinction is, it becomes reductive when applied to the multiplicities of African writings in English.

In fact, the variations in the Anglophone African novel – essentially a hybrid of a European invention, the novel, and African oral traditions, orature – demonstrates that such reductive taxonomies are inadequate. For example, the literary works of Nadine Gordimer have a heavy dose of what can pass for Eurolect influences, yet she writes primarily from an Africa-centred consciousness even as she writes within white-settler codes, and her works also contain some Afrolect features. In this regard, a language such as English and its literary tradition cannot operate in a space with African languages and cultures and remain unaffected by these. Moreover, many postcolonial African texts still have Afrolect influences despite lacking a significant presence of African oral traditions, mainly because of social heteroglossia – or the range of social dialects – in nation-specific contexts.

Social heteroglossia, as Mikhail Bakhtin explains in *The Dialogic Imagination*, constitutes the basic distinguishing feature of the stylistics of the novel. The novel 'orchestrates all its themes' through 'the social diversity of speech types and by differing individual voices that flourish under such conditions', which include 'uthorial speech, the speeches of narrators, inserted genres, the speech of characters' (Bakhtin 1987, 263). This ability makes the novel form a useful literary device that facilitates the interaction of English and indigenous African languages, cultures and beliefs in literary discourse. When nation-specific, these distinctive features can usually serve as useful indicators of a national literature. In Africa, of course, demarcating such 'national literatures' within the arbitrary colonially-drawn boundaries, thanks to the Berlin Conference, can prove problematic. However, it suffices here to say that those national boundaries can serve as a starting point but not an end itself. Nevertheless, when the national particularities, coupled with the consciousness of the author, are applied to art, the resultant literary works are identifiable with certain locales of the traditionally non-English contexts.

Overall, the introduction of English in many of the African linguistic communities has also helped to develop literary-linguistic features mostly amongst the educated elite specific to particular national contexts. Hence, in Achebe's novels we find Nigerian Pidgin English, a product of the intermingling of English and indigenous African languages. As Bakhtin explains, languages 'do not *exclude* each other, but rather intersect with each other in many different ways' (Bakhtin 1987, 291), and Nigerian Pidgin English emerges out of such an intersection. Against this backdrop, the term 'Afrolect' therefore needs a broad-based scope to reflect the heteroglossic literary-linguistic picture of African Anglophone literatures.

The thematic orientation of Achebe's fiction, the third aspect I consider in this chapter, constitutes an integral part of his linguistic and literary agenda. Achebe's preoccupation with the questions of leadership and political instability stems largely from events in his restive native country of Nigeria, a nation that has seen at least six coups in its first thirty years of post-independence existence, and a devastating 1966 civil war that pitted his native region of Biafra (seeking secession or autonomy) against federal forces (seeking to keep Nigeria united as a unitary nation). The close affinity between the nature of discourse embodied in the novels of a particular nation and the state of nationhood justifies the attention we pay to the socioeconomic and political context. Achebe's literary language and narration variously represent and critique such a post-colony, a process the writer compares to a masquerade he talks about in *Arrow of God*, which allows one to 'keep on circling the arena' to 'catch glimpses' and have a 'complete image' of the event (Wilkinson 1987, 145). The context helps us grasp some of the literary devices in Achebe's novels.

Nigeria, like many so-called Anglophone African countries, retained English at independence from Britain in 1960 as the official and national language in the absence of a pan-Nigerian indigenous language. Such political linguistic support has helped to entrench Anglophonism in Nigeria's national literary discourse, and comparatively few African nations can rival its literary output in English. Consequently, the continued use of English in Nigeria's national discourse allows the language to serve as a vehicle for transcribing and assimilating beliefs and values of disparate groups for this multicultural, multi-ethnic and multireligious nation, an environment conducive to the emergence and sustenance of an Anglophone literary-linguistic continuum. Achebe's contribution to this Anglophone African literary-linguistic tradition, therefore, can be seen in terms of how he engages with the English language and its tradition to portray the Igbo society – as a representative group of the pre- and post-nation Nigerian societies – for a mostly non-Igbo audience.

Chapter 2

F. Abiola Irele confirms the place of English in Achebe's literary contribution when – in his 'Homage to Chinua Achebe' to mark Achebe's seventieth birthday – he lauds Achebe's 1958 *Things Fall Apart* because of the way this archetypal Anglophone African novel engages with the colonial encounter and the way it reformulates English, 'the inherited imperial language,' to give 'a special expressiveness to the novel's enactment of a decisive moment of the African experience' (Irele 2001, 2). This reformulation of the English language, then, becomes an integral part of Achebe's aesthetics and helps to place his contribution in the Anglophone literary-linguistic tradition. Indeed, the way Achebe localises English to enable his Anglophone literary project to reflect the local literary-linguistic context orients his works towards African (not necessarily European) aesthetics. In other words, the English medium used does not necessarily compromise his attempt to produce a work of art identifiable with Africa primarily because the values expressed, among other things, are typically African.

One of Achebe's accomplishments stems from his ability to produce *Things Fall Apart* in largely uncharted territory. Achebe embarked on his literary career at a time when modern African literatures – in this case in the English language in which Achebe opted to write – lacked an established written literary tradition despite many African writers having already published before him in English. His fellow Nigerian, Amos Tutuola, a messenger-turned-author, had published *The Palm-Wine Drinkard* in 1952 and *My Life in the Bush of Ghosts* in 1954 before him.[3] However, many African literary critics had for many years ignored his fitting place amongst pioneering modern African writers regardless of his obvious genius. In fact, Tutuola's books had received favourable criticism abroad and a denunciation at home in Africa. As Bernth Lindfors notes, 'Nigerians disliked Tutuola for the same reasons that Europeans and Americans treasured him: his subject matter was exotic and his grammar atrocious' (Lindfors 1972, xiii). Not surprisingly, Tutuola's works did not feature in the discussions during the landmark 1962 Conference of African Writers of English Expression in Kampala, Uganda. Later, his Western supporters also became critical of his works because they grew 'tired of his fantasies and fractured English' and his 'inability to develop new themes and techniques' (Lindfors 1972, xiii). What comes of this cold shoulder is the suspicion that only the English of a certain standard was acceptable, forgetting that in a continuum there would be varieties, some closer to the standard English variety than others. In the case of Tutuola, his writing was so much influenced by Yoruba syntax and idiom that it was hard for a traditional Anglophone reader to decipher what he was trying to convey. Despite being a writer of English expression, the absence of Tutuola's work at the 1962 conference indicates how many African writers of the time either overlooked or disregarded his work.

If Tutuola operated on one extreme of so-called sub-standard English, then

Achebe was on the other side of the spectrum of standard English. With *Things Fall Apart*, Achebe exposed another dimension of Anglophone African literatures that many critics could not ignore. Whereas they could belittle Tutuola's literary contribution, they could not do so with Achebe's. With a university education (as opposed to Tutuola's six years of elementary education), Achebe had more options at his disposal regarding how to approach his Anglophone literary project than Tutuola had. This chapter will not go into the merits of Tutuola's contribution since few can question his place in the African canon. After all, Achebe's literary contribution augments Tutuola's in the Anglophone African literary tradition in terms of integrating the particular, such as traditional lore, syntax, idiom and orality in general. Achebe helped to refocus our attention on an African discursive alternative to the denigrating colonial imperial adventure fiction.

Duality of purpose in Achebe's literary-linguistic project

Apart from helping to raise the profile of modern African literatures, Achebe's inaugural *Things Fall Apart* and his subsequent novels constitute an engagement with an already established Anglophone mainstream tradition. In his presentation, Achebe directly and indirectly engages with colonial and postcolonial texts. This is evident in *Things Fall Apart* and *Arrow of God*, novels that dramatise the penetration and entrenchment of British colonial hegemony in convoluted ethnicities. The allusion to colonial discourse in these novels situates Achebe's literary contribution as a counter-discourse. Achebe alludes to the nature of colonial discourse at the end and beginning of both novels, respectively. Towards the end of *Things Fall Apart*, a District Commissioner (DC) muses that in the book on Africa 'he planned to write', he would stress the 'story of this man who had killed a messenger and hanged himself' since it would 'make interesting reading':

> One could almost write an entire chapter on him. Perhaps not a whole chapter but a reasonable paragraph, at any rate. There was so much else to include, and one must be firm in cutting out details. He had already chosen the title of the book, after much thought: The Pacification of the Primitive Tribes of the Lower Niger. (Achebe 1958/1992, 179)

The District Commissioner's reductive process typifies the treatment of Africans in some Eurocentric colonial literature. The DC would in this case reduce into a paragraph material Achebe has used for an entire novel. By including this passage in *Things Fall Apart*, James Snead observes, Achebe 'pre-empts an attempted white usurpation of his story and his culture, trapping the "official" version within a more sympathetic history' (Snead 1990, 242). What Snead overlooks is the fact that such texts already existed in the form of colonial treatises and the imperial adventure fictions of Joseph Conrad and Joyce Cary. Since Achebe's novel responds to a discourse already in place, Achebe appears to undermine an established colonial tradition that perpetuated a negative representation of Africans. In this regard, Achebe attempts to de-marginalise Nigerian characters by creating an authentic voice that could otherwise have remained muted or distorted in typical Eurocentric texts.

The difference lies in the treatment and presentation of details, particularly what to emphasise and subordinate in a literary discourse. This same title, *The Pacification of the Primitive Tribes of the Lower Niger*, reappears as published work of one George Allen in Achebe's *Arrow of God*.[4] The book is presented as a colonial relic left behind after the 'pacification in these parts of the world was done' (Achebe 1964, 32). As colonial discourse tended to marginalise and distort the image of the colonised peoples, their culture and their history, Achebe's early novels engage with the West in a dialogue on Africa, seeking to provide an alternative voice to what appeared to be a monologue[5] on representing both Nigerians and Africans. In other words, Achebe's choice of literary language has a lot to do with the exoteric rather than esoteric discourse he engaged in.

Achebe's desire to produce a counter-discourse results from his exposure to colonial writings. While at the University College of Ibadan, Achebe found Cary's depiction of Africans in *Mister Johnson* of 1939 – set in 1923 colonial Nigeria – offensive to the sensibilities of Nigerians. Though Molly Maureen Mahood notes in *Joyce Cary's Africa* that the novel, 'like almost every masterpiece … has been misunderstood from the day of publication', mainly because of its 'African setting' (Mahood 1965, 170), Cary's characterisation of the novel's romantic hero, whom the author describes as derived from 'some intuition of a person' and not 'from life' (Cary 1939/1995, 257), leaves a lot of room for discontent among Nigerians in particular and Africans in general. Mister Johnson, a Nigerian character, is a child-like, mission-educated, comical character, whose incomplete Western education makes him a misfit among his fellow Nigerians and British colonial expatriates. Mister Johnson's mimicry of Western values ultimately leads him to his death after a series of mishaps. Despite being 'black as a stove, almost a pure Negro, with short nose and full, soft lips' (Cary 1939/1995, 1), Mister Johnson – a flawed romantic hero – lacks an African sensibility necessary to reflect a Nigerian character, which Harris (1992) calls a 'classic colonial stereotype' and Korang (2011) describes as a 'botched African product' of the colonial enterprise.

Of the many texts on Africa that Achebe disapproved of, he has continually singled out this one. Achebe accuses Cary, who once worked and lived in Northern Nigeria as a colonial administrator, of failing to see the Hausa 'like a proper Nigerian' would and for producing what is 'more of a caricature than a true description' (Afrique

1962/1997, 7). Achebe – as he has reiterated in a series of interviews – found this novel to have painted 'a most superficial picture' of both Nigeria and 'the Nigerian character', prompting him to consider writing and 'look[ing] at this from the inside' (Nkosi 1966/1997, 3–4). Looking at the Nigerian character 'from the inside' suggests a different approach to thematic treatment of the Nigerian subject matter in terms of representation as well as English usage. As an insider, Achebe attempts to show the disparities in the representation and knowledge of the coloniser and the colonised. This approach also commits the writer to engaging in the traditions, language and beliefs of his people, which are reflected in his English discourse, already indicating that the language he uses has to be different for it to capture the essence of the mannerisms, the place and the culture of his people in English writing.

Achebe chose to write in English both as a linguistic strategy to respond to colonial discourse, and as an aesthetic effort aimed at carving out a space for authentically African Anglophone literary expression. This resolve has implications for his Anglophonism as well. Such literary attempts in Achebe's preferred medium, English, make his Anglophonism specific enough to address Nigeria's literary needs but also broad enough to be acceptable to a broader audience beyond the scope of national boundaries or particularities. In fact, two scenarios regarding the function of English in Achebe's novels emerge: as an alternative voice in international discourse, it allows others to read about Nigeria and learn about the views 'from the inside'; as a voice of Nigerians within Nigeria, it allows Nigerians to look at the mirror reflection of themselves – or a segment of themselves. In either case, English serves as a communication bridge in a world of much cultural, ethnic, linguistic and religious diversity.

The Nigeria that emerged from British colonial intervention had at independence over four hundred languages (Cozier and Blench 1992). Of these languages, only English and Nigerian Pidgin English are not associated with specific indigenous peoples. They are therefore the only ones that are Pan-Nigerian 'in the sense that no ethnic group can claim rights to them to the exclusion of other ethnic groups' (Onwuemene 1999, 1055). The major languages in Nigeria, with at least 10 million speakers, are Hausa (also a cross-border language), Igbo and Yoruba. In this linguistic context, English as a *national* and *neutral* language enjoys a special privilege as the official language of administration as well as the medium of instruction. As the lingua franca of Nigeria alongside Nigerian Pidgin English, English allows indigenous political and linguistic groups to engage in national communication, ironically one of the positive outcomes of the colonial heritage. Generally, in Africa and elsewhere the colonial experience had been bitter. English is also a product of that bitter experience. Thanks to the arbitrary borders created at the Berlin Conference, the same colonial languages that were used to colonise Africans have served as languages of national unity in many African countries. Though in some parts of Africa colonialism divided up a single ethnic group among two or even three powers, it also brought together many peoples that had hitherto been separate entities under one nation, with English serving as a national language, as in Zambia for example.

For Achebe, who argues that he has 'been given a language and intend[s] to use it' (Achebe 1975, 102), the question has not been whether to abandon English but how to apply the language so that it reflects the local context and fulfils his literary rhetorical agenda. The outcome is Nigerian characteristics that Achebe introduces into the English language without desecrating the base language. An African writer, Achebe insists, should aim 'to use English in a way that brings out his message best without altering the language to the extent that its value as a medium of international exchange will be lost' (Achebe 1975, 100). This statement is important in understanding how African writers approach writing in English. Implicit in Achebe's argument is the fact that writing in English for Africans also imposes certain restrictions on how far they can manipulate the language without making it incomprehensible and inaccessible to traditional Anglophone readers.

Often overlooked in this observation is the fact that a language has a way of regulating a literary tradition that uses that language to retain its functional value. On the other hand, language is elastic enough to absorb non-traditional materials such as languages and cultures it comes into contact with or, as in this case, those it seeks to embody. In fact, Achebe draws a line between using a kind of English that reflects the local linguistic context and cultural experience, and distorting the language to the point where English – as a trans-national and international language – forfeits its function as the base (acrolect) of the Anglophone African literary-linguistic tradition. This partly explains why despite the seemingly over-use – and some would say extreme use – of Igbo words in *Arrow of God*, Achebe still manages to retain comprehensibility. Consider the following passage from *Arrow of God*:

> Ezeulu rose from his goatskin and moved to the household shrine on a flat board behind the central dwarf wall at the entrance. His *ikenga*, about as tall as a man's forearm, its animal horn as long as the rest of his body, jostled with faceless *okposi* of the ancestors black with the blood of sacrifice, and his short personal staff of *ofo*. Nwafo's eyes picked out the special *okposi* which belonged to him. It had been carved for him because of the convulsions he used to have at night. They told him to call it Namesake, and he did. Gradually, the convulsions left him. (Achebe 1964/1969, 6)

Disturbing as the Igbo words may appear to a non-Igbo reader in this intercalation, Achebe provides enough textual context for a traditional Anglophone reader to grasp the gist of the intended meaning. The Igbo words in the excerpt above also remind the readers of the indigenous language that Achebe introduces into the text. These words are also markers of the particular elements found in the linguistic repertoire of the Igbo.

Such anthropological details that Achebe introduces in his novels have attracted criticism, especially from Anglophone readers in the West. Snead, for one, observes that the European reader who is not familiar with Igbo traditions may find 'the presence of 'anthropological' detail in Achebe' a 'veritable declaration of war on the practice of dividing cultures and fictions into strictly national groupings' (Snead 1990, 241). Snead wonders whether Achebe and Tutuola were aware of the implications of the 'most casual manner in which they present African norms' in their narratives depicting the first encounters between Africans and European colonialists 'to primarily non-African readers', mainly due to the 'interpretative confusions resulting from their disregard of earlier segregations' (1990, 241). Snead further observes that Achebe's novels do not 'merely insinuate the unaware reader into a foreign and positively inferior consciousness' but also 'suggest a natural and indeed actual place for African cultures alongside or even admixed with European ones' (1990, 241). Though Snead refers to *Things Fall Apart*, *No Longer at Ease* and *Arrow of God*, all of Achebe's novels – to a certain extent – use traditional norms as part of the rhetorical strategy. The plurality of voices in these novels provides complementary explanations that make up for whatever is lost in some of the traditional forms that Achebe uses in his writings. What Snead appears to overlook is that the West is only a segment of Achebe's audience. Furthermore, Achebe has provided sufficient context to allow the plot and the major themes of the novels to be communicated without necessarily losing his diverse readers.

Ironically, Snead's observation can also be true for the bulk of Achebe's primary readership – non-Igbo Nigerians and other Africans. They, too, may varyingly not be as familiar with Igbo traditions – or the anthropological details Snead refers to – as the Igbo. As Achebe aims at 'presenting a total world and a total life as it is lived in that [Igbo] world', he 'cannot do that in a vacuum' and hence he creates 'for [his characters] the world in which they live and move and have their being' (Ogbaa 1997, 64). These *anthropological* details turn out to be part of Achebe's 'total world' and reinforce the values of the Igbo in an Anglophone discourse. Writing in a local context does not necessarily mean being a slave to clarifying everything about that context. This has been relatively true in non-traditional English contexts where English has been used as a vehicular language. The least an artist can do is provide enough social and textual context to jog the imagination and let the reader follow what is being said. After all, as the passage above demonstrates, the Igbo words intercalated in the text do not make us fail to follow the story.

Another dimension of this cross-cultural and inter-lingual contact is that the host language has terms that cannot be translated verbatim. Igbo words used in Achebe's novels such as *ogbanje* (a child who repeatedly dies and returns to its mother to be born over and over again) are culturally loaded specific terms without equivalents in English. Retaining such words in an Anglophone text allows English to borrow without altering the word and meaning from the host language.

There are also cases where Achebe uses words that can be substituted by English equivalents. Words such as *ilo* (the village green, where assemblies for sports and discussions take place), *nno* (welcome) and *osu* (the outcast who, having been dedicated to a god, becomes taboo and is not allowed to mix with the freeborn in any way) are translatable, but only *just*, since direct translation of these culturally-loaded words could make them lose the subtleties of the local belief system. Then there is also the age-old problem of translation, whereby different translators might translate a particular word or term differently. For a word such as *chi*, the text provides 'personal god' as its English equivalent, but the meaning lacks the philosophical depth of the Igbo word that reflects the local belief system. In fact, the use of *chi* exposes some of the shortcomings of translation, as Lindfors (1972) demonstrated. For example, Donatus Ibe Nwoga, an Igbo, in 'The *Chi* Offended' supports Achebe's translation of *chi* as 'personal god' (Nwoga, 1964), whereas Austin Shelton in 'The Offended *Chi* in Achebe's Novels' prefers to translate the term as 'God within' (Shelton 1964) and Victor Uchendu, an Igbo anthropologist, explains it in *The Igbo of Southeast Nigeria* as 'the Igbo form of guardian spirit' (Uchendu 1965). These varied translations of the same word justify Achebe's use of the Igbo word in English discourse. These personal gods serve as guardian angels that can also bring bad luck and occupy one of the lowest ranks in the cosmos of Igbo deities. Some words may also receive a general translation that lacks the specific reference: *ekwe* (Achebe 1964/1969, 51) translates into drum, but the Igbo have many kinds of drums, including *udu*, a drum made from pottery. All these Igbo words become an integral part of Achebe's rhetorical strategy since they attempt to persuade the reader to accept them as part of the literary-linguistic context that feeds his Anglophone African novels.

Achebe further appropriates traditional modes of storytelling and oral literary expressions in the form of Igbo proverbs (in translation), local idiom, or Nigerian pidgin in his novels to reinforce the presence of Nigerian characteristics in his discourse, but also because of their persuasive potential. In fact, the influence of the host culture and language goes beyond issues of language usage: it extends to representing the host culture's mannerisms and ways of life. For example, early in *Things Fall Apart* we read:

> Having spoken plainly so far, Okoye [a musician whom Okonkwo's father owes a debt] said the next half a dozen sentences in proverbs. Among the Ibo the art of conversation is regarded very highly, and Okoye was a great talker and he spoke for a long time, skirting around the subject and then hitting it finally.

> In short, he was asking Unoka to return two hundred cowries he had borrowed from him more than two years before. (Achebe 1958/1992, 4)

This passage introduces the context in which the Igbo use proverbs and establishes their role in discourse. Okonkwo says: 'I am not afraid to work. The lizard that jumped from the high Iroko tree to the ground said he would praise himself if no one did' (Achebe 1958/1992, 18). The proverb carries more weight and meaning than all the words that he uses to explain his need for borrowing yams for planting. As Egar (2000, 229) notes, Achebe 'sees, in proverbs, a means to persuade the Western European reader of the authenticity of the traditional African language – a language that is clear, transparent, and quintessentially innocent', and uses them to demonstrate 'the drastic difference between African rhetoric and the Western European'. Whereas proverbs constitute an art of persuasion, it is erroneous to assume (as Egar does) that Western Europeans are the primary audience, since the context of these proverbs is representative of the situations in which they were used. Moreover, all kinds of readers can appreciate such a portrayal, whether African or non-African. We have been conditioned to accept the assumption that because Achebe is writing in English, his audience must be Western European, which is far from the truth and needs qualification as it can be misleading.

This explains why Egar – as noted above – appears to insist on Achebe using proverbs as a 'means to persuade the Western European reader of the authenticity of the traditional African language'. Yet, there is evidence to support the view that, despite their being written in English, the primary audience of these African works was not necessarily in the West. In fact, as Ruth-Hamilton Jones (1998) and Becky Clarke (1998), editors of the African Writers Series (AWS) at Heinemann, noted in their respective talks 'The African Writers Series' and 'The African Writers Series: History, Development and Effect of the Series on African Cultures and Publishing' affirm, the primary audience for the AWS was Africa, as the books were mainly to be sold in African bookshops which dealt exclusively in educational books. In fact, the severe economic depression on the continent in the mid-1980s hit the series hard because its major sales were in Africa. Moreover, as Achebe (1975, 68) illustrated, his books were initially primarily sold in Nigeria, Africa and the West, in that order of importance. To illustrate his point, Achebe pointed to the 1964 sale figures of *Things Fall Apart*, which in cheap paperback edition sold about 800 copies in Britain, 20 000 in Nigeria and 2 500 in the rest of the market. The same pattern was true of *No Longer at Ease*. Now the series is mostly sold in the US, mainly to students of literature, politics and social studies.

Chapter 2

Beyond stereotyping: The implication of Achebe's aesthetics

There is a further mistaken belief that proverbs are typically African or are the prerogative of the African literary domain. Everywhere – Asia, Europe, the Americas – people have used proverbs since time immemorial. Even in traditional English literature the use of proverbs is not a novelty. In performance genres, for example, the use of proverbs has been 'maintained in popular cultural forms as diverse as mystery novels, American country songs and parlour games' because proverbs are 'a witty unit of discourse' (Abrahams and Babcock 1977, 413, 415). The difference in this case is the particularised way in which Achebe uses Igbo proverbs generated in a specific social context but reproduced in an Anglophone text in a manner that makes the meaning discernible to non-Igbo readers. The proverbs have been removed from the oral context in which they were produced and immortalised in written discourse in the text. Thus 'these generic devices' of proverbs become severed 'from the interactional situation they have come to "name"', so leading to '*de-situation*' and '*de-contextualization*' since the proverb 'now exists in a different medium' (Abrahams and Babcock 1977, 418) devoid of the actual social situation and context. Outside the Igbo and oral literary context, Achebe grafts these proverbs into his text not only to reflect the role they play in a traditional Igbo social context but also to appropriate them and turn these adages into rhetorical tools for his fiction. Such usage denotes a convergence of the oral literary culture of the Igbo and the Anglophone mode of expression. As proverbs are an integral part of the discourse of his linguistic community, Achebe appropriates and makes them part of his literary project because of the way they help develop the themes of his novels. These proverbs perform both a stylistic and rhetorical function in Achebe's narratives. This latter part of using proverbs as a rhetorical strategy in national discourse confirms how adaptive artists and languages can be in pan-, trans-, and international discourse. Overall, an initially esoteric literary and communication tool for the Igbo transforms into a communication tool in Anglophone African literary discourse aimed at an exoteric audience.

At one level, proverbs reflect local literary-linguistic and cultural expression; at another, the proverbs in Achebe's writing serve as a rhetorical and literary device. Apart from Achebe's creativity, these proverbs are also ready-made literary and rhetorical tools appropriated from local lore. Irele (2002) classifies them as a 'genre' that has been concretised and passed on in cryptic form over generations. This demonstrates that indigenous languages and cultures are not inert in Anglophone African literary discourse. Achebe must be credited for being inventive and for exploiting the potential of these proverbs in his fiction. The rhetorical value of the proverbs in Achebe's writings has been well documented. Here a brief attempt is being made to consider how Achebe deploys these proverbs both as literary tools and as a rhetorical strategy for addressing issues pertaining to his country Nigeria and, by extension, Africa as a whole. In particular, these proverbs are used to summarise or carry the novel's major themes.

Another dimension that makes Achebe's writing unique in Anglophone African literary discourse lies in the way he manages to reflect linguistic nuances of one language (ethnic), that is Igbo, in another (trans-national), in this case English. Achebe succeeds in doing so partly through a process known as localisation, by successfully transferring the local idiomatic expressions of his characters into English speech without diluting the original nuances. In *Anthills of the Savannah*, for example, an illiterate elder at the head of the delegation from Abazon – who 'does not know ABC' (Achebe 1987, 113) – explains:

> *The people who were running in and out* and telling us to say yes [to Life Presidency] came one day and told us the *Big Chief* himself did not want to rule for ever but that he was being forced. Who is forcing him? I asked. The people, they replied. That means us? I asked, *and their eyes shifted from side to side.* And I knew finally that cunning had entered the matter. […] I called my people and said to them: The Big Chief doesn't want to rule forever because he is sensible. Even when a man marries a woman he does not marry her forever. […] So my people and I said No. (Achebe 1987, Anthills of the Savannah,115–6; emphasis added)

This speech, represented in vernacular idiom – like the one by the old man quoted earlier in this chapter – bridges the linguistic gap between the perceived original in Igbo (in this case) and the transliterated version in English. In this regard, Achebe succeeds in transmitting the common man's indigenous speech in English without losing the ethnic wisdom and nuances of the elders in his society.

Those who reproduce speech from one language in another tend to do so in a modified manner. Since the writer transcribes local idiomatic expressions in another language, he or she must ensure that the reported speech remains discernible to the reader while reflecting the local oral forms of expression. Similarly, Achebe maintains the distinctive manner of speech of Igbo elders in his fictional universe, creating a new form of idiomatic expression in English, which Bernth Lindfors (1972) dubs 'vernacular style' or a simulation of Igbo idiom in English. Achebe maintains such vernacular style even in his later novels. On this Achebe admits:

> There is a way in which the vigour of one language, its imagery and metaphors, can be transferred across. And there is a certain irreducibility in human language anyway, which is what makes translation possible […] you make this extra effort to get as close as possible to what you have in your mind. (Searle 1987/1997, 163)

Though writing in Igbo can solve this problem, doing so would not help a writer such as Achebe who envisages an audience beyond the scope of one's ethnicity, an esoteric linguistic audience. In many ways, it is the ability of English to accommodate nuances from other languages and cultures and still communicate the intended message that makes the language effective as a vehicular language of many ethnic groups in their attempts to reach out to others beyond the scope of their own ethnic groups.

In many literary studies, this process has come to be known – for lack of a better expression – as transliteration. Transliteration constitutes 'the rendering of the letters or characters of one alphabet in those of another' (Oxford English Dictionary 2010), which Onwuemene (1999, 1057) interprets as 'literal translation'. The word 'transliteration' first appeared in 'African critical discourse as part of practical advice to African literary artists writing in English' to 'condition' them to 'imprint the "signatures" of their natal tongues or cultures on their English language literary expression' (Onwuemene, 1999, 1057). In his press report on the 1962 Conference in Kampala, Uganda, Ezekiel Mphahlele, renowned South African writer and scholar, wrote: 'It was generally agreed that it was better for an African writer to think and feel in his own language and then look for an English transliteration approximating the original' (as cited in Wali 1963, 14). In other words, transliteration is a deliberately induced process aimed at communicating something in English that was first thought out in an indigenous African language. Whereas this could be true to a certain extent, there is also evidence that some of the literary features that appear in Achebe's novels are readily available in the cultural context of the Igbo transcribed for a non-Igbo audience.

Moreover, these characteristics in *No Longer at Ease*, *A Man of the People* and *Anthills of the Savannah* create a realistic portrayal of a changing Nigerian sociocultural linguistic context rather than merely constituting a manipulation of English. Mphahlele's explanation appears to ignore the fact that the very nature of African national audiences in many African nation-states demands such transliteration. Any intercourse between languages begets new linguistic characteristics. Onwuemene (1999, 1059) lists three outcomes of such transliteration: (a) the target-language expressions cast in the formal mould of source language counterparts; (b) source-language loanwords introduced into the target language texts by means of transliteration; and (c) source-language idioms and tropes introduced into the target-language text by means of transliteration.

The 'source-language idioms and tropes' Onwuemene refers to can translate into one of the ways through which Achebe embodies the social heteroglossia of the Nigerian linguistic and social context in his fiction in utterances such as:

> 'Let them eat,' was the people's opinion, 'after all when white men used to do all the eating did we commit suicide?' (Achebe 1966/1989, 145)

> '...Their intentions are good, their mind on the right road. Only the hand fails to throw as straight as the eye sees...' (Achebe 1987, 211)

> 'But fighting will not begin unless there is first a thrusting of fingers into eyes. Anybody who wants to outlaw fights must first outlaw the provocation of fingers thrust into eyes.' (Achebe 1987, 212)

Here Achebe represents the speech from the local language into English. These sentences demonstrate that local contexts influence Anglophone literary situations in literary discourse. Either in translation or in 'Nigerian' English, the use of local idiomatic expressions introduces nation-specific elements into English. Though the language structure may be the same, the meaning differs from what may be assigned to the same utterances in England, for example. Therefore, literary semantics cannot overlook the local contexts of the linguistic expressions that the new cultural and linguistic communities bring to English. In this regard, the words might be the same, and sometimes even the syntax, but the meaning differs because the resultant literary semantics is influenced by the cultural experience of a given speech community, in this case Nigerian. Such English usage does not represent a departure from standard English as generally spoken and understood, but demonstrates how local contexts influence meaning. After all, such local contacts reflect the emergence of idiomatic expressions that may appear strange to native English speakers.

In Achebe's later novels, we also find diglossic – and sometimes polyglossic – situations because the representations traverse beyond those of one ethnic group, the Igbo in this case. Such representations lead to a complex linguistic environment that cuts across traditional conversational modes. These linguistic situations include the use of standard English among educated Nigerians, Nigerian Pidgin English, and a combination of traditional and modern speech. In fact, narratives in English also reflect the linguistic influences pertaining to the local context. On this point, Achebe notes:

> [T]his English, then, which I am using, has witnessed peculiar events in my land that it has never experienced anywhere else. The English language has never been close to Igbo, Hausa, or Yoruba anywhere else in the world. So it has to be different, because these other languages and their environment are not inert. They are active, and they are acting on this language which has invaded their territory. And the result of all this complex series of actions and reactions is the [English] language we use. (Rowell 1989/1997, 176-7)

Achebe refers to nativisation of the English language as it encounters Igbo, Hausa, Yoruba – all Nigerian languages. This 'nativisation' of English is an inevitable consequence of the contact between English and indigenous African languages. Kachru (1992, 235) defines nativisation as 'the linguistic readjustment a language

Chapter 2

undergoes when it is used by another speech community in distinctive sociocultural contexts and language contact situations'. The outcome of this confluence is twofold. The first is transliteration, as already discussed, and the second, Nigerian Pidgin English.

Here a brief mention of Nigerian Pidgin English is essential. It is one of the manifestations of social heteroglossia in Achebe's novels representing modern as opposed to traditional Nigeria. The exceptions, of course, in Achebe's oeuvre are *Things Fall Apart* and *Arrow of God*, which represent an earlier period before the development of such a language variation. This form of language also demonstrates that a language used in a particular locale cannot escape the linguistic influences of the host languages. For Achebe, this does not constitute a medium in which he could express his writing but rather one of the dialects to be included in his writing to reflect social heteroglossia without necessarily alienating the reader in the overall discourse. In *A Man of the People*, we find a conversation involving Chief Nanga, a corrupt Nigerian cabinet minister, Odili, the narrator, and Elsie, his girlfriend:

> 'If somebody wan make you minister,' said Chief Nanga, coming to my support, 'make you no gree. No be good life.'
> 'Uneasy lies the head that wears the crown,' said Elsie.
> 'Na true sister,' said the Chief.
> 'I think I tell you say Chief Nanga de go open book exhibition for six today,' I said.
> 'Book exhibition?' asked Elsie. 'How they de make that one again?'
> 'My sister, make you de ask them for me-o. I be think say na me one never hear that kind of thing before. But they say me na Minister of Culture and as such I suppose to be there. I no say no. Wetin be minister? No be public football? So instead for me sidon rest for house like other people I de go knack grammar for this hot afternoon. You done see this kind trouble before?'
> (Achebe 1966/1989, 62)

In Achebe's novels, this Nigerian Pidgin English brings Nigerian characters to a common linguistic level on the one hand; on the other, it introduces non-Nigerian English readers to distinctive Nigerian modes of speech. In fact, such pidgin serves as a sub-discourse within the main narrative frame of standard English. At the linguistic level, it shows the outcome of language intermingling. Achebe could have made this pidgin English the main language of his novel but desisted from doing so by ensuring that his novels remained accessible mainly through the employment of standard English infused with elements from the indigenous language, culture and social milieu.

Attempts at realistic portrayals can be defended by the fact that the absence of pidgin in *Things Fall Apart* and *Arrow of God* – Achebe's earlier novels – reflects the linguistic reality of the period so represented, and thus does not constitute a stylistic deviation – or deficiency. Those who raise the question of whether Nigeria has a national character (Sullivan 2001, 74) must examine some of these literary-linguistic features. Each nation, each ethnic group, has some peculiar characteristics that tend to be introduced into localised versions of English. The absence of pidgin English in *Things Fall Apart*, therefore, is compensated by the transliteration evident in the way Achebe transcribes Igbo speech in English for his Anglophone readers. Doing so results in some form of particularism that anchors these local expressions in a specific social context.

In other words, speeches of characters in *Things Fall Apart* and *Arrow of God* are English translations from Igbo or their equivalents because at this stage the speakers have yet to become assimilated into the new linguistic community of the new Nigeria. The variations in their speech acts occur in terms of how many proverbs and anecdotes they use to demonstrate rank and rhetorical prowess within the Igbo society of the novels. These conversations appear in standard English with occasional words of wisdom in translation. The same translation technique is deployed in Achebe's later novels – *No Longer at Ease*, *A Man of the People*, and *Anthills of the Savannah* – particularly when the characters are communicating with each other in local tongues, or they happen to be outside the Anglophone linguistic community. The use of pidgin also marks a shift from solely focusing on the Igbo – as the focal point of national discourse – to a multi-ethnic and more broad-based national outlook.

These novels – *No Longer at Ease*, *A Man of the People* and *Anthills of the Savannah* – represent a shift in the language usage in modern Nigeria. On the ground, the linguistic situation evolved whereby the Nigerians not only used English for communication but also transformed it to suit their own social and communication needs. Achebe was aware of this linguistic dynamism and captured it in his narrative to represent how Nigerians speak in addition to introducing elements of heteroglossia in his novels, in congruence with the complex national linguistic situation. Notably in this regard, Nigerian pidgin English constitutes an integral part of his narrative in *No Longer at Ease*, *A Man of the People* and *Anthills of the Savannah* because the novels project an era when Nigerians use standard English if they are well-educated and pidgin English if they are not, or when they are educated but want to converse with those with less education.

As mentioned earlier, this *brand* of English could be used to produce a distinctively Nigerian literary discourse, but this would be a *low* variety of the language (in the context of Bickerton's [1973] conception of a language continuum) that would only be accessible to an esoteric audience, something Achebe opted against by choosing to write using standard English. His restriction of this variety only to certain parts of the novel's discourse where characters actually use it in their dialogue demonstrates that Achebe wants standard English to be the primary conduit of his narrative. Functionally, this pidgin also brings together the uneducated, the semi-literate and the university educated to the same linguistic level in Achebe's novels.

Another significant dimension of Achebe's writing that demonstrates the way traditional elements enrich the literary output produced in another language is the appropriation of rhetorical techniques from a specific context to convey national themes in English. In *A Man of the People*, for example, Odili, who is almost of the first-generation Nigerians – as Achebe was – employs the same narrative technique deployed in Igbo conversational acts to explain complex problems:

> A man who has just come in from the rain and dried his body and put on dry clothes is more reluctant to go out again than another who has been indoors all the time. The trouble with our new nation […] was that none of us had been indoors long enough to be able to say 'To hell with it.' We had all been in the rain together until yesterday. Then a handful of us – the smart and the lucky and hardly ever the best – had scrambled for the one shelter our former rulers left, and had taken it over and barricaded themselves in. And from within they sought to persuade the rest through numerous loudspeakers, that the first phase of the struggle had been won and that the next phase – the extension of our house – was even more important and called for new and original tactics; it required that all argument should cease and the whole people speak with one voice and that any more dissent and argument outside the door of the shelter would subvert and bring down the whole house. (Achebe 1966/1989, 37)

In this passage, Odili follows the traditional way of developing an argument. He starts with an anecdote, or saying, in a traditional mode of speech before progressing to tell a story to explain what is happening in his post-independence Nigeria. The fusion of the oral and the written literary modes appears to constitute an attempt on the part of Achebe to deploy traditional and modern literary means at his disposal to reach the general readership. He borrows from the informal traditional mode of teaching and makes it a part of a broader literary discourse. Achebe, it appears, wants to exploit the same rhetorical devices employed in his native Igbo society to address the complex problems besetting his nation. It is towards such ends that he also uses proverbs. Anglophone African literary discourse did not sprout in a literary-linguistic vacuum; it benefits from many cultural and literary aspects of the host languages that, as Achebe would put it, serve as 'tributaries' feeding the main river.

Conclusion

As Achebe has demonstrated in anglicised African discourse, we cannot anglicise without integrating local traditions, lore and cultural values available in the universe of particular local contexts, hence the diverse variants of literary and linguistic

elements introduced into the Anglophone text. Since standard English remains the foil against which literary expressions are measured and the main conduit for the narrative frame for the creative effort, whatever aspects are introduced into the language do not necessarily represent a complete break – or departure – from the main Anglophone literary-linguistic tradition, but rather a literary-linguistic continuum with peculiar characteristics and divergences imposed by a localised context. Writing in Nigerian Pidgin English would be fine as far as writing for a particular audience in Nigeria is concerned. However, it would defeat the purpose of producing a work of art that is accessible outside the esoteric framework of a given linguistic community with a shared language. By opting to write in standard English, Achebe helps to support the argument that such language application in a traditionally non-English context facilitates rather than limits pan- and trans-national discourse. In fact, the various manifestations of the particular in the discourse of his novels demonstrate how varied writing in English can be. Indeed, Achebe demonstrates that English has utilitarian value, even in traditionally non-English contexts. Achebe's example also shows that an English usage continuum makes a mockery of earlier attempts to describe the application of English in colonial Africa as merely an abrogation and appropriation. Perhaps one of the counter-arguments in Anglophone national discourse is that it is generally elitist and exclusionary. But this ought to be explained in terms of demographic statistics, not in spatial terms. It is in this context that the next chapter focuses on Ngũgĩ, whose nativist project has ruffled feathers in the debates on the language of African literature. However, the chapter does not seek to reinforce Ngũgĩ's ideas but goes beyond the polarising linguistic debate to consider how both his English and Gikuyu texts engage with the Anglophone tradition to reveal the Anglophone African literary-linguistic continuum in much more meaningful ways. In this regard, the chapter situates both sets of books in the Anglophone African literary-linguistic continuum by examining how they deploy translingualism, and how the Gikuyu texts constitute a deeper form of engagement with the same Anglophone tradition Ngũgĩ appears to repudiate.

Notes

1. This chapter is an adaptation of my article entitled 'When 'the Centre Cannot Hold': Achebe and Anglophone African Literary Discourse', originally published in *LWATI: A Journal of Contemporary Research*, 8(2), 106–126, 2011.
2. Achebe states this explicitly, explaining that he wanted Kangan to be more representative of African nation-states rather than of Nigeria only.
3. By then Nadine Gordimer and Alan Paton had already published novels; however, being white, their writings were at that stage seen as part of mainstream English discourse, not African.

Chapter 2

4 *Arrow of God* is Achebe's third novel but second to *Things Fall Apart* in terms of the chronology of events. The novel is also set in Igboland.

5 I use 'monologue' to refer to the domination of Eurocentric colonial discourse even when it comes to representing colonial subjects.

3

Ngũgĩ, nativism, English and translingualism[1]

Introduction

When it comes to the issue of the language of African literature, Kenya's Ngũgĩ wa Thiong'o is never far from courting controversy. After all, the East African writer epitomises the view that African literature can only be written in indigenous African languages, which Obi Wali had initially championed from the early 1960s. Paradoxically, Ngũgĩ also holds the key to understanding the relationship between 'transliteration' and 'translation' in Anglophone African literature, two concepts that have come to shape the production of modern African literature written in English. Whereas transliteration refers to a process of thinking in one's mother tongue but writing in English and to an imprint of the natal tongue on the English language, translation is the process of converting words or text from one language into another. As Ezekiel Mphahlele (Wali 1963) once quipped at the 1962 Makerere Conference of African Writers of English Expression, translation refers to the act of making a literary production in an indigenous language available in English. More significantly, Ngũgĩ brings together these two aspects to reveal his contribution to understanding the Anglophone African literary-linguistic continuum in Africa. This chapter contends that his Gikuyu fictions (also in English translation) are as much an integral part of Ngũgĩ's engagement with the Anglophone tradition as his earlier works published in English. Cumulatively, they reveal the relation between English and indigenous African languages in the literary discourse of traditionally non-English contexts.

Negotiating through various critical issues raised on Ngũgĩ and his articulations on the language of African literature, the chapter uses his works to show that those originally written in English and those in Gikuyu benefit from similar processes of translingualism. The chapter further addresses the subject of the relationship between translation and minor languages, arguing that translation involves an inevitable and continuous manipulation of texts in which the subjectivity, ideology, visibility and power of the words complicate the very process of translation and reception

Chapter 3

of texts from minor languages to major languages. Finally, the chapter shows that Ngũgĩ's Anglophone and Gikuyu novels (in translation) are complementary in the exploitation of various manifestations of translingualism, despite arguments to the contrary.

Ngũgĩ had already published four novels over the course of 13 years before he started writing in his native Gikuyu in 1977. His shift from writing in a major colonial language, English, to writing in a minor indigenous language, Gikuyu, has attracted a great deal of attention, perhaps more than African writers with illustrious publishing track records in indigenous African languages. For example, Stephen A Mpashi, a Zambian writer writing in Bemba since the 1950s, has remained largely unknown outside his own Central African country, and Gakaara wa Wanjaũ, Ngũgĩ's countryman, has been publishing in Gikuyu since 1946, with little international acclaim (Pugliese 1994). The difference is that the latter two largely write and operate outside the Anglophone African literary tradition, whereas Ngũgĩ writes his fiction in an indigenous African language, but with an eye on an international audience. In fact, Ngũgĩ's novels in Gikuyu also exist as Anglophone novels in translation, a deliberate design on the part of the author, who personally translates his own works.

Ngũgĩ's novels have generated a great deal of controversy, partly because of the author's ambivalent stand on the question of language, and partly because of critics' failure to find common ground between his novels originally written in English and those written in Gikuyu and now being read in English translation. Ngũgĩ complicates the issue by making contestable statements about his oeuvre, which he calls 'Afro-European novels'. For example, Ngũgĩ (2004, 4–15) claims: 'I knew about whom I was writing but I did not know for whom I was doing it', as '[t]he people about whom I wrote so eloquently would never be in a position to read the drama of their lives in their own language'. Ngũgĩ's view appears to overlook the multiplicity of linguistic landscapes in Kenya, and the even more complex mosaic of ethnic languages in Africa. Because many Kenyans (Ngũgĩ's 'own people') cannot read Gikuyu, the phrase 'their own language' only becomes meaningful when his Gikuyu texts benefit from translation. But the translation of Ngũgĩ's Gikuyu novels, as Gikandi (1991, 164) has observed, 'seems to fall short of its epistemological and narrative ambitions', as 'readers of the English translation cannot fail to notice the extent to which Ngũgĩ's novel is imprisoned by the very Europhone tradition he was trying to disavow'. Gikandi (1991, 166) refers to Ngũgĩ's second Gikuyu novel, *Matigari ma Njiruungi*, whose 'eloquent English translation', he says, 'defeats [his] intention of restoring the primacy of the African language as the mediator of an African experience', since the translation serves as 'a double-edged weapon' that 'allows Ngũgĩ's text to survive and to be read' and yet be 'read and discussed as if it were a novel in English'. On the one hand, Ngũgĩ has issues with his novels originally published in English; on the other hand, his critics appear to have problems with his Gikuyu novels in translation.

In light of this opposition, this chapter seeks to answer two key questions in relation to Ngũgĩ's work: To what extent is Ngũgĩ right when he says 'I knew about whom I was writing but I did not know for whom I was doing it'; and, what do Ngũgĩ's Gikuyu novels in English translation reveal about his continued engagement with the same Anglophone-African tradition that he repudiates? The first question invites revisiting the original Anglophone novels Ngũgĩ dismisses as Afro-European; the second seeks to place his Gikuyu works in English translation alongside their English predecessors, exploring how they complement each other in exploiting various forms of translingualism. Part of the agenda of this chapter is to illuminate what these two literary projects reveal about translation in its broader sense in relation to minor languages. It further explores how any form of translation – in its wider sense – involves an inevitable and continuous manipulation of texts, which can obscure the popular belief that the translator acts as a bridge between linguistic traditions.

As an African writer, Ngũgĩ feels that if he does not write in a native language, he 'is deracinated and de-cultured', but if he 'write[s] in the imperialist's language' he 'risks absorption into the imperialist's culture' (Williams 1991, 54). Yet one can write in a former colonial language without necessarily being absorbed into it; inversely, one can write in an indigenous African language and still be 'deracinated and de-cultured'. The use of 'former colonial languages' in this chapter, as opposed to 'European' or 'language of the oppressor', is more fitting in the African context or, indeed, in any non-traditionally but formerly colonised nations than the latter. African writers may produce their literary work either in an indigenous African language or former colonial language since, as Mwaura (1980, 27) explains, 'Language influences the way in which we perceive reality, evaluate it and conduct ourselves with respect to it', as it 'controls thought and action, and speakers of different languages do not have the same worldview or perceive the same reality unless they have a similar culture or background'. The first contact language in which one conceptualises the world, however, does not necessarily have to be the same language in which one communicates that reality. It is perhaps with this in mind that Mazrui (1993, 360) suggests that the 'liberatory power' of language 'must be based, not on a reversal of values accorded to European versus African languages on the basis of a preconceived paradigm of linguistic determinism, but on disalienation that seeks to pose new terms of reference altogether', with language serving as 'an instrument of communication'. In this regard, the first contact language remains primary in shaping the consciousness of an African writer, whether one is writing in Gikuyu, Hausa, Kiswahili, Zulu or English.

Often overlooked in the analysis of Ngũgĩ's English works and those in Gikuyu (now in English translation) is how both sets of novels benefit from similar processes that can be dubbed 'translingualism', which Scott (1990, 75) defines as 'the purposive and artful reproduction within one language [...] of features from another language'. Although the terms 'translation' and 'transliteration' are often used loosely as inherently different concepts, they can also be treated as variants of the broader term 'translingualism' when it comes to the production of literatures from minor languages. The traditional term 'translation' – direct or syntax-directed – amounts to what Jakobson (1959/2000, 114) calls 'interlingual translation', which he defines as translation from one language to another.

Paradoxically, even indigenous African languages themselves are not immune to colonial influence, as Ngũgĩ himself has pointed out: 'in "The Language of African Fiction" his Gikuyu language also has "traces of colonial violence"' (Nicholls 2010, 195). African literary discourse, therefore, falls generally into two types. The first type refers to traditional forms of translation. The second, presented as transliteration (or what Gyasi calls 'creative translation'), 'manifests itself in African writing in the authors' transposition of African oral and traditional literary techniques of storytelling into the European written genre' (Gyasi 1999, 85). Broadly speaking, Gyasi (1999, 80) sees translation as 'encompass[ing] the process through which African writers incorporate oral and traditional literary techniques such as proverbs, repetition, folktales, etc., into the foreign medium'. Furthermore, Gyasi (1999, 82) notes that 'African writers are creative translators in the sense that in their works, they convey concepts and values from a given linguistic, oral culture into a written form in an alien language'. Gyasi's description applies readily to Ngũgĩ's writings in English and in Gikuyu, since the author consciously engages with other linguistic landscapes in Gikuyu, knowing that his writing will also be translated into English. This explains why he personally translates his first novel in Gĩkũyũ, *Devil on the Cross*, and his later novel, *Wizard of the Crow*. Ngugi's awareness of his dual (or even multiple) readership – in both Gĩkũyũ and English – is made explicit in his translation note in *Devil on the Cross* when he quips: 'In the original work, written in Gĩkũyũ, certain words and phrases appear in English, French, Latin and Swahili. In this translation all such words and phrases are printed in italics' (Ngũgĩ 1977, 10). This is an author who is fully aware of not only the power of translation but also the international nature of his audience.

Because of the complex nature of issues associated with translation, this chapter will rely on the more appropriate term of translingualism as defined by Scott (1990), which is a broad-based term that essentially refers to the phenomena relevant to more than one language that highlight the inter-relationship of languages in the communication realms as diverse people negotiate meaning. Indeed, translingualism can also refer to something that shares some meaning in multiple languages, or that works within various frameworks of different languages. One can even go a step further and place what Batchelor (2009) describes as translation under translingualism, since she does not simply refer to what Jakobson (1959, 233) calls 'interlingual translation' or translation proper. Batchelor (2009, 65) approaches translation in its intersection with linguistic innovation such as 'visible traces', or 'idiosyncratic' borrowings from African language in the Francophone narratives, and 'traces within traces', which indicate the presence of French lexical borrowings and adaptations in African languages. We get a similar picture in Ngũgĩ's Anglophone, or English-speaking, Africa. One can also consider Bandia's (2008) 'Translation as reparation: Writing and translation in postcolonial Africa', in which he proposes a new perspective for postcolonial literary criticism informed by theories of translation, underscoring the centrality of oral culture and artistry in modern African fiction. Bandia provides new insights into the ethics of translation relating to the politics of language, ideology, identity, accented writing and translation, and the place of translation theory in literary criticism, and affirms the importance of translation in the circulation of texts, particularly those from minority cultures in the global marketplace.

The first assumption on which this chapter is based is that there is a very thin line between transliteration, which Ngũgĩ relies upon in his earlier works originally written in English, and translation, which his Gikuyu works undergo, placing them within Anglophone African literary discourse. This commonality is what will eventually determine the place of both his Anglophone African novels and his Gikuyu African novels (in translation) in the Anglophone African literary-linguistic continuum. It can also help us to understand the relationship between the two sets of texts. Ngũgĩ is engaged in the process of negotiating between and among languages through translingualism. Ngũgĩ's first-contact language and dominant culture remain central in both his Anglophone and Gikuyu fictions, with his rhetorical agenda shaping his literary output.

The second assumption is that because the Anglophone and Gikuyu novels are both products of the same African writer who cannot, as he puts it, 'invent [his] own history or a new world' and thus 'write[s] from [his] social perspective, from [his] class perspective' even 'in a marginalised language' (Rodrigues 2004, 163), Ngũgĩ's Anglophone and Gikuyu novels (whether in translation or not) are not as far apart as we or even Ngũgĩ might believe. This second assumption opposes some of Ngũgĩ's misgivings about writing in English, a former colonial language, which he nevertheless embraces at the level of translation. Whereas in his earlier Anglophone novels Ngũgĩ subordinates feeder languages such as Gikuyu and Kiswahili to English, in his Gikuyu fiction he subordinates other languages, including English, to Gikuyu.

For convenience and partly because of Ngũgĩ's ideological developments over the years, which have influenced his attitude towards the language of African literature, I base this analysis on three phases of Ngũgĩ's illustrious writing career and contribution to the Anglophone tradition. These three phases also highlight the tensions and implications of his writing in English and finally in Gikuyu. The first phase covers the early years, when English remained the main conduit for his literary expression, and when he published *Weep Not, Child* (1964) and *The River Between* (1965). Then comes the intermediary phase when he published *A Grain of Wheat* (1967) and *Petals of Blood* (1977). During this period, Ngũgĩ became convinced that writing in English constituted a betrayal of the masses he seeks to represent, which led him into a linguistic crisis evident in *Petals of Blood*. It is during this phase that he also experimented with traditional dramatic forms in Gikuyu, resulting in the production of a Gikuyu play, *Ngaahika Ndeenda* (*I Will Marry When I Want*), co-authored with Ngũgĩ wa Mirii in 1977, the same year *Petals of Blood* was published. This experiment paved the way to what many critics describe as Ngũgĩ's 'post-English' period, when Gikuyu novels *Caaitani Mutharaba-ini* (*Devil on the Cross*, 1982), *Matigari ma Njiruungi* (*Matigari*, 1987) and *Murogi wa Kagogo* (*Wizard of the Crow* 2006) appeared. Since 1977, when he published his last novel in English, Ngũgĩ has also written three children's books and a number of essays in Gikuyu, and edited a Gikuyu journal, *Mutiiri*. However, the 'post' does not necessarily mean 'without' English, since the author has gone to great lengths to translate two of his three novels in Gikuyu into English himself. It should also be noted here that Ngũgĩ is in self-exile in an Anglophone country, based as he is in the US at the University of California in Irvine, and thus far from his ideal Gikuyu readership in Kenya, even as he continues with his crusade of writing in that language.

Apart from sharing colonial and postcolonial themes, all Ngũgĩ's novels in Gikuyu and English draw on his people's oral traditions, song, dance and – to a certain degree – mime, features that are retained through translingualism. This chapter also implicitly accounts for Ngũgĩ's hardening ideological and literary-linguistic stand in his engagement with Anglophonism. Anglophonism is a tradition of actively or passively using English as a medium of literary discourse in traditionally non-English cultures because of socioeconomic and colonial and neocolonial encounters.

The original Anglophone project

McLaren (1998, 390–391) contends that Ngũgĩ's 'notion of the centre is tied to his creative process and his conception of audience' and hence, in his early novels in English he 'practiced the kind of narrative strategies that grew out of his writing for the West', using English and Western novel forms that he later found to be 'counter to his political goals' and hence 'led to a shifting of his literary centre to influence a *Gikuyu-speaking Kenyan audience*' (added emphasis). This observation is reductive because it presupposes that writing in English amounts to writing solely for the West; furthermore, writing for a 'Gikuyu-speaking Kenyan audience' ignores the fact that Kenya is 'inherently polyglot' (Gikandi 1997, 136). Kenya has between 30 and 40 ethnic groups, including the Gikuyu, Luhya, Luo, Kamba, Kalenjin, Maasai, Asians, and a small group of European settler descendants. In many cases, members of these ethnic groups speak another language in addition to their own first language, either English or Kiswahili, or both. To familiarise all Kenyans with Gikuyu traditions and values, Ngũgĩ relied on the English language, which came with British colonialism. Ngũgĩ started to write in English because the language suited his anticolonial pan-Africanist and trans-national rhetorical agenda. Unlike the literature of any European country, which 'is first and foremost national and expresses the intelligence and the sensitivity of one specific people', African writing has 'an essentially hybrid nature imposed upon it by the diversity of the African realities it represents' and 'cultural realities of a large number of different countries and peoples' (Kane 1966 cited in Gyasi 1999, 83). Similarly, Adejunmobi (1999, 593) says that

> the development of a literature characterised by its own authors as 'African' is closely interwoven not only with the use of European languages, but also with the experience of colonialism and acculturation in Africa [whereby the] pan-Africanist and nationalist impulses at work in the emergence of this literary tradition necessitated reliance on a select number of common languages – common, that is, to the members of the movement rather than to the African populace at large.

In sum, the context in which Anglophone African literature developed created conditions that allowed for the emergence of an Anglophone African literary-linguistic continuum as defined in Chapter 1.

When Ngũgĩ started writing in the 1960s, he was aware of the advantages of the English language. Gikandi (1997, 132) reminds us that Ngũgĩ 'claim[ed] in his juvenilia that writing in English had advantages over African languages because the European language had a larger vocabulary', and that 'the identity and function of African literature depended on appropriating the colonial language to represent the African experience', which is a key to understanding the language of his earlier novels. And Ngũgĩ's engagement with the Anglophone tradition from the 1960s and the post-1977 period, when he chose to write primarily in Gikuyu, reveals the extent to which Anglophonism can serve the interests of non-native speakers, whether in a trans-national, pan-national or pan-African context. Ngũgĩ's first novel, *The River Between* (written first but published second, after *Weep Not, Child*), first manifests Ngũgĩ's attempt to reproduce literary-linguistic features from Gikuyu and Kenyan society in English discourse, and this also paves the way for his deeper engagement with the Anglophone tradition in his Gikuyu writings. The novel, which covers the immediate pre-colonial phase in Kenya, attempts to rewrite in English the history of the Gikuyu people as colonialism unsettled their social organisation. Since the novel depicts the effects of colonial intervention on Kenya generally and the rapid change it triggered, it sets the tone for Ngũgĩ's subsequent English or Gikuyu novels.

At this early stage of his career, Ngũgĩ experimented with the English language and the European realist novel form in the mould of Chinua Achebe of Nigeria. Ngũgĩ considers Achebe's *Things Fall Apart* as particularly important to him (Sicherman 1989) because of the way the novel engages with the English tradition. Irele (2001, 2) also refers to the reformulation of English, 'the inherited imperial language', when talking about this archetypical African novel's engagement with the colonial encounter. From Achebe's *Things Fall Apart*, Ngũgĩ gained a template for his own Anglophone African novels. This reformulation, grounded in an African cultural and linguistic context, had a different orientation from the one sourced from Europe. Early readers of Ngũgĩ's first two novels, such as Knipp (1967, 394), note that in *The River Between* and *Weep Not, Child*, Ngũgĩ attempts to 'communicate the characteristic thought of the African' by 'employ[ing] short simple sentences free of idiom and, for the most part, of transition words' with 'simple and monosyllabic' vocabulary. Knipp claims that this 'simplistic technique' enables Ngũgĩ to achieve certain effects by reducing statements and situations to 'the basic' as a way of 'communicat[ing] a kind of African mental process' but ends up making 'Africans appear rather naive'. But Knipp (1967), as one of Ngũgĩ's early critics, misses the complexity that lies in this simplicity. Indeed, as some of these early readers approached Ngũgĩ's works largely from a European literary tradition, they generally overlooked many particular African nuances typical of African aesthetics, including features in both form and content inherent in literatures from traditionally non-English or non-European contexts. In fact, some of these critics have tended to identify Ngũgĩ's *The River Between* and *Weep Not, Child* with an 'English aesthetics', mainly because of Ngũgĩ's adaptation of the European realistic novel form, the perceived 'radical discontinuity between Ngũgĩ's early and later fiction', and 'Ngũgĩ's apparent embrace of "Englishness"' when the extent of such 'embrace in his earliest fiction is riddled with ambivalence, ambiguity, and slippage' (Amoko 2005, 35). No doubt these two novels benefited from the aesthetic models of writers such as Joseph Conrad, DH Lawrence and Thomas Hughes, with the additional influence of Dickens, whom Ngũgĩ greatly admired; however, Ngũgĩ's original use of the elements of fiction indicates how the African sensibilities respond to prevailing realities. Amoko explains this ambivalence, inherent in Ngũgĩ's early works, in terms of 'colonial mimicry' (Bhabha 1993, 86), by saying Ngũgĩ's early novels might 'mimic canonical English texts', but they 'are almost the same but not quite, almost English but not quite' (Amoko 2005, 35). Generally, an Anglophone text produced in an African context by an African writer influenced by a different set of linguistic and cultural traditions cannot simply be classified as belonging to English aesthetics.

The language of honour in death that the narrator accords the female character, Muthoni, is anything but simple. Under missionary teachings, Muthoni, a Christian, deludes herself by stating that she has seen Jesus in an apparent case of suicide since she willingly undergoes an abominable rite of female circumcision to become 'a real woman, knowing all the ways of the hills and ridges' (Ngũgĩ 1965, 26). Dying of complications resulting from the genital incision, Muthoni cries out: '*I am still a Christian, see, a Christian in the tribe.* Look [...] I see Jesus. And I am a woman, beautiful in the tribe' (Ngũgĩ 1965, 53; added emphasis). Muthoni wants to embrace both Christian and traditional values, something missionaries discouraged. Ngũgĩ, who appears to oppose the rite because of the inherent danger but sanctions its didactic and rhetorical function, uses indirect discourse to criticise the West for its bigotry. He treats language as a cultural system in paradoxical ways, playing with his readers, to highlight the fact that familiarity with the language does not necessarily mean familiarity with the cultural context in which the language has been deployed.

The seemingly simple and direct language used in the passage does not disguise the contentious issues the narration reveals. The novel allows Muthoni to find the sublime in a controversial rite that traditional Christians would denounce. To accomplish this effect, Ngũgĩ juxtaposes the sacred, Christian liberation with the supposedly barbaric rite of female genital mutilation. Gikandi (2001, 66) says this should be read 'as a commentary on the tragedy of biculturalism in a colonial situation'. Amoko (2005, 44), on the other hand, treats this portrayal as the 'lesson to be learnt', since the building of 'cultural bridges' needs to be 'contingent on more substantive and critical terms than are presented in Muthoni's tragic biography'. This fusion may have a shock value for readers from a different sociocultural background. Thus, the reductive nature of the classification cited by Ngũgĩ's early critics overlooks both the local particularities that influence the novels and the authorial aesthetic and rhetorical agenda. Ngũgĩ's texts are informed by Gikuyu sayings, myths, legends and beliefs, as well as socioeconomic realities in Kenya in relation to Christian beliefs and European values introduced in the African landscapes.

Apart from the obvious influences from the oral tradition, we also witness three other issues at play in Ngũgĩ's Anglophone texts: an imposition of his native tongue and thought processes on an Anglophone text; the undermining of popular and misguided Eurocentric beliefs on Africa; and the incorporation of pluralism in novels that does not necessarily create a whole meaning that is universally accessible, even when a common major language has been employed. The imposition of indigenous language features within English literary discourse allows Ngũgĩ to include already-translated Gikuyu sayings verbatim for a traditional Anglophone audience, such as

'*Kagutui ka Mucii gatihakagwo Ageni*; the oilskin of the house is not for rubbing into the skin of strangers' (Ngũgĩ 1965, 3; added emphasis). Why go to such extremes if, indeed, the primary audience was the West, as some commentators have noted? The indigenous literary-linguistic feature Ngũgĩ imposes on English makes his discourse context-specific. Ironically, one of the complaints often raised against Ngũgĩ's translation has to do with the tendency to distort the meanings of proverbs. With reference to *Matigari*, Gikandi (1991, 166) notes:

> [T]here are moments when the eloquence of this translation depends on the translator's decision to suppress certain unique aspects of the Gikuyu language which, because they have no equivalents in English, might either prove difficult to the English reader or render the text less fluent. Such difficulties apply particularly to proverbs and sayings.

By retaining the Gikuyu original alongside the English equivalent, Ngũgĩ sidesteps this argument. Ngũgĩ not only acknowledges the significance of the first contact language his literary English attempts to embody, but also provides Gikuyu readers with the message in its undiluted form. The same claim can be extended to the use of vernacular words alongside their English equivalents, since they tend to stress the non-English context in which the non-English-speaking characters reside: '*Tiitheru*, of a truth' (Ngũgĩ 1965, 14; my emphasis). Miller (1990, 6) calls this process 'anthropological rhetoric', which provides the reader with 'necessary cultural information'. African writers writing in any of the shared former colonial languages are aware of the need to provide 'necessary cultural information' via linguistic and cultural translation. Thus, Ngũgĩ's early fiction can be said to have been 'conscious of itself as linguistic act' (Jackson 1991, 5), geared towards promoting a particular anticolonial agenda. In this regard, Ngũgĩ's dismissal of his own works written in English as Afro-European letters seems rather misplaced, since it ignores the intricate process that he, as the author, goes through in his negotiation between Gikuyu and other languages and cultures to produce African novels in English.

Novels in transition: On the threshold to nativism

Ngũgĩ's shift in his attitude towards English, which he had earlier placed on a pedestal, had more to do with his hardening ideological stance than with not knowing for whom he was writing, let alone the English language's failure to represent an African sensibility. At this stage, he had become politicised and embraced many of the socialist beliefs that he thought were largely a panacea to Kenya's and Africa's crises resulting from the dominance of Western-induced capitalism. Ngũgĩ's third novel, *A Grain of Wheat* (1967), highlights the problem of reconciling the conflict between the message, the language used and what Ngũgĩ sees as his target audience. His embrace of socialist ideals makes him realise that powerful anticolonial heroes promoting the cause of the common man, such as Kihika in *A Grain of Wheat*, would remain isolated from the very people they represent because of the elitist language they use. However, the question of audience is not as simple as Ngũgĩ would have us believe. As Mbele (1992, 148) points out, African society is also made up 'of other social groups, including intellectuals' and many of these are also sons and daughters of peasants and workers. Furthermore, Indagasi (1997, 197) sees Ngũgĩ's 'writing for peasants and workers who speak the language' (that is, Gikuyu) as 'wishful thinking', since 'writers write for whoever wants to read their works'. Indagasi (1997, 197) identifies Ngũgĩ's ideal reader as someone 'whose emotional vibrations move in the same direction as that of the author's intention', whom the author describes as once a 'complex, sophisticated persona of the 1960s, attempting to understand the multidimensionality of human experience', who has now presumably been reduced to 'a fairly simple, uncomplicated individual in search of quick and clear-cut solutions to the world's most intricate problems' (Indagasi 1997, 200). Indagasi's dismissal of Ngũgĩ's readership of his Gikuyu novels, as this chapter demonstrates, generally overlooks the influence of the more direct employment of oral forms and their implication for his writing and literary appreciation as well. Certainly, the novelist's readership, in both Gikuyu and English, is anything but 'fairly simple, uncomplicated'. Part of the reason is Ngũgĩ's conscious use of language and manner of presentation in his effort to promote his African-centred anticolonial and anti-neocolonial agenda.

A Grain of Wheat centres on the struggle to free people's minds from the constraints of colonialism in preparation for the assertion of national integrity and individual human identity. Stylistically, this novel does not constitute a radical departure from its predecessor, *The River Between*. Indeed, one sees African aesthetics at work even in this novel. For example, Harrow (2001, 243) observes:

> In many ways Ngũgĩ utilised the elements of fiction in *A Grain of Wheat* in a distinctively African way. War and its nightmarish consequences form much of the substance of the novel's themes, all of which are grounded in the specifically Kenyan experiences of the violent times that led to independence. The imagery draws upon the African environment, geography, and seasons in accordance with fundamental patterns that have little correlation to the archetypal values attached to them by European traditions.

Like *The River Between*, this novel falls within an Anglophone African tradition. Ngũgĩ, who had been depending on transliteration to incorporate cultural and linguistic elements in his Anglophone novels, here realises the limits of his artistic endeavour when writing in English, primarily because of his now strong belief in the liberating power of socialism. This political, rather than linguistic, inclination also explains Ngũgĩ's belated embrace of Obi Wali's fervent pro-nativist argument and constitutes more of a political manoeuvre than one based on the complex African linguistic situation. Wali strongly supported African writing in indigenous African languages. In fact, Ngũgĩ's present views on language have been very much influenced by Wali, whose article 'The dead end of African literature', which received a lot of mostly negative criticism, declared:

> [T]he uncritical acceptance of English and French as the inevitable medium for educated African writing is misdirected, and has no chance of advancing African literature and culture. In other words, until these writers and their Western midwives accept the fact that any true African literature must be written in African languages, they are merely pursuing a dead end, which can only lead to sterility, uncreativity, and frustration. (Wali 1963, 14)

Ngũgĩ came into initial contact with this article much earlier in his literary career; however, he was strangely 'unable to respond', despite being 'struck by the forcefulness of [Wali's] argument' (Owusu 1986, 1734). The article first appeared in *Transitions* and the editor, Rajat Neogy, gave Ngũgĩ a pre-publication copy. Then, Ngũgĩ appears to have been comfortable establishing himself as an Anglophone African writer. Nevertheless, what Ngũgĩ calls the 'Obi Wali challenge of 1963', which he later refers to as a 'historic intervention' (Ngũgĩ 1986, 72, xi), haunted him throughout his initial phase of writing primarily in English. He first expressed doubts about writing in English in a 1967 interview, the same year *A Grain of Wheat* was published. But it is in the subsequent *Petals of Blood*, published 10 years later, that his hardening linguistic stance starts to manifest itself in more concrete terms.

Petals of Blood redefines the direction of Ngũgĩ's literary career. In retrospect, the novel serves as a bridge between Ngũgĩ's fiction in English and in Gikuyu. As Ngũgĩ's last novel published originally in English, *Petals of Blood* demonstrates the linguistic crisis that steered Ngũgĩ towards writing in Gikuyu. Though the novel largely retains the same realistic form, it features more traditional songs in translation than Ngũgĩ's earlier novels. The novel also contains more folktales, oral history, mythology, proverbial wisdom and traditional lore than its predecessors. Furthermore, it is the least accessible of Ngũgĩ's works originally written in English. Mwangi (2004, 63) notes that *Petals of Blood* 'contains numerous untranslated taboo words' that are mainly 'expressions that are not used in polite society because they refer to intimate parts of the body, infallible beings, or phenomena whose mention would portend bad luck', mainly 'transcription[s] from a pre-existing oral text'. Mwangi (2004, 66) explains the problem of the 'untranslated language in the text and the novel's structural contradictions' thus:

> [U]nlike [the novel's] predecessors, in which non-English expressions are stylistically integrated into English and subordinated to the English discourse,

> *Petals of Blood* contains numerous non-English expressions that are left either untranslated or loosely hanging in the sentence structure in a way that would suggest the narrative's ideal reader to be a person competent in both English and Gikuyu [as well as Kiswahili].

The narrator in *Petals of Blood* presents the events from the point of view of Munira, one of the key characters in the novel, as follows: 'They also sang: *Kamau wa Njoroge ena Ndutu kuguru*' (Ngũgĩ 1977, 10; added emphasis). No linguistic aid has been provided, whether in the text, through translation or transliteration, or footnoting, as Ngũgĩ does for *Uhere* (measles) and *Mutung'u* (smallpox) elsewhere in the novel. In fact, a footnote sometimes only provides partial meaning: 'She shrieked out, *auuu-u, Nduri ici mutuike muone*, and fled in flight' (Ngũgĩ 1977/1991, 7). For the Gikuyu expression, the footnote simply says 'a curse expressing shock', something that could be picked up from the textual context. Mwangi explains that this orientation in terms of the anticolonial discourse in *Petals of Blood* is 'so haunted by a deep sense of Englishness that the Gikuyu of the text is coterminous with the colonial language, indicating the ubiquity of colonialism in the post-independence present' (Mwangi 2004, 72).

Since both languages address the same topic in the anticolonial rhetoric, one does not expect them to be so separate. Mwangi also notes Ngũgĩ's 'use of untranslated terms [as] conform[ing] to the narrative's desire to forge a decolonised English' and 'also ironically reveals how deeply colonial and patriarchal hegemonies are entrenched in the very articulations against them' (Mwangi 2004, 66, 67). De-colonised English, yes, since this has been Ngũgĩ's goal all along; however, the use of the untranslated terms also hints at something much bigger: Ngũgĩ's hardening stand and need to impose African languages more strongly on English discourses to promote his anticolonial and anti-neocolonial position. In this regard, Niang (1989, 130) notes that Ngũgĩ 'shifted very late in his career from an idiomatic standard usage of English to a contextualised one', whose discourse Jackson (1991, 8) sees as 'essentially a featureless standard English' in 'a "culturally realistic" style in which narrator and speakers alike sound like Kenyans'. These observations overlook the fact that Ngũgĩ's earlier writings, though largely in standard English, do not by any means lack context and neither are they as 'featureless' as these critics appear to suggest. On the other hand, these statements could also imply that the discourse in Ngũgĩ's later fiction is more overtly grounded in the linguistic and cultural ambiance of Ngũgĩ's society than in his earlier fiction. *Petals of Blood* shares the same radical anti-neocolonial themes with the Gikuyu play *Ngaahika Ndeenda*, along with a heightened use of oral literary features.

The context of the play's production in Kenya in 1977 and its impact amongst the ordinary Gikuyu convinced Ngũgĩ that Gikuyu should take precedence over

English for him to communicate effectively in the language and forms that the Gikuyu could readily identify with. *Ngaahika Ndeenda*, developed at Kamiriithu Village, demonstrates the influences of oral literary forms when published in an indigenous tongue. The play consolidates the use of the three principal ingredients of the Gikuyu oral tradition: song, dance and mime. The play utilises both revolutionary and traditional songs and dance to galvanise ordinary Kenyans – the Gikuyu speakers among them, at least – towards self-assertiveness and consciousness in a non-elitist language. As Ngũgĩ (1981/2006, 78) explains in his prison memoir *Detained*:

> I saw how the people had appropriated the text […] so that the play which was finally put on […] was a far cry from the tentative awkward efforts originally put together by Ngũgĩ [wa Mirii, the co-author] and myself. I felt one with the people. I shared in their rediscovery of their collective strength and abilities.

Thus, Ngũgĩ saw writing in an indigenous African language as a solution to the dilemma he had been wrestling with in *Petals of Blood*. Common Kenyans generally talked about the politically-motivated play *Ngaahika Ndeenda* (*I Will Marry When I Want*) on the streets, so much so that the authorities were anxious; the government feared that continued staging of the play could lead to violence. The play attacks capitalism, religious hypocrisy, and corruption among the new economic elite of Kenya. Subsequently, the government detained Ngũgĩ without trial in December 1977. In 1976, Ngũgĩ had co-authored a play with a university colleague, Micere Githae Mugo, called *The Trial of Dedan Kimathi*, but the English play, written in an elitist language, did not generate as much interest among the people and the authorities as the Gikuyu play. This play in English was based on the exploits of Kimathi, who had led the Mau Mau uprising, and was executed for it by British colonial authorities in 1957.

Following his arrest in 1977, Amnesty International named Ngũgĩ a Prisoner of Conscience. The subsequent international campaign spearheaded by Amnesty International eventually secured him his release in 1978 after a year in incarceration. In December of the same year, Ngũgĩ announced that he would henceforth be writing in Gikuyu. While in detention, Ngũgĩ had also drafted early versions of *Caaitani Mutharaba-ini* on toilet paper. The prison authorities seized the materials, but Ngũgĩ could recreate the Gikuyu narrative later translated into *Devil on the Cross*. Arguably, the ambivalence in Ngũgĩ's Gikuyu articulations on language in relation to his fiction feature more prominently in the aftermath of his bidding farewell to English symbolically in *Decolonising the Mind* (1986/1997): he felt that he had to write creatively in Gikuyu and translate (or be translated) into English for his non-Gikuyu audience. On the surface, Ngũgĩ might argue that he is contributing to Gikuyu literature; on the other hand, he knows that his works in a minor African language can only reach his now broad-based readership once translated into a major language.

The Gikuyu project and translation

This brings us to the second question based on Gikandi's critical response to Ngũgĩ's works in translation. As already pointed out, Gikandi (1991, 164) notes that the translation of Ngũgĩ's Gikuyu novel *Matigari* 'seems to fall short of its epistemological and narrative ambitions', as 'readers of the English translation cannot fail to notice the extent to which Ngũgĩ's novel is imprisoned by the very Europhone tradition he was trying to disavow'. As translations, can these Gikuyu novels escape the intricacies of translation, and, indeed, the fact that they were being reproduced in English at all? Here there are two points to consider. First, the major target-language (English) has its own rules and traditions that have to be negotiated to communicate meaning. Second, the distinct cultural-specific and linguistic elements survive the translation through various forms and translingual processes inherent in translation. Thus, these translated novels cannot be read as though they were originally written in English; conversely, the texts originally written in English cannot be read as though they were archetypal productions belonging to English or European letters. Both English and African text must be deciphered for context-specific cultural and literary-linguistic elements in order to be understood. Ngũgĩ's Gikuyu texts can, of course, be studied without any recourse to their English versions. In his Gikuyu novels, largely a mixture or a series of oral tales, Ngũgĩ makes no pretence that he is still courting the realistic mode. He sees the oral narrative as having a 'symbolic dimension' and hence his novel *Matigari* constitutes 'a symbolic poem with multiple references' (Ngũgĩ and Jaggi 1989, 248). McLaren (1998, 395) notes that Ngũgĩ's exploration of orature in these Gikuyu novels, now in translation as *Devil on the Cross* and *Matigari*, allows 'song and story [to] supplant the devices of the Western novel', even though we find such evidence in his English novels as well. Some critics also see these novels as representing 'a decisive break with middle-class intellectualism' (Lazarus 1990, 207) to end what Ngũgĩ (1985, 152) terms as 'self-colonisation' as he strives to identify himself more with the common people.

Since Ngũgĩ largely has to rely on translation, many of his critics question his seriousness in raising the profile of writing in African languages. Hauptman (2005, 5), for one, sees Ngũgĩ's writing in Gikuyu as merely 'a symbolic act', which 'serves no one except the author [...] and perhaps a handful of Gikuyu speakers', with 'no effect on the vast majority of his readers'. Also, Hawley (1992, 173) cautions that 'resistance like Ngũgĩ's condemns an individual writer or a resistant culture to irrelevance in the global village'. Arnove (1993, 293), for his part, treats Ngũgĩ's stand as 'fundamentally idealist', which 'fails to take into account the complex set of practices and structural relationships […] that define one's standpoint and sense of the world, practices which are often oppositional to or relatively autonomous of the language of imposition'. These accusatory views notwithstanding, Ngũgĩ's choice to write in Gikuyu is not necessarily the problem. The truth is that what Ngũgĩ says about Gikuyu writings as authentic African texts can also be true about his writing in English. His statement in *Decolonising the Mind*, 'I believe that my writing in Gikuyu language, a Kenyan language, an African language, is part and parcel of the anti-imperialist struggles of Kenyan and African peoples' (Ngũgĩ 1986/1997, 28), for example, applies to his writing in English and his Gikuyu works in English translation as well: they are also 'part and parcel of the anti-imperialist struggles of Kenyan and African peoples'.

If Ngũgĩ's argument had been restricted to tapping his literary genius in Gikuyu and producing what he would rather classify as 'true African' novels in his native Gikuyu, then his argument might have stood. Indeed, writing in Gikuyu offers him some advantages. By first writing in Gikuyu, Ngũgĩ makes it easy to experiment further with the traditional oral literary forms such as songs and the remodelled oral methods of storytelling that Gikuyu readers can identify with without necessarily worrying about 'the restrictive jacket of a realist portrait' (Ngũgĩ and Jaggi 1989, 248). After all, many of the critics of Ngũgĩ's so-called post-English phase have pushed him towards disengagement with European-inspired forms. Although writing in English may not be as effective as writing in Gikuyu in terms of direct representation of the local sociocultural and linguistic values, it does succeed at the level of representation to concretely embody these values through translingualism. Indeed, Ngũgĩ now admits that 'it is possible to achieve orality in English or other European languages'. Such possibilities are expansive: 'It seems to me that the possibilities of an oral literature or the verbal arts [are] so vast that African literature be it in European languages or African languages can only gain from that reliance' (McLaren 1998, 396). In effect, this realisation demonstrates that his original Anglophone and Gikuyu African novels (also available in translation) are complementary.

In this regard, Gikandi's (1997) observation on the contradictions inherent in Ngũgĩ's literary-linguistic theory and arguments on language ought to be acknowledged with caution. Gikandi (1997, 139) identifies 'three (Europhonic) theoretical positions that Ngũgĩ needed to resolve if he hoped to regenerate his writing [in Gikuyu] and to sustain its function as a mode of social criticism': one, 'confront[ing] his unquestioning belief in the efficacy of the nineteenth-century European novel, its conventions of realism, and its modes of linguistic representation'; two, of language 'resolv[ing] the tension between his materialist theory of language and his nationalist inheritance as an instrument of nativism'; and, three, 'propos[ing] a new program that would mediate the ambivalent relation between language and national identity' on whether the nation 'depend[s] on a single unifying language to sustain its identity' or 'the national space [is] inherently polyglot', a situation that 'continues to haunt cultural production in Africa'. Both Ngũgĩ's Gikuyu and Anglophone texts appear to provide some answers to the questions that Gikandi raises, particularly on the issue of national space as 'inherently polyglot'. Ngũgĩ's *Caaitani Mutharaba-ini* (*Devil on the Cross*) not only includes Kiswahili lexical borrowings, but also untranslated English expressions.

Also, Ngũgĩ's more ambitious and adventurous use of orature, as many have noted, offsets some of the blows he has received for his use of the European realist form. Otherwise, one would wonder why an author who had perfected his art of storytelling with *A Grain of Wheat*, or even *Petals of Blood*, should embrace largely traditional forms of storytelling in *Devil on the Cross* and *Matigari*, which some readers are not comfortable with. In fact, Ngũgĩ does acknowledge that what shapes fictional narratives is the question of language and how one 'use[s] words, imagery', with matters of form being secondary (Rao 1999, 165). In addition, as Williams (1991, 61) notes, 'His Gikuyu-language novels are rich examples of magical realism and allegory with clear debts to a variety of European and African literary traditions. Historically, literature borrows across linguistic boundaries.' Williams' observation confirms the interdependency of literary forms – that is, African and the Western-derived aesthetics – and especially how they inform and interrogate each other.

Ngũgĩ's novels in Gikuyu are more firmly oriented towards the politics of commitment he highlights in *Writers in Politics* and *Detained* than his earlier novels in English. Lovesey (2000, 65) observes that *Devil on the Cross* 'perhaps too stridently for some Western readers, at least, declares its message about neocolonialism and the means to correct it, so boldly and relentlessly, in places nearly choking on its expression of outrage'. This, however, should not come as a surprise, since Ngũgĩ can afford such bold terms and even licence through such direct address to his so-called common readers in their language. The 'common people' may not feel offended by the direct condemnation of exploiters and exploitation because they are victims of such exploitation. And yet, Ngũgĩ also wants to reach other, more diverse, readers with his Gikuyu novels in translation. After all, he always has one eye on the broader, exoteric, diverse international audience, even as he writes in Gikuyu. It is, therefore, important to consider the context-specific literary-linguistic and cultural features that survive in the translations through translingualism and their effect on readership. In this regard, *Devil on the Cross* assumes a special place amongst Ngũgĩ's Gikuyu novels in translation for two reasons: as his first Gikuyu novel, it sets the framework for his subsequent efforts; and the fact that the author translated the novel himself facilitates the comparison of the two versions of it, and their relationship to the Anglophone African tradition. Ngũgĩ's translation provides us with a glimpse of what he sees as the relationship between the Gikuyu original and its translated English version (although one can argue – as some have – that Ngũgĩ may have written two texts, with one based on the other). In his footnote to *Devil on the Cross*, Ngũgĩ (1982/1987) explains that 'in the original work, written in Gikuyu, certain words and phrases appear in English, French, Italian, Latin, and [Ki]Swahili, and thus in translation all such words and phrases are printed in italic type'. If the audience is really primarily made up of peasants and workers who happen to be Gikuyu speakers, as Ngũgĩ implies, then how would these 'simple' folk be able to understand all of these languages?

In Ngũgĩ's Gikuyu original, many context-specific features lose their nuances when translated. For example, Gikandi (1991) in 'The Epistemology of Translation' notes that the Gikuyu title *Matigari ma Njiruungi* loses its allusions to the Mau Mau, Kenya's freedom fighters who were dreaded by the white settlers, and simply becomes the central character's name. *Matigari* is the only Gikuyu novel by Ngũgĩ not translated by the author. The novel was translated by Wangui wa Goro a year after it went out in print. But there are also gains. A good example can be drawn from Mwangi's interpretation of the original Gikuyu text *Caitaani Mutharaba-ini*, in which a character's bulging stomach is described in terms of a dead metaphor for victimisation, whose very familiarity suggests that 'victimisation has become commonplace in postcolonial Kenya' (Mwangi 2004, 38). As Mwangi (2004, 37–38) further explains, Ngũgĩ presumably knows that this dead metaphor – which concerns an invading hyena – 'would appear novel and fresh in an English transliteration'. Just as he has proven through transliteration in his original Anglophone novels, Ngũgĩ, as translator of his own works, is a conscious craftsman, negotiating between the minor language of Gikuyu and the target major language of English to communicate through the manipulation of the language of his texts. Indeed, Ngũgĩ, as author and translator, maintains sight of the rhetorical agenda that he promotes so well through language. In his Gikuyu novels, Ngũgĩ is always aware of what to expect from an Anglophone audience, since he makes translation an integral part of his agenda.

Despite its orientation towards the oral, *Devil on the Cross* has to be treated as written literary output (like Ngũgĩ's previous Anglophone novels). In fact, the novel also reproduces some of the features available in the local context in the English version. Generally, the Gikuyu language allows Ngũgĩ to make some adjustments to his writing. Both *Devil on the Cross* and *Matigari* deploy the journey and quest motif common in oral tales. Moreover, novels in Gikuyu thrive on allegory, typical of fabulist literature, even as they strive to represent the realistic concerns of Kenyans and other Africans. The plot of *Devil on the Cross* centres on the tragedy of a beautiful female character, Wariinga, who symbolises the nation (just as the female protagonist, Wanja, does in *Petals of Blood*). The character is taken advantage of by male characters, who are largely portrayed as leeches. In this regard, the storyteller uses this symbolic character to narrate a tragic story of contemporary Kenya, raped and abused by the devil, who represents the face of capitalism in the novel. The use of allegory and traditional forms of storytelling constitute a choice that Ngũgĩ has to make, whether he writes in English or Gikuyu.

In their linguistic analysis of *Devil on the Cross*, Kasanga and Kalume (1996, 44) conclude that 'more than solely being a result of translation, the use by Ngũgĩ in his novel of "idiosyncratic forms" of English, replete with Gikuyu and Kiswahili syntactic and lexical borrowings, forms of African narratives and biblical language' serves to communicate 'African culture and art in an unaltered manner and in a medium which might be perceived as close to the Gikuyu and Kiswahili idioms used by Kenyans'. They also note Ngũgĩ's 'Africanisation of English', which he accomplishes by 'inserting items from Gikuyu and Kiswahili and forms of African narratives in English' as 'a deliberate use of hybrid forms of language that would be more relevant to the oral tradition than to the written form' (Kasanga and Kalume 1996, 44). In other words, Ngũgĩ contextualises English in the Kenyan environment to ensure that the stylistic, syntactic and lexico-semantic forms relevant to Gikuyu (and to Kiswahili to a certain degree) should appear not only in the English translation, but also in all other translations. (It is possible that had Ngũgĩ written this novel directly in English, he might still have been able to fulfil the same rhetorical agenda.) Because of the specific context in which this language has been nativised, the resultant literary language inevitably increases the burden of interpretation on readers from different linguistic and cultural backgrounds. It is apparent that Ngũgĩ writes consciously for a diverse audience: the Gikuyu readers who read his original stories in Gikuyu, and the non-Gikuyu readers who read his works in translation. Ngũgĩ also places certain demands on his Gikuyu readers to be familiar with his key languages – Kiswahili and English – in addition to Gikuyu. For example, the author leaves some well-known English quotations from the Bible untranslated in the original Gikuyu text. After introducing the Parable of Five Talents in Gikuyu, the narrator tells the rest of the parable in English (the words in emphasis):

> She heard the voice of Mwireri wa Mukiraari soothing them to sleep with the story of the man who was about to travel to a far country and who called his servants and delivered unto them five talents, two talents, one talent [originally in Gikuyu, with the following italicised words in English in the Gikuyu text] [...] *Then he that had received the five talents went and traded with the same, and made five talents more. And likewise he that had received two, he also gained another two. But he that had received one went and dug in the earth and hid his lord's money. After a long time, the lords of those servants returned, and reckoned with them, and he that had received [...] talents.* (Ngũgĩ 1982/1987, 98)

The parable is familiar to readers of the New Testament. The rhetorical agenda is not clear until the master of ceremonies reminds the gathered foreign guests in the cave, in English, 'The flag of independence can be likened unto a man travelling unto a far country, who called his own servants, and delivered unto them his goods' (Ngũgĩ 1982/1987, 174). Here, the speaker directly connects the parable to the much maligned 'flag independence', which refers to the political independence African nation-states received from their former colonial administrators, but without getting concomitant economic liberation, to illustrate how such teachings 'send their souls and minds to sleep' (Ngũgĩ 1982/1987, 81). The English expressions and other intercalated words left untranslated in the Gikuyu text raise questions about whether Ngũgĩ really wanted Gikuyu readers without any access to these languages to read these texts. For non-Gikuyu readers these expressions do recover certain rhetorical functions in the English version, thus affirming the claim that Ngũgĩ kept his international audience in sight when writing this novel in Gikuyu.

Conclusion

This chapter primarily set out to answer two questions: To what extent is Ngũgĩ right when he says, 'I knew about whom I was writing but I did not know for whom I was doing it'; and, what do Ngũgĩ's Gikuyu novels in English translation reveal about his continued engagement with the same Anglophone African tradition that he repudiates? The first question invited us to revisit the original Anglophone novels Ngũgĩ dismisses as Afro-European novels; the second question helped to situate Ngũgĩ's Gikuyu works in English translation alongside their English predecessors to explore how they complement each other in exploiting various forms of translingualism. From the discussion, several conclusions can be drawn. Rather than focus on the ambiguity associated with Ngũgĩ's arguments towards the language of African literature, it is better to spotlight what we learn about translation and transliteration, or simply translingualism, from his works. Such an approach broadens the horizon of our understanding of literatures produced in the so-called minor languages and their rhetorical agenda, as well as their connection to translation. To begin with, it has been observed that any writing that targets a trans-national readership, whether in translation or transliteration, is understandably tied to the rhetorical agenda of the author. Ngũgĩ remains conscious of multiple audiences, even as he transliterates or translates his works. Also, local particularities in language and culture have a way of retaining their presence in a work of art that has been informed by a minor language, even when reproduced in a major language through translingualism, since minor languages and cultures are not inert in this process. Indeed, Ngũgĩ varyingly retains context-specific cultural and literary-linguistic features in his novels, whether originally produced in English or translated into that language. Furthermore, translingualism helps to retain the cultural and linguistic features of one language in another, whether directly written in a major language (through transliteration) or translated from a minor language. In fact, there appears to be a close affinity between translation and transliteration. Ngũgĩ, in either process, reinforces his literary/rhetorical agenda by negotiating between his local culture and language on the one hand and the target-language on the other, to ensure that particular literary-linguistic and cultural features are not lost in the major language.

Because of the thin borderline between translation, transliteration, and even translingualism, there is a close relationship between Ngũgĩ's fiction in English and in Gikuyu (in translation). Ngũgĩ, even in his Gikuyu fiction, appears to be writing for a particular esoteric as well as a general exoteric audience. Many of Ngũgĩ's critics, therefore, should concentrate on what we learn about Ngũgĩ's contribution not only to translation studies, but also the relationship between minor and major languages through his use of translingualism. In short, to fully grasp Ngũgĩ's complementary African Anglophone and Gikuyu novels, both in themselves and in translation, we must consider elements of translingualism variously at play in the novels in English, where transliteration dominates, and the Gikuyu versions in English, where translation and other forms of translingualism occur. As Ngũgĩ's works illustrate, there is a great deal that we still can learn about the processes of transliteration, translation and translingualism in general, particularly as they relate to minor language literatures, such as those originally produced in Gikuyu, that are subsequently transliterated or translated into major languages.

Note
1   This chapter is an adaptation of my article entitled 'Beyond Nativism: Translingualism and Ngũgĩ's Engagement with Anglophonism', originally published in *Perspectives: Studies in Translation Theory and Practice*, 22(2), 179–197, 2014.

4

Gordimer, English, race and cross-cultural translation[1]

Introduction

The race card has often been used to exclude African writers in Africa from the African canon. Though Nadine Gordimer has been publishing since the late 1940s, with her first novel, *The Lying Days*, appearing in 1953, some five years before Chinua Achebe's *Things Fall Apart*, because of her white skin she has only grudgingly been accepted as an African writer. Born of a Jewish father and a mother of British descent, Gordimer, who died in Johannesburg, South Africa on 13 April 2014, used to write largely within white settler codes. Yet, her writing in English, in a South African landscape, is one example of the manifestations of Anglophone African writing from which we can learn about additional dimensions of modern African literature. Moreover, her writing exhibits what Bamiro (2000) would call predominantly 'Europhone' literary influences but with African authenticity. Traditionally, as Gérard (1981) highlights, the literatures in the formerly colonised territories written in English are shaped by the cultural policy of the conquerors and the cultural substratum – that is, the cultural remnants in the post-contact period. For Gordimer, this was not so straightforward. It remains indisputable that her English encountered the African space, languages and cultural milieu; moreover, and more significantly, the language that Gordimer used sought to embody the languages and cultures of the African landscape. Unlike many of her contemporary African writers, she also represents a cross-section of African writers who do not have to justify writing in English (white settlers being one group and Creole intellectuals in Liberia and to a certain extent Sierra Leone being another). On the whole, Gordimer's writing is but another manifestation of the literary Anglophonisms prevalent in Africa that can help us learn about the nature of the Anglophone African literary-linguistic continuum.

Gordimer's delicate, perceptive, and often idiosyncratic treatment of controversial issues has received considerable critical enquiry. Scant attention, however, has been paid to how Gordimer's critical appraisal of apartheid policies emerges from her attempt to embody, concretely, African languages, discourses and cultures in her fiction. This chapter revisits Gordimer's apartheid-era fiction to examine how the representation of a range of discourses constitutes a means and a treatise through which she embodies African discourses and appraises apartheid power relations and the effects of divisive policies in her apartheid-era fiction. This embodiment is also a manifestation of how inextricably linked her writing is to the African landscape and discourse. Foucault defines discourse as

> ways of constituting knowledge, together with the social practices, forms of subjectivity and power relations which inhere in such knowledges and relations between them ... [d]iscourses [that] are more than ways of thinking and producing meaning.... They constitute the "nature" of the body, unconscious and conscious mind and emotional life of the subjects they seek to govern.
>
> (Cited in Weedon 1987, 108)

They are also 'a form of power that circulates in the social field and can attach to strategies of domination as well as those of resistance' (cited in Diamond and Quinby 1988, 185). Both definitions refer to discourse not as an innocent act, but one that conditions subjects in their social, cultural and economic interactions.

Thus, although we can situate Gordimer's African writing within white settler codes, she writes from an African consciousness, which Achebe described as writing from within, and which Gordimer (1973) would describe as writing from Africa, not from the world. In particular, Gordimer's apartheid fiction offers some useful insights about English, race and Anglophone writing. Unlike the post-apartheid period, the apartheid period raises intriguing questions regarding Gordimer's placement in African Anglophone discourse.

To present its argument, this chapter uses as primary examples three of Gordimer's nine novels written at different points in the apartheid era: her debut novel, *The Lying Days* (1953), her sixth, *The Conservationist* (1974) and *July's People* (1981), the eighth. Part of the reason for focusing on her novels rather than her numerous short stories is personal preference, though as André Brink (1998, 8) notes in 'The Language of the Novel', 'The remarkable shifts in language theory in the twentieth century made it possible for the novel to dramatise and exploit its relationship with language much more self-consciously than ever before.'

The choice of three apartheid novels representing different times of Gordimer's long literary career can also partly be justified by Stephen Clingman's observation:

> Each shift of consciousness in Nadine Gordimer's fiction is made in response to external developments and to the way in which these clarify the weaknesses of earlier positions; each therefore bears some significant relationship to South African historical development as a whole ... [T]his relationship is mediated

> at each point by the determinations of her social and ideological position, and in that the response of each novel emanates from such a position, the historical consciousness each manifests may be used as representative: of the class of people to whose understanding, options, and choices it corresponds, at each particular juncture. (1981, 169)

Indeed, Gordimer's novels demonstrate a maturation process in her engagement with indigenous voices and discourses. Her three post-apartheid-era fictions add another dimension to this growth and representation; for example, in *The House Gun* (1998), Gordimer brilliantly adopts the narrative style encountered earlier in *July's People*. Therefore, one can question Stephane Serge Ibinga's (2010) contention that in her post-apartheid-era fiction Gordimer now 'focuses on the Marxist dialectics of class division with very little comment on politicised racial dialectics', with her 'work epitomis[ing] the transition from racial dialectics to the dichotomy of class' (n.p.). Ibinga's reading of Gordimer's post-apartheid-era fiction is somewhat problematic because it appears to overlook the prospect of Gordimer's novels operating as part of a continuum. However, these post-apartheid novels lie outside the scope of this chapter on English, race and cultural translation as informed by the apartheid era.

The interest in the representation of language and discourse in Gordimer's novels has been influenced by Brink's (1998, 9) adaptation of Bakhtin's idea regarding the 'concept of language as a system, as a phenomenon, as a practice, as a process, in every novel'. According to Brink, Bakhtin's conception of the dialogic nature of language as *heteroglossia* has to do with 'the multi-tongued consciousness' that underscores 'the actual plurality of language forms activated in any novel' (Brink 1998, 15). This idea situates different discourses that Gordimer seeks to embody and what they reveal about the social and cultural relations under apartheid. Another justification stems from the pernicious nature of apartheid that permeates the nation's social fabric. As Gordimer (1976, 132) notes,

> All writers everywhere … are shaped by their own particular society reflecting a particular political situation. Yet there is no country in the Western world where the daily enactment of the law reflects politics as intimately and blatantly as in South Africa. There is no country in the Western world where the creative imagination, whatever it seizes upon, finds the focus of even the most private event set in the overall social determination of racial laws.

The representation of discourse in apartheid South Africa mirrors the social strata the divisive apartheid policies engendered. As such, Gordimer's apartheid discourse cannot be extricated from South Africa's socio-political context. Susan Pearsall (2000, 95) is of the same view when she observes that Gordimer's novels 'render accounts of the intrusions of the political into the everyday'. The manifestations of this intrusion are apparent in the inter-racial and cross-cultural intercourse and discourses of *The Lying Days*, *The Conservationist* and *July's People*, as well as other novels in Gordimer's apartheid-era oeuvre. Gordimer uses the problematic and often limited cross-cultural exchange to both expose the debilitating effects of divisive policies and politics and force the reader to interrogate those same issues to seek a schema for interpreting the novel. In her apartheid-era fiction, Gordimer generally presents characters from across the racial divide facing difficulties in having meaningful cross-cultural exchange despite being well-intentioned. Her narration then creates contexts in which the reader can consider the mitigating circumstances. This is true of Helen, the protagonist in *The Lying Days*, and Mary Seswayo, a black character she befriends; Mehring, the protagonist in *The Conservationist*, and Jacobus, the man in charge of his farm; and Maureen, a protagonist, and her apparent nemesis, July, in *July's People*.

In transcribing trans-cultural discourse, Gordimer acts as a 'translator' whose primary duty Susan Bassnett (2002) sees as seeking to create a text in the target language that can be appreciated by readers while at the same time demonstrating a respect for the source. In this connection, I find Tina Steiner's (2010, 302) explanation of 'translation' as an 'interlingual transfer' that 'involves all kinds of stages in the process of transfer across linguistic and cultural boundaries' rather useful. Steiner also dismisses the distinction often accorded to linguistic and cultural translation as a 'false one', since 'the mediation of language(s) entails the mediation of culture(s) and worldview(s)' (Steiner 2010, 303). In fact, Gordimer in her novels appears to benefit from what Steiner calls 'the paradoxical nature of translation as intercultural transfer, which first "involves appropriation, stereotyping and the negation of difference and otherness" and then provides opportunities for "contact and dialogue"' (Steiner 2010, 305), particularly on the part of readers in their negotiation of meaning with the text. Also, the colonial legacy and the confluence of cultures it engendered made cultural translation an integral part of cross-cultural interaction, albeit in a lopsided manner that favours the centre. In the context of the novels under discussion, cultural communication under divisive colonial subjectivities tends to limit meaningful cross-cultural exchange. It is against this backdrop that this chapter discusses Gordimer's apartheid-era fictions.

They 'Spoke and Shouted in a Language [She] Didn't Understand'

The Lying Days is, in many ways, naive in incorporating African discourses and less hard-hitting in its reproach of the apartheid system than Gordimer's subsequent apartheid-era novels. This novel also suggests, however, how Gordimer's later fiction would embody African indigenous voices, discourses and cultures.

Chapter 4

As Alan Lomberg (1976, 2) notes:

> In her first novel, *The Lying Days*, Nadine Gordimer established a pattern which all the other novels were to follow; ... it signifies a process inherent in her overall vision of life, and is reinforced by her style, which embraces two large principles ... particularising and generalising. ... a capacity for microscopic observations of human behaviour [and] the capacity for discerning general features and principles objectively, and from a distance.

Yet, early critics largely ignored *The Lying Days* as a South African novel because they believed it had 'far too little of South Africa and far too much of the coming-of-age of an adolescent', as Nathan Rothman observed in the 3 October 1953 issue of the *Saturday Review* (as cited in Heywood 1983, 19). Whereas the novel can 'often barely [be] distanced from the autobiographical' and is one in which Gordimer 'is almost literally finding her own voice' (Clingman 1981, 169), its scope is greater than critics have acknowledged. Also, Gordimer was writing with little precedent to fall back on, if one leaves aside the settler tradition set by Olive Schreiner's 1883 *The Story of an African Farm*. Indeed, as John Cooke (1985) observes, at the beginning of her career Gordimer was primarily occupied with what can be considered as the limitations a colonial writer faces, including the severely limited body of literature on which to build. Here the minimal body of literature refers to one relevant to the new contexts of the white settlers in South Africa, which differed in scope and preoccupation from the literatures of the parent European literatures anchored in the European space.

What has often been overlooked by critics about this work, however, is first, how it deliberately seeks to distance itself from traditional English literature from which it emerged, and second, how it employs indirect discourse to represent what the narrator lacks access to, but which the reader can infer from the text. To begin with, *The Lying Days* questions rather than affiliates itself with the mainstream European literary tradition. This deliberate attempt to align with Africa, rather than Europe, is a crucial step for Helen, the novel's protagonist and narrator, and for Gordimer as well. Helen can only effectively engage with her native South Africa after 'emerg[ing] from the trappings of colour-consciousness that were as "natural" to the white South Africans "as the walls of home and school"' (Gordimer 1973, 110). Gordimer, on the other hand, appears to see her fiction, even at this early stage, as rooted in Africa, not in Europe. On the whole, the questioning of the relevance of the 'gentle novels of English family life' and 'stray examples of the proletarian novel ... about the life of the poor in England' (Gordimer 1953/2000, 31, 32) to a child in South Africa constitutes the first step in Helen's unlearning process, which also has implications for the placement of the novel itself in postcolonial discourse.

Generally, the reading of South Africa's apartheid-era fiction through the prism of postcolonial theory presents problems because of the 'colonial structure' in place, despite the country having become a Union in 1910, a self-governing autonomous dominion of the British Empire and subsequently a 'republic' in 1961. In this regard, Nicholas Visser's (1997) 'Postcoloniality of a Special Type' explores the intricacies of South Africa's appropriation of postcolonial theory by examining both 'the centralist' and 'moderate' versions, whose acceptance of 'We were colonial [and now] we have become postcolonial; no further fundamental transformations are required' appears to coincide with the 1994 inclusive and democratic elections (as the 'now'). These versions base their analyses 'on colonialism' and treat 'race' as 'the primary factor in South African affairs' (Visser 1997, 92, 93).

Although Visser concludes that South Africa's appropriation of postcolonial theory 'is unlikely to be accomplished by any theoretical orientation prefixed by post-, whether hard or soft, strong or weak, excessive or moderate' (Visser 1997, 94), postcolonial theory is useful in interpreting Gordimer's apartheid-era fiction on two grounds. First, Gordimer attempts to reorient, for instance, *The Lying Days* beyond the trappings of Eurocentricism (the colonial) towards 'our Africa' (the postcolonial). Second, the convoluted nature of cultural exchange in South Africa – whether colonial or postcolonial – can also be informed by a 'tendency to essentialize race', which 'underlies much postcolonial thought' (Visser 1997, 86), even though Gordimer attempts to subvert such racialised dichotomies by interrogating their root causes and effects. The application of postcolonial discourse in this chapter has been largely based on Simon During's (1990, 115) definition of 'postcolonialism' as 'the need, in nations or groups which have been victims of imperialism, to achieve an identity uncontaminated by universalist or Eurocentric concepts and images'. Both white and black characters in Gordimer's apartheid-era fiction have been cast as 'victims of imperialism' on account of divisive policies, hence the resultant convoluted cross-cultural exchange.

Helen faces a challenge of developing an Afro-centred consciousness. Although Helen's mother is 'sometimes a little uncertain' about the 'stray examples of the proletarian novel' dealing with 'the life of the poor in England', she felt it would not 'do her any harm if she want[ed] to read it.' This was because she did not 'believe a girl should grow up not knowing what life is like' (Gordimer 1953/2000, 32). According to Dominic Head, Helen's mother is 'not consciously trying to radicalize her daughter' but wants 'to help her discover "what life is like"' (Head 1994, 37, 38). Helen is 'brought up into the life of a South African mine' and, thus, she finds some of the stories of children enjoying upper-middle-class English family domesticity 'weird and exotic' as well as alienating, primarily because she cannot 'read a book' in which she herself is 'recognizable'; in which there is a 'girl like Anna', the African servant, 'who did the housework and the cooking and called the mother and father Missus and Baas'. The 'real world' for Helen lies outside the insularity of her white homestead in 'this unfamiliar part' of her town, which constitutes her 'own world' that 'did not exist in books'. Then the intrusive adult persona explains that 'if this was the beginning of disillusion, it was also the beginning of Colonialism', that is, 'the identification of the unattainable distant with the beautiful' as well as 'the substitution of "overseas" for "fairyland"' (Gordimer 1953/2000, 11). It is this very association that the novel appears to recant. This is where indirect discourse comes in. What Helen does not state directly makes the reader interrogate what she misses.

Moreover, at this stage of her career, Gordimer, as a white South African, found herself writing against colonisation and its effects within white settler codes. Indeed, as a white writer, Gordimer found herself in an awkward position where she had to attack the colonial attitudes with which black Africans would otherwise identify her. Abdul JanMohamed (1985, 65) explains this dilemma for Gordimer as follows:

> Genuine and thorough comprehension of Otherness is possible only if the self can somehow negate or at least severely bracket the values, assumptions, and ideology of [one's] culture. As Nadine Gordimer's and Isak Dinesen's writings show ... this entails in practice the virtually impossible task of negating one's very being, precisely because one's culture is what formed that being. Moreover, the colonizer's invariable assumption about his moral superiority means that he will rarely question the validity of either his own or his society's formation and that he will not be inclined to expend any energy in understanding the worthless alterity of the colonized.

Gordimer was aware of this limitation when she noted that 'the one thing [a white man] cannot experience is blackness, with all that implies in South Africa', just as it is conversely true for a black man because '[e]ach is largely outside the other's experience-potential', and the 'identification of class with colour means that breaching class barriers is breaking the law' thus 'limiting the writer's intimate knowledge of his society' (1976, 148). Gordimer's writing cannot be categorically classified as colonialist in the same sense as the imperial adventure fiction in the mould of Joseph Conrad's *Heart of Darkness* or H Rider Haggard's *She* or *King Solomon's Mines*. Gordimer makes an attempt to 'understand [...] the worthless alterity' in the discourse of her novels (JanMohamed 1985, 65). In fact, her first novel rejects the romanticised notions about Africa as the home to 'the great rivers, the savage tribes, the jungles and the hunt for huge palm-eared elephants'. Instead, it presents romanticised Eurocentric notions of Africa as having nothing to do with the reality of 'the sixty miles of Witwatersrand veld that was our Africa' (Gordimer 1953/2000, 91).

The linguistic representation of *The Lying Days* mirrors South Africa's apartheid policies of exclusion – of 'whites-only' enclaves – since the indigenous African languages and discourses operate on the margins of what on the surface appears to be a whites-only discourse. Gordimer would later explain that the 'cultural isolation of whites who left their Europe' coupled with the 'cultural upheaval of blacks under conquest' has resulted in a 'compartmentalization of society' that condemns the white writer to a life in which s/he remains 'buried in his [sic] segregated cemetery', and 'cut off by enforced privilege from the greater part of society in which he [sic] lives' (Gordimer 1976, 131, 148). This enforced separateness makes Helen visualise black women's moods only from 'one's experience of Europeans' since there is 'no way of knowing' (Gordimer 1953/2000, 186). She has 'grown up, all [her] life among strangers', the black Africans whose language had been in her ears 'like the barking of dogs or cries of birds' (Gordimer 1953/2000, 186), both frightening images, associated with the adverse effects of social exclusion. In fact, the absence of African languages also reflects Helen's limited cross-cultural interaction.

To transcend such linguistic apathy and indifference, Gordimer attempts in the novel to make up for what Helen – and Gordimer's own early consciousness – lacks through the deployment of indirect discourse, which alerts the reader to what the narrator does not know. In this regard, the novel presents the discourse in African languages by implication, as the narrator lacks access to indigenous languages. Maureen simply watches as 'dozens of natives along the path' exchange some words in an indigenous language: 'Quite often the exchange lasted for half a mile, bellowed across the veld until one was too far away to do more than wave a stick eloquently at the other' (Gordimer 1953/2000, 9). She has no way of transcribing their spoken words, let alone their culture, to which she remains an outsider, cut off from it socially and linguistically. The reader, on the other hand, can infer some of what is missing and fill in the gaps. Gordimer uses this contrast to expose the effects of apartheid policies on cross-cultural human relations.

Also, Helen can communicate only in English with Mary Seswayo, a black character whom she befriends at university, the house-servant Ann, and other black characters, regardless of their linguistic competence. Helen's communication with blacks operates largely at the level of a master-servant discourse, with severely limited social and cultural interaction. Ironically, Helen has 'long lived surrounded by natives who simply attended our lives in one function or another' and as a child saw them 'as animals in a zoo' (Gordimer 1953/2000, 159). As a child, Helen experiences fear due to her ignorance of indigenous South African languages. She may find 'Native boys […] harmless and familiar' because they were 'servants', or 'delivery boys', 'Mine boys', or 'garden boys', but she also fears them because they are 'mysterious' and 'spoke and shouted in a language [she] didn't understand' (Gordimer 1953/2000, 4). Helen suffers from both linguistic and cultural alienation. The apartheid system condemns her to the status of an outsider despite being surrounded by indigenous African languages and cultures.

On the whole, this European *bildungsroman* imperative hints at Gordimer's nascent awareness of the critical need to incorporate indigenous African voices. In this novel, important black voices that might otherwise enrich the narratives anchored in an African setting remain underrepresented, a limitation Gordimer addresses in her subsequent fiction. As Head (1994, 36) concludes: '[T]he indeterminacy and ambiguity' about the stage Helen reaches at the end of the story 'affects the formal effects and devices of the novel', an indication that 'Gordimer is already making headway in her pursuit of appropriate forms to encompass her message of requisite cultural and political change'. What emerges in *The Lying Days* is that Gordimer's novels cannot satisfactorily reflect 'our Africa' without considering the languages and beliefs of the indigenous African voices.

'In the Safety of Their Own Language'

Compared to *The Lying Days* and some of Gordimer's earlier novels such as *Occasion for Loving* (1960/1991), her sixth novel, *The Conservationist*, is more forthcoming not only in attacking the apartheid system but also in incorporating African speech, whether in indigenous African languages or in translation.

The manifestations of African languages, or discourses, and cultures within the novel assume a higher profile in this novel than they do in *The Lying Days* and other earlier novels, albeit in a convoluted sense. This problematic linguistic relationship is best captured by the signposting to the farm owned by Mehring, the protagonist– 'NO THOROUGHFARE/ GEEN TOEGANG/ AKUNANDLELA LAPHA' (Gordimer 1974,140). The signposting deploys two languages of power in apartheid South Africa – English and Afrikaans – and one indigenous African language. The two languages of power take precedence over the indigenous African language. Yet, this 'absurd' but also 'hopeful claim that can never be recognized' (Gordimer 1974, 141) is primarily designed to discourage black South Africans – speakers of indigenous African languages, and the majority of those who will read the sign – from trespassing onto the property.

The discourses in *The Conservationist* are much more inclusive as well. The novel takes on board the perspectives of black African characters by exploring their thoughts and experiences. In fact, *The Conservationist* has two parallel thought processes covering two distinct worlds in the story: that of the indigenous Africans (whose perspective is embodied in the epigraphs relating to the *amatongo* in Zulu), and the white settlers (whose point of view is captured by Richard Shelton's poem 'The Tattooed Desert', which is used as an epigraph). Jacobus and other black characters represent the former, and Mehring and other whites the latter. The parallel presentation of these thought processes helps to undercut Mehring's seemingly dominant perspective, while providing the reader with access to both sides of the conflict to grasp the novel's treatise on the effect of divisive apartheid policies.

The grafting of the *amatongo*, or this 'ancestor motif', into the narrative structure is 'central to the complex ironies' presented in *The Conservationist* (Thorpe 1983, 184). In all, the novel draws ten quotations from Rev Henry Callaway's nineteenth-century book *The Religious System of the Amazulu*, and these provide some insights into the Zulu traditional belief system. This alignment with the African tradition is also significant because, as Gitte Postel (2007, 49) asserts, the 'Historical, Biblical, and Zulu myths are all part of the discourse of this focalization' that 'frames both Mehring's observations and the reader's interpretations'. Furthermore, the placing of the *amatongo* at the centre of the narrative acknowledges the centrality – rather than the marginality – of black presence on the land that Mehring prefers to ignore. The presentation of parallel linguistic and cultural systems is designed to expose and interrogate the effects of the apartheid system upon the lives of different social groups. The use of two parallel thought processes creates room for presenting two cultural traditions – white and black – in opposition to each other.

Furthermore, the intercalations – or the insertion – of indigenous African language words in English discourse acknowledge directly the presence of other linguistic landscapes and cultural systems subordinated to the main narrative discourse. These indigenous language words are linked to the Zulu spirituality at the heart of the narrative. Phineas's wife, the most spiritual character in the novel, speaks of 'snakes she had dreamt she was going to turn into', the '*Umthlwazi, Ubulube, Inwakwa, Umzingadhlu*; of *imamba* and *inyandezulu*, the snakes that are men and if killed will come to life again', and also of 'the ugly and rough-skinned lizard, the *isalukazana* (the lizard that is a little old woman) that is the "*itongo* [spirit] of an old woman"' (Gordimer 1974, 165–6). As a traditional seer, Phineas's wife connects various occurrences in the novel to highlight the fact that black characters see Mehring's farm as haunted because of the presence of the unnamed man who is buried on the farm. Eileen Julien (2011) uses the term 'ornamentalism' to describe the tendency by African writers to authenticate their writing through the shorthand of indigenous words, the incorporation of oral practices or references to ritual. However, in Gordimer's case, the conscious use of these elements appears geared towards alerting the reader to the parallel worlds that dominate the discourse of the novel. In this novel, for example, the reader cannot digest what Mehring says without recourse to the views of the black characters, a process that tends to undermine Mehring's seemingly dominant perspective.

In fact, Mehring, who considers himself the *master* of the farm, opts to remain an outsider, linguistically and socially, in his relationship with black characters and their languages and cultures, despite claiming ownership of the 400-acre farm forty

Chapter 4

minutes' drive from town on which the blacks live mainly as squatters. Indubitably, Mehring turns himself into a pariah, and black characters talk about him 'in the safety of their own language' to which they retreat and 'can say what they like' (Gordimer 1974, 75). As in the case of Helen, the black characters can communicate with him in English, the language of power, but he cannot do the same with them in their indigenous languages. Furthermore, the level of intimacy the black characters enjoy in the indigenous African languages further estranges Mehring from the land and the people to which and to whom he is only partially committed. Jacobus and other black characters on the farm 'greet […] each other with "brother", "sister", "mother", "uncle", a grammar of intimacy that went with *their language*' (Gordimer 1974, 35; emphasis added). The narrator remains conscious of the linguistic gap and uses it to expose the cosmetic nature of the ties Mehring has with the land and its people. Mehring's isolation, when contrasted with the camaraderie of black characters, exposes his lack of interaction with those on his farm.

In the novel's troubled cross-cultural exchange, English is presented as an imposed language for the black characters, who are more at home speaking their indigenous languages. In English, Jacobus's 'words were different' and he 'also stuttered', but in his native tongue, 'the language they all spoke' (Gordimer 1974, 64), he 'talk[ed] again, fast loud' and 'they all listened' (Gordimer 1974, 65). In both *The Conservationist* and *July's People* (discussed a little later), Gordimer avoids creating what Ngũgĩ calls 'this English-language speaking peasantry and working class, existing only in novels' (Ngũgĩ 1986/1997, 22). The novel distinguishes the speech black characters utter directly in English and the speech they produce in their indigenous language, but which is presented in the narrative supposedly in translation, as the following two passages illustrate. The first is between Jacobus and another black farmhand, and the second between Mehring and Jacobus.

First passage:

– Like the India's dogs at the shop. Something everybody will be afraid of. I'll keep it chained up all day, then it will get mad at night. That's the way to have a good dog. –

– Ask him. –

– I told you – many times. I have said it to him. –

– What can you do then. –

– Many times. You know how it is. You say one thing, and they just use it to say another. He looks past my face: how many dogs already on this farm? … (Gordimer 1974, 32)

Second passage:

– Jacobus, I was coming to find you. How's everything? –

– No – Everything it's all right. One calf he's borned Friday. But I try to phone you, yesterday night –

– Good, that's from the red cow, eh? –

– No, the red cow's she's not ready. This from that young one, that ones you buy last year from Pietersburg – (Gordimer 1974, 11)

Jacobus's speech is free and natural in his African language but laboured, constrained and ungrammatical in English. As in the case of July in *July's People*, this English is functional; he learns it primarily to communicate with Mehring and other non-indigenes.

Similarly, the South African pidgin, a hybrid language, does not promote mutual cross-cultural exchange. It, too, has been tainted by the divisive discourses that apartheid engendered. This African *lingua franca* of the mines and farms is 'the pidgin white people understand' in *The Conservationist*, or 'bastard black *lingua franca*' in *July's People*, largely deployed in a vain attempt to bridge the linguistic and cultural gap amongst racially and linguistically stratified communities. Yet, this language's 'vocabulary was limited to orders given by whites and responses made by blacks' (Gordimer 1981, 45). Characters use 'the few necessary words of their language in the pidgin form that evolved in the mines', such as '*Mina funa lo job*' [I am looking for a job] and '*Yinifuna*' [what are you looking for] as well as 'pidgin Afrikaans and English used by blacks on the farms' (Gordimer 1974, 119) to facilitate communication. The social stigma to this low hybrid language prompts Maureen, a primary character in *July's People*, to be 'ashamed… of a father who had talked to his "boys" in a dialect educated blacks who'd never been down a shaft in their lives regarded as an insult to their culture' (Gordimer 1981, 45).

This skewed apartheid intercultural exchange is reinforced by the failure of those with white privileges to learn indigenous African languages. In itself, such language acquisition may not necessarily foster intercultural communication. First Helen in the *Lying Days*, then Mehring in *The Conservationist* and then Smales in *July's People* fail to acquire indigenous languages and to foster meaningful cross-cultural communication and their knowledge gap is exposed. The elevation of the languages of power to a status where the indigenous African must learn them to communicate with their conquerors reduces the motivation for these characters to learn indigenous African languages as well. Mehring's inability to learn an indigenous African language is particularly notable, considering the fact that he is a polyglot. Eleni Coundouriotis (2006, 5) observes that Mehring's 'white privilege lends him the air of a more conventional cosmopolitanism' as 'he travels, speaks many languages'. And yet, none of these languages is an indigenous African language. The apartheid social system made the acquisition of the language of power mandatory for the blacks, who needed these languages to communicate with whites across the colour-bar; conversely, there was no such pressing demand for whites, hence Mehring's life in his comfort zone, learning only the languages he believes matter.

The failure to cultivate a meaningful relationship with the blacks makes Mehring suffer from colonial delusion as he 'think[s] in time there's something between [him] and the "simple" blacks [he doesn't] have to talk to' (Gordimer 1974, 177–8). Furthermore, Mehring misreads their complexity because of his limited understanding of their world and culture. The 'languages and cultural difficulties' (Gordimer 1974, 180) he faces stem from his deliberate policy of keeping a distance from the so-called 'simple' blacks. As a result, Mehring can only 'imagine someone speaking as the [blacks] speak' (Gordimer 1974, 180). His failure to identify with the people on his farm, their languages, and their culture is a matter of choice for him. Postel (2007, 54) underscores the 'mythical inter-textuality' in Gordimer's *The Conservationist*. But one can go a step further: the 'mythical spaces' that 'define boundaries between different parts of Mehring's farm, or between farm and city' or 'insiders and outsiders' that Postel (2007, 54) refers to also implicitly account for Mehring's witting or unwitting refusal to interact effectively with the legitimate owners of the space he wants to appropriate.

Mehring represents what Thorpe (1983, 190) calls 'the bankrupt white order whose possession rests upon an amoral assertion of power'. And yet, he cannot control the farm without recourse to the services of the Jacobuses he disregards. Thus, even as Mehring walks alone in the 'vlei' – an Afrikaans word that grew out of the local environment – he persists in distancing himself from the blacks on what he sees as 'his' land. This failure is evident in his disjointed and poor discourse with the black people. Although he does an honourable thing by sanctioning the reburial of the unnamed dead man, he opts not to attend the ceremony. This refusal confirms his alienation from the land he claims to own and those who people it, along with their language and culture. As a social recluse, Mehring has no way of knowing how to live with the 'squatters' on the land, who are here to stay.

'Speaking an African Language was Simply a Qualification'

July's People, which attempts to bring together whites and blacks under reversed roles on the verge of a revolution to usher in majority black rule, demonstrates the perniciousness of the cultural divide created by centuries of divisive policies. The well-intentioned liberal white protagonists fail to interact effectively with their black South African hosts, despite being more committed to the land than the naive Helen in *The Lying Days* or the self-serving Mehring, a sojourner on the farm. The Smales, a family of white liberals in *July's People*, on the other hand, fully commit to the African land and, presumably, to its people. However, they turn out to be victims of powerful forces they are unable to control. Erritouni (2006, 74) observes that *July's People* 'expose[s] the impasse to which apartheid condemned interracial relations' and 'equally envisions a utopian future in which South Africans try to overcome their intractable social and economic problems'.

The novel represents this 'impasse' at the level of intercultural discourse, illustrating the linguistic limits and problematic politics of identification. Indeed, the Smales are let down by the rather limited linguistic and cultural interaction they have with their indigenous hosts. As Brink (1984, 193) aptly notes, 'Gordimer exposes this group of floundering Crusoes in their efforts to adapt to "us and them … an explosion of roles", which involves an explosion of language'. The difficulties the characters encounter in the 'village' of their once loyal servant, July, as the tables turn are most clearly reflected in their failure to communicate effectively. In the *Grammar of Identity*, Clingman (2009) notes that the 'village' setting in *July's People* (and the desert in Gordimer's post-apartheid-era novel, *The Pickup*) is central to grasping the relationship between both the existential and literal settings of the novel and the novel's rhetorical agenda on the contestable identity represented through language.

This difficulty is also activated by the ambiguity in the novel's title, *July's People*, which readers must grapple with. It raises a question: who are 'July's People'? The term applies to both the village people (to whom July is naturally affiliated, linguistically, culturally and ethnically) and the white people he has brought to the village, and with whom he has spent fifteen years of acculturation that has helped to map his dual identity. But July is also Mwawate in his native African language: 'July', as the chief explains, 'was a name for whites to use' and for 'fifteen years they had not been told what the chief's subject really was called' (Gordimer 1981, 120). In other words, the Smales have not been aware of July's true identity in those fifteen years. Moreover, this indigenous name shows that July retains his language and ethnic identity despite years of acculturation under apartheid. The indigenous African name Mwawate identifies July with the village of his birth, which gives him an Afro-centred identity. His Euro-centred acculturation thus remains partial, even as it conditions him to a life of subservience, linguistically and socially. The reversal of roles in the 'village' devoid of the modern luxuries critiques white settler ideology in South Africa. As Paul Rich (1984, 365) observes:

> White settler political ideology in South Africa has traditionally seen itself as the embodiment of some form of 'civilization' against the threatened 'barbarism'

of African majority rule. The term has a significance both in its Victorian imperial roots and in its facility for acting as a kind of common ideological denominator binding the political discourse of both Afrikaner and English settlers into a common defence of 'white civilization'.

July's People places the liberal white characters in the African 'village', or a country under black Africans, the supposed centre of this 'barbarism', to test how they will hold on to their values. This village setting is the bedrock of African cultural identity, where the languages of the Smales – English and Afrikaans, represented by Maureen and her husband Bam respectively – prove inadequate. In linguistic and cultural terms, the African village is the cornerstone of indigenous African languages and cultures, where the languages of power spoken by the Smales have little value.

Language lies at the heart of both the struggle and the envisaged redemption that the novel suggests may lie within the strictures of apartheid divisive politics. The fictional world of the novel thrives in polyglot space; however, there is limited meaningful cross-cultural interaction between the races because of linguistic and hence cultural barriers. The failure of communication between the characters from the two racial groups points to a wider social communication problem: none of the women that Bam encounters can 'speak his languages' (Gordimer 1981, 39), English and Afrikaans, and neither can he speak their indigenous languages. In a group of drinkers, Bam makes himself understood only because one 'could speak a few words not of English but of Afrikaans' and another 'some English' (Gordimer 1981, 39). Also, Maureen tells her son Victor that they 'don't understand our language' (Gordimer 1981, 14). The Smales know only the languages of power, but these have little value in a society where the majority speak indigenous languages.

Paradoxically, the whites 'who speak their languages are never people' like Bam and Maureen, but 'always the ones who have no doubt that whites are superior' (Gordimer 1981, 44). These are 'Whites in the pass offices and labour bureaux who used to have to deal with blacks all the time across the counter', to whom 'speaking an African language was simply a qualification' (Gordimer 1981, 4). Learning indigenous languages boosts their credentials to work in offices that further entrench white domination. Thus, the political commitment of the liberal Smales, who do nothing to learn the languages of the people they purport to side with, comes under scrutiny. Even for outside communication they rely on the radio in this rural outpost whose 'voice spoke English only to the white pair, only for them', not the 'other radios in the community, bellowing, chattering, twanging pop music, the sprightly patter of commercials in a black language' (Gordimer 1981, 25). They simply cannot extricate themselves from the cultural barricades erected by apartheid.

The novel is quick to remind the readers of the problematic nature of the marriage of convenience between Maureen Hetherington and Bamford Smales. Their union symbolically links two acrimonious groups who also happen to be the two dominant white linguistic groups in South Africa: those of British and Dutch (Afrikaner) extraction. The Afrikaans and Anglo-Saxon historical connection to apartheid is also reflected in their gender roles – Bam, a male, and Maureen, a female, the former more rooted in the soil than the latter. From a linguistic point of view, Maureen, an Anglophone and conveyor of the dominant language of power in Africa (thanks to the British conquest of the Afrikaners), is the central consciousness through which the events in the novel are told. The cracks of this marital relationship emerge as the narration progresses.

The presentation of the Smales (an apparent pun for Smells, whose use is tinged with irony in the novel) as 'white pariah dogs in a black continent' (Gordimer 1981, 8) allows the novel to revisit the primary theme of Gordimer's (1959) essay 'Where do Whites Fit in?' in Africa. As Africans, these whites are 'not Americans, or Europeans of other European nations' (Gordimer 1981, 126). That the Smales refuse to flee abroad when an opportunity arises makes it clear that they see Africa as their home. Michael Chege in 'Africans of European Descent' presents two possible reasons for this: they are either 'white foreigners who play the expatriate game' released 'from any feelings of sympathy or any real obligations toward the people [they] are among' and see Africa as 'less a place or a people than a standard of living – a better way of life than most of them would enjoy back home'; or whites who 'recognize the necessity of facing Africa, and to seriously imagine themselves' (and here Chege borrows a phrase from Nelson Mandela) as 'proud sons and daughters of Africa' (1997, 82). Although the latter scenario applies to the liberal Smales, the novel undermines this dichotomy. The inability of the Smales and their black hosts to understand each other is as much a product of limited linguistic and cultural exchange as it is a product of many years of divisive colonial and apartheid policies. It also exposes how cosmetic has been the cultural exchange between the liberal Smales and their servant July (alias Mwawate) under apartheid policies.

Not knowing indigenous languages creates wide gaps in the Smales' knowledge and understanding of July's 'village' world. For the *gumba-gumba*, the traditional gathering, the Smales children, Victor, Gina and Royce, 'kn[o]w the name in the village people's language but not in their own' (Gordimer 1981, 140). On the one hand, this indigenous African language complements their knowledge of 'our Africa'; on the other, the *gumba-gumba* exposes the limitations of the linguistic and cultural knowledge of the Smales. This becomes even more apparent when July asks a man on the roof

> in the way his people did, teasing and encouraging, the first part of what he said gabbled and rapid, the syllables of the last word strongly divided and drawn out, the word itself repeated. *Mi tat wa tu ku nadziha ngopfu, swi famba a moyeni.*

Chapter 4

> *Ncino wa maguva lawa, hei – i...hei – i!* [...] The *gumba-gumba* was itself the occasion. (Gordimer 1981, 141)

Gordimer's narrator leaves the Zulu expressions untranslated, attesting to how the Smales operate outside the social, linguistic and cultural circle of the indigenes in whose nest they have come to roost. Inevitably, as Steiner aptly points out, 'instances where the narrative withdraws its translation nevertheless invite translation' (Steiner 2010, 303) on the part of the reader. Such translation would then make the cross-cultural communication much more meaningful.

Apart from not knowing the indigenous languages, the Smales also shun this meaningful social event. The *gumba-gumba* presents them with a cultural learning opportunity, yet when the event starts, the 'white people wander [...] away': the father 'did not want to drink that stuff and did not want to offend' (Gordimer 1981, 141) and 'the mother thought there were pleasanter sights for the children than – in particular – some of the women [...who] get [...] drunk with their babies on their backs, and [...] pee only as far as their staggering would carry them' (Gordimer 1981, 142). This attitude amounts to self-imposed exile. Retrospectively, Gordimer notes that '[i]n spite of all the vile and terrible things that have been and continue to be done in the name of all whites here', South Africa 'has been the single African country where whites once had the chance to enter into a changing – and that is to say mutual – indigenous culture' (Gordimer 1981, 45). The Smales wittingly pass up this opportunity for white and black characters to come together, and this reveals more about the Smales' attitude to things African than their failure to acquire an indigenous African language. As a result, the Smales reduce themselves to outsiders looking in. Not surprisingly, Maureen refers to 'his [July's] people'. One encounters the same usage at the beginning of the novel: 'July bent at the doorway and began that day for them as *his* kind has always done for *their* kind' (Gordimer 1981, 1; emphasis added).

Because of the turbulent colonial experience of conquest, black characters also treat whites as essentially different, as the superior other. July's mother, for example, compliments Bam for the game-meat he has provided by calling him '*mhani*' (Gordimer 1981, 81) – a white man – just as she uses 'mhwanyan' (or 'my lady'), an expression 'that had come down to her attached to any white female face, from the conquests of the past' (Gordimer 1981, 132). These terms perpetuate the idea of otherness that attended the colonial encounter, and are also sustained in a number of indigenous languages. As Bam reminds his black hosts, they also use '*umlungu*', 'white baas' (the latter word in Afrikaans), '*nkosi*', '*morema*', and '*hosi*' (Gordimer 1981, 117) to refer to the almost cult-like status that white people had come to assume in their African settlement. Bam's intervention here is particularly revealing since he appears to suggest that the cultivation of otherness cuts both ways, implying that undoing this damage is also a shared responsibility. The novel thus suggests that black characters are, to a certain extent, also culpable in the lopsided cross-cultural exchange.

Both Maureen and July, for example, are at an impasse because of the adverse colonial and apartheid conditioning. In his essay 'The Black Writer's Burden', Chinua Achebe (1966, 135) describes the enduring effects of the colonial encounter thus: 'In terms of human dignity and human relations, the encounter was almost a complete disaster for the black races. It has warped the mental attitudes of both blacks and whites'. *July's People* exposes these 'mental attitudes of both blacks and whites' through their problematic social intercourse. As a result, Maureen fails to understand July and his state, whether in the town under her wings or in the village where he gives her sanctuary. When Maureen 'didn't understand [July] it was her practice to give some noncommittal sign or sound, counting on avoiding the wrong response by waiting to read back his meaning from the context of what he said next' (Gordimer 1981, 97). This reaction defines the nature of their communication back in town. Bam is even worse off because he 'often irritated [July] by a quick answer that made it clear, out of sheer misunderstanding, the black man's English was too poor to speak his mind'. July 'might mean "place" in the sense of role, or might be implying she must remember she had no claim to the earth – "place" as territory' (Gordimer 1981, 97). July and Maureen can 'assume comprehension' between them only if the latter keeps 'away from even the most commonplaces of abstractions' because his 'was the English learned in kitchens, factories and mines' (Gordimer 1981, 95–6). In this bumpy relationship, three issues emerge.

First, July has acquired an English limited to his socioeconomic dealings with white South Africans. The apartheid system teaches July to communicate what is necessary for him to perform tasks for his 'masters'. Maureen knows that July is 'not a simple man'. After all, 'they could not read him ... back there, for fifteen years; but at the time, they had put it down to the inevitable, distorting nature of dependency' (Gordimer 1981, 60). Failure to 'read' July stems from the limited nature of the apartheid English at his disposal, and hence the limited meaningful cross-cultural interaction he has with the Smales. The identification of English with subservience is also evident when the village chief feigns lack of competence in the language. Initially, he pretends to 'kn[o]w no white man's language' because it 'was not for him to work as a servant or go down the mines' (Gordimer 1981, 115). He identifies English with the servitude associated with white domination. However, when he realises that the balance of power has shifted in favour of black South Africans (the Smales are on the run and basically at his mercy), the chief decides to address the Smales directly in English without July's suspect translation. 'They want to kill you', he suddenly says in

English, 'without any explanation' and 'with a face that stopped short of any surprise' before speaking 'again [...] in his own language' (Gordimer 1981, 117, 118).

Secondly, July is trapped in the language of subservience, even as he attempts to assert his newly-found power. Hence his statement: 'Your boy who work for you' whom 'you trusted there in town for fifteen years' (Gordimer 1981, 69). This 'absurd "boy" [falls] upon [Maureen] in strokes neither appropriate nor to be dodged' (Gordimer 1981, 69–70). It was a word that Maureen's father 'had used' as part of the vocabulary in apartheid South Africa but 'was never used in *her* house'. As a white liberal, Maureen 'priggishly shamed and exposed others who spoke it in her presence' and had 'challenged it in the mouths of white shopkeepers and even policemen'. However, the novel exposes her commitment as surface-deep since inside of her, she still accepts the idea of July as he is defined by the apartheid policies, not as a person, with his own culture and humanity. It is not until July warns her that he is 'not thinking all the time for your things, your dog, your cat' (Gordimer 1981, 71) that Maureen realises that he chooses 'what he wanted to know and not know', and as the 'present was his; he would arrange the past to suit it' (Gordimer 1981, 96). Back in his village, July asserts his wants more freely than under apartheid in town. Indeed, apartheid conditions have trained July to be non-committal, so his statement remains largely 'unqualified, [as he] did for every kind of commitment: to a burial society, a hire purchase agreement, their thumbprints put to a labour contract for the mines or plantations' (Gordimer 1981, 152). Thus, the July Maureen believes she knows is actually a lie, not the Mwawate she now has to contend with. Third and most significantly, Maureen accommodates only what comfortably fits her liberal beliefs, ignoring the notion that July is more than the servant she had assumed him to be. In fact, the more July asserts his power before Maureen, the more untenable it becomes to sustain their rapport in English.

Their conflict stems from a misunderstanding based on the word 'dignity'. Once Maureen 'drop[s] fifteen years of the habit of translation into very simple, concrete vocabulary' in English, she wonders whether 'he understood the word' and had avoided using 'the word "dignity" to him' before 'not because she didn't think he understood the concept' or 'didn't have any', but because she feared 'the term itself [...] might be beyond his grasp of the [English] language' (Gordimer 1981, 72). Before 'she came here', she had not realised that 'the special consideration she had shown for his dignity as a man, when he was by definition a servant, would become his humiliation itself, the one thing there was to say between them that had any meaning' (Gordimer 1981, 98). When their roles are reversed, Maureen finally comprehends the nature of July's humiliation even as he opts to speak eloquently in the native language she cannot understand:

> Suddenly he began to talk at her in his own language, his face flickering powerfully [...] She understood although she knew no word. Understood everything: what he had to be, how she had covered up to herself for him, *in order for him to be her idea of him*. But for himself – to be intelligent, honest, dignified for *her* was nothing; his measure as a man was taken elsewhere and by others. She was not his mother, his wife, his sister, his friend, his people. *He spoke in English what belonged in English.* (Gordimer 1981, 152; emphasis added)

Their social interaction had hitherto been steeped in falsities, with Maureen complicit, as she safeguarded the privileges that came with her white status. In this regard, Erritouni sees 'Maureen's liberal views and her humane treatment of her servant before the revolutionary war' as 'cosmetic' because they 'leave intact the economic discrimination of apartheid' (2006, 74). She has yet to grow into mutually beneficial relations that can make her understand the wants and aspirations of her black servants both in relation to her and with themselves as a people whose lives have become intertwined with hers. However, Maureen's problems go deeper than that as Gordimer retrospectively explains her situation:

> I see Maureen as, in a way, the last colonial woman. She has been handed from father to husband. And she has had, in effect, two husbands – though she didn't realize it – because July does so much for her. July is so protective of her, takes care of her, takes all sorts of burdens off her. This is ... a typically colonial attitude – that the white woman has a man who looks after her. In the classic colonial situation, she wouldn't even have worked. She just would have been the graceful consort of the husband. And then there would be soft-footed servitors running around – male. So, in effect, you have two husbands there. And then, of course, both husbands turn out not to be able to protect her anymore ... her own husband, Bam, without his car and his gun and his office, is absolutely unable to do anything for her ... And July turns out to belong to his own people. (Bazin 1995, 581)

The changed circumstances in the 'village' not only cause Maureen to fail to relate effectively with July and Bam, they also render meaningful dialogue, particularly with July, almost impossible.

This wide gulf between the two social groups, however, does not mask the fact that their fates remain inextricably linked. Hence, Bam questions the categorisations of 'Us and them. Who is us, now, and who them?' There is 'an explosion of roles' in which the 'Union Buildings' – symbolising Afrikaans-Anglo-Saxon unity – and 'master bedrooms' (Gordimer 1981, 117) are gutted. The old establishment teeters on the brink of an inevitable collapse, but the fates of these two peoples are nevertheless somehow linked, a message also affirmed by the novel's title. Moreover, in July's dark profile there lies 'a contempt and humiliation that came from their blood and his', 'a feeling brutally shared, one alone cannot experience it, be punished by it, without the other' (Gordimer 1981, 62), even though the 'validities' that determined 'the absolute nature of intimate relationships between human beings' were 'decided by "We," the whites' (Gordimer 1981, 64–5). The onus finally falls on both races working together to bridge the cultural divide that has kept them apart for centuries. Even as Bam warns against possible black-on-black violence due to ethnic tensions, Gordimer focuses on the search for a cultural bridge between two races set apart by both colonial and subsequent apartheid policies. Only then can they deal with the problems they face: failure to communicate, failure to relate, and failure to understand their common humanity.

In essence, 'them and us' belong to the same side – victims of colonialism and apartheid policies that hamper effective communication. Gordimer suggests that the Smales have been given another chance to learn and understand not only the language of Mwawate but also his culture, so that they can be effectively integrated in the society dominated by black culture. Of the Smales, only the 'colonial' Maureen remains too rigid to seize this opportunity, and hence runs towards a helicopter, uncertain whether she is running towards death or redemption. This ambiguous ending also underlines her untenable situation in the absence of 'unlearning' the apartheid conditioning to adapt and adjust to the African culture. Gordimer implies that people like the chief and July will have to accommodate the Smales, whose survival under the changed circumstances and long-enforced cultural ignorance depends on the receptiveness and flexibility of black culture. After all, the Smales did not create the cultural divide engendered by apartheid. All concerned must live.

Conclusion

On the one hand, the incorporation of African languages, cultures and discourses in Gordimer's apartheid novels helps to expose the extent to which the divide between 'them and us' fostered by the colour bar hinders the emergence of a situation in which whites can 'merge [...] with an indigenous culture' (Gordimer, 1980, 46). On the other hand, this incorporation also reveals how English in Africa is never immune from embodying the indigenous African languages and cultures that not only surround it but also shape it. Also, the novels discussed in this chapter suggest that it is only through mutually beneficial interactions that the wounds from a shared painful history may be healed – whether that interaction is through the medium of indigenous African languages or carefully edited English. In the case of the latter, the communication has to be geared towards equitable relationships, rather than perpetuating linguistic, cultural and economic gaps. On the whole, Gordimer's apartheid-era novels demonstrate how problematic cross-cultural communication can become when social entities remain insulated behind the privileges sanctioned by divisive laws and sustained by the language of power. They also demonstrate that cross-cultural interaction is more essential than the artificial barriers created by the apartheid policies. In her apartheid-era fiction, Gordimer exposes the limited and convoluted cross-cultural exchange between black and white through her representation of African discourses. She thus represents the debilitating effects of the divisive apartheid policies on both blacks and whites. The reader is left with the task of negotiating between what is either directly or indirectly stated in the various discourses of the novel to grasp the seemingly paralysing effects of divisive politics and policies that Gordimer so strongly attacked.

Note
1   This chapter is an adaptation of my article entitled '"Imagine Someone Speaking as They Speak": Linguistic Divide and Convoluted Cross-Cultural Exchange in Nadine Gordimer's Apartheid-Era Work', originally published in Postcolonial Text, 8(1), 1–21, 2013.

5

Farah, English and cosmopolitanism[1]

Introduction

This chapter analyses the intricacies of using English in a traditionally non-English context such as Somalia through the work of its foremost Anglophone writer, Nuruddin Farah. Farah uses English to re-imagine the nation and promote intra-, pan-, and trans-national discourses within and outside Africa. The analysis of Farah's work has been informed by the articulations of Ernest Renan (1996), Ernest Gellner (1987) and Benedict Anderson (1991), within the view of Somalia's now-contested exceptionalism. In Farah's hands, English becomes a vehicle for bringing together diverse linguistic, literary, cultural and religious expressions into a genre that facilitates trans-national discourse. Thus, the chapter contends that the Anglophone African literary tradition that Farah embraces gains the capacity to transcend national boundaries and broadens – rather than limits – the scope and coverage of national and trans-national literatures.

The intricate relationship between language and nation that African nation-states contend with was foregrounded by Ernest Renan in the nineteenth century. In his famous Sorbonne lecture 'What is a Nation?' in 1882, Renan said, 'Language may invite us to unite, but it does not compel us to do so' (Renan 1996/1882, 41). In his analysis of that lecture many years later, Ernest Gellner (1987, 6) observed that Renan's 'main purpose' was to 'deny any naturalistic determinism of the boundaries of nations'. '[T]hese are not dictated by language, geography, race, religion, or anything else', Gellner wrote, since 'nations are made by human will'. Similarly, Benedict Anderson (1991, 133) points out that it is 'always a mistake to treat languages' as 'emblems of nation-ness', because the 'most important thing about language is its capacity for generating imagined communities, building in effect particular solidarities'. It is as though these writers had foreseen the crisis of identity now associated with African nation-states carved out of boundaries arbitrarily drawn during the Berlin Conference that took place in 1884–85. This chapter re-reads the Somali novelist Nuruddin Farah against the caution that Renan, Gellner and Anderson have raised about misunderstanding the relationship between language and nation in a bid to reaffirm the role of literary Englishes in their various manifestations in promoting national and trans-national discourse within traditionally non-English contexts. Farah's Somalia has over the years been considered unique because of Somali exceptionalism (Ahmed 1995), which emphasises the country's supposed homogeneity and coherent cultural and linguistic national identity in Africa.

This discourse was, perhaps, never unproblematic, but Somalia's subsequent fragmentation as a unitary state from the 1990s onwards raises further questions regarding its exceptionalism. It has been argued that not many African countries could claim national identity as they lacked 'the unity they need to clearly identify them in terms of language, social structure, the economy, religion, etc.' (Menang 2001). Somalia, on the other hand, could do so in the pre-national disintegration days. Uncle Hilaal, one of the characters in one of Farah's 1986 *Maps*, alludes to such exceptionalism when he says, 'Somalia is unique' as it is named 'after Somalis, who share a common ancestor and who speak the same language – Somali' (Farah 1986/1989, 155). However, in the face of the current collapse of the Somali nation and dispersal of the Somali people in the diaspora, this Somali exceptionalism seems contentious. In fact, recent scholarship on Somalia grapples with the question of how such an apparently homogeneous nation, whose Somali national character had been enshrined in national lore and immortalised in books by both Somali and non-Somali scholars, could degenerate into 'mosaic fiefdoms', leaving its supposed homogeneity in tatters (Ahmed 1996). Yet, Farah has been contesting the question of Somali national homogeneity in practically all his fiction from the 1970s onwards.

Contrary to logical expectations, the most famous novelist from this seemingly ethnically and linguistically homogenous African nation has largely been writing not in Somali but in English, which is Farah's fourth language after Somali, Amharic and Arabic. Farah received his formal written education in Amharic in the Ogaden, a Somali enclave in Ethiopia; in Arabic at the Koranic academy; and only then in English and Italian, both languages introduced to the Somali during colonialism. Somali is his first contact language. Farah claims he chose English for practical reasons: he only had access to an English typewriter. He started 'toying with the idea' of writing in English at sixteen, a 'practical thing that has nothing to do with the politics of language' (Jussawalla and Dasenbrock 1992, 47). But his choice of language was also influenced by what he saw – from a cosmopolitan perspective – as his audience: not only 'our people', 'those who speak the same languages as we do', but also all 'Africans and Third World people' (Jussawalla and Dasenbrock 1992, 45). This exoteric view is very much in line with Farah's largely cosmopolitan approach to his writing, in which Somalia is the epicentre even as he writes from exile.

Farah's cosmopolitan perspective can be explained with reference to Appiah's analysis in *Cosmopolitanism*, which calls for the redrawing of the imaginary boundaries to focus on the powerful ties that connect people across religions, cultures, and nations:

> [T]here are two strands that intertwine in the notion of cosmopolitanism. One is the idea that we have obligations to others, obligations that stretch beyond those to whom we are related by the ties of kith and kind, or even the more formal ties of shared citizenship. The other is that we take seriously the value not just of human life but of particular human lives, which means taking an interest in the practices and beliefs that lend them significance. People are different, the cosmopolitan knows, and there is much to learn from our differences. (Appiah 2006, xv)

Appiah's (2006) universalist concerns also accommodate respect for difference. In literary terms, such cosmopolitanism aims to extend writing beyond the confines of any one nation, and it does so in the service of a broadly humanistic agenda. As such, Farah has much in common with James Joyce, an Irishman (though writing mainly as part of the English-speaking world) who wrote about his homeland in English. Moreover, like Farah, Joyce wrote from exile. As Ian Adam notes, Joyce 'stretches its [the English language's] resources to capacity', 'adding to them those of other tongues' and cultural experiences (Adam 1984, 34). Both Farah and Joyce write about their respective cultures' strengths and limitations from cosmopolitan perspectives. Such affinity, Adam (1984, 34) further explains, stems from an attempt to reconcile 'a dualism which comes from writing in a language which has a powerful literary tradition, and out of a culture removed from that tradition in varying degrees through peculiarities of history, geography, social structure, dialect or language'.

It is also worth noting that, although Farah has been writing in English for years, he has not done so uniformly. His maiden efforts, for example, to write in Somali were curtailed prematurely in 1972, the same year the official Somali orthography was introduced, by the government censors of President Mohammad Siad Barre, who found Farah's work 'seditious' (Wright 1994, 10). Apart from denying him an opportunity to build on his Somali writing, this intervention by a despotic ruler also condemned Farah to a life in exile, from where he has continued writing in English. Farah does not believe writing in English is a hindrance, as long as what he writes 'will be translated back into Somali or […] into all other languages' (Jussawalla and Dasenbrock 1992, 48). To explain his position on language, Farah, in an award lecture aptly titled 'Celebrating Difference', appears to provide a plausible explanation for this linguistic dilemma:

> I asked myself if, in the opinion of my father, I was subversive, because I wrote in foreign tongues, or because, in my writings, I challenged the authoritarian tendencies of Somali tradition? I could say, in self-defence, […] that writing in cosmopolitan settings, in foreign tongues, is, to my mind, more forward-looking, ultimately more outward-looking, than much of the writing done in the indigenous languages in Africa and elsewhere […]. (Farah 1998b, 712)

Francis Ngaboh-Smart (2000, 86) has argued that this 'disavowal of the strong position on nation and ethnicity' must be 'located in what could be called a new postcolonial discourse, namely, the emphasis on cultural diversity, which has emerged as a repudiation of the nationalists' obsessive concern with indigenous values as a mark of identity'. Thus, Naomi Chazan (1988, 139), for example, rules out the existence of 'pure' ethnic groups in an African national space because of the growing 'fluctuation around the situational pre-eminence of the territorial framework' on the continent, whereby even 'the architecture of power' shows 'diverse locations of concern and interconnection'. Thus, Farah emphasises cultural diversity even as he writes about Somalia, which at first sight seems to be a homogeneous space, composed of people apparently sharing the same language, territory and even culture.

Farah also makes one of the most audacious claims on the use of English in a non-native context by claiming that one can acquire a language and develop it into one's first language, at least from a literary point of view, since he draws a distinction between possessing a language as a native speaker and making articulate uses of that language through the written word. Farah explains that 'millions of people in various parts of the world […] really have no language as such' since 'they have never put any effort in highlighting their experiences by writing' (Jussawalla and Dasenbrock 1992, 48). These include 'native speakers of English' who 'don't make any articulate use of the language' as 'one becomes conscious of using a language, and one may give it a status of a first language, although one may have learned such a language later' depending on 'the effort one has put in' (1992, 48). This statement by Farah is controversial because native speakers of a language do not have to make 'articulate use of the language' through writing since language can also be literary in the spoken form. Second, native speakers, perhaps, experience a language differently from non-native speakers. However, many Anglophone writers tend to treat English in written discourse as though it were their first literary language, often at the expense of other languages, as it appears in the case of Farah, and indeed many writers who write in English as though it were their first contact language.

The question of readership appears to have primarily influenced Farah's linguistic choice of writing in English, which in turn also affects the way he writes in that language. Whereas in the case of Achebe and Ngũgĩ we may cite historical reasons, and linguistic heritage for Gordimer, for Farah the situation appears more related to readership. As both Italy and England colonised Somalia, Farah could have chosen to write in either former colonial language, but he chose the latter. Moreover, since he has a rich heritage in the Somali language, Farah cannot argue for using the language because of the absence of a pan-national language as is the case of Achebe's Nigeria. In fact, in exile Farah remains cut off from the bulk of Somali readers; however, this assertion would simplify the reasons behind his embarking on writing in English since he decided to do so long before he went into exile. We can also conclude that his writing in English has more to do with readership because of what he considers his audience. For Farah, not only 'Somalis are [his] people, but the whole of the continent of Africa', India, and 'the Arab world, which has also influenced me culturally' – simply those 'in any part of the world who have been colonized and have been deprived of their own self pride' (Jussawalla and Dasenbrock 1992, 45). The question of readership also seems practical for someone who has lived in exile for so long and far from his own Somali audience.

The primary argument of this chapter stems from my dissatisfaction with the existing scholarship in relation to the questions of linguistic play and/or syncretism in Farah's work, particularly regarding language and national representation. Farah remains an enigma in Anglophone African literary discourse, as his literary work 'does not demonstrate the explicit Africanist commitments of language or style of writers such as Ngũgĩ or Achebe' (Jussawalla and Dasenbrock 1992, 43), the two voices that for many years symbolised the major sides of the African literature/language debate: pro-nativism and pro-English. Lately there has been a marked shift towards recognition of linguistic diversity as articulating the 'complex and many-sided' features of Africa's identity, accepting the use of indigenous African languages on the one hand, and adopted former colonial languages on the other. In consequence, '[A] literature that is both a factor and a product of that identity should also exploit and reflect the complementary relationship that already exists between Africa's native and non-native languages' (Menang 2001). This is where Farah's fiction fits in.

This approach further helps to resolve some of the binaries associated with African writing, which Edmund Bamiro (2000) classifies as having either 'Afrolect' or 'Eurolect' literary influences. Bamiro defines Afrolect as a 'linguistic experimentation in variants of an imperial language' to mirror 'characteristics of African oral traditions', and Eurolect as 'literary productions that exhibit considerable influences from European literature in content, language, and style' (Bamiro 2000, 72). Such distinctions do not have to be used to separate African literatures in English, for their strength lies in their plurality and diversity. In fact, Farah fuses them. This chapter, therefore, examines how Farah's cosmopolitan position shapes and complicates his contribution to Anglophone African literary discourse. It also explores how his works shed light on the complexity and plurality of Anglophonisms not only in

Africa but also in other non-native English-speaking contexts. The core argument is that Farah's works demonstrate that the Anglophone African tradition transcends national boundaries and broadens – rather than limits – the scope of national and trans-national literatures. Indirectly, it also interrogates the importance attached to nativism in determining authentic African literatures and extends Menang's (2001) more inclusive view of this theme.

Born in 1945, Farah grew up in the Ogaden in present-day Ethiopia, where his father worked as an interpreter to the British Governor of the area. After the Ogaden came under Ethiopian administration, his family stayed on until the 1963–64 border skirmishes forced them to return to Somalia proper. During a long self-imposed exile since 1976, Farah has taught in the United States, Germany, Italy, India and a number of African countries. He visited his country for the first time in 1996 after 22 years in exile. He currently divides his time between Cape Town, South Africa, where he moved in 1998, and Minneapolis, the United States, where he holds an endowed chair in liberal arts at the University of Minnesota. Despite his long physical absence from Somalia, Farah's writing is fiercely attached to the realities on the ground there. As he observes in *Yesterday, Tomorrow: Voices from the Somali Diaspora*:

> As a people, we've been at the mercy of traffickers in human misery, cowboy politicians, who have cut up our country into fiefdoms run by a cabal of criminals who claim to have the mandate of the clan as their constituency. (Farah 2000, viii)

Moreover, Farah contends, 'Somalia survives better in my mind when I write about it' (Jussawalla and Dasenbrock, 1992, 61). Somali culture, myths, lore, and traditional and religious beliefs inform Farah's Anglophone writings along with the diverse cultures and linguistic influences with which he has come into contact. For Farah, culture remains elastic and transcends national boundaries, hence the inherent difficulty in situating his novels within traditional geographical and national classifications of literatures. As Jace Weaver (1997) notes, 'worldview' is 'what may distinguish any people's literature from that of any other group' (48), regardless of the language they write in. In this regard, Weaver argues that 'the self-appointed status of the writer is, and must be, one of those things that makes us understand our accountability to Native community' (1997, 51). Yet, as Itala Vivan (1998, 787) notes,

> Language is not a means to decode the puzzle and solve the enigma but, rather, a key element in the enigma itself. [...] The novels [of Farah] are written in English, but as they are all set in Somalia and have Somali characters, it is obvious that the English used here is a sham to cover up an underlying and secret language [...]. [A]t a fictional level, Somali appears in the disguise of a foreign language, or, rather, as a language capable of being foreign to somebody and so excluding him or her.

Chapter 5

The English Farah deploys is rooted in Somalia. How he deploys that English to imagine his nation raises contentious questions.

In presenting the subject matter, I focus primarily on three of Farah's eleven novels: *From a Crooked Rib*, his first novel published in 1970; *Maps*, the first volume of his second trilogy *Blood in the Sun*, published in 1986 (the others being *Gifts* [1993/1999] and *Secrets* [1998a]); and *Links*, the first book of his third trilogy, Past Imperfect, published in 2004 (the others being *Knots* [2007] and *Crossbones* [2011]). *From a Crooked Rib* is set in the 1950s pre-independence Somalia and introduces differences regarding clanship and linguistic variations within the seemingly homogeneous Somali nation, issues that Farah's later novels develop further. *Maps*, which Alden labels as Farah's 'most difficult and interesting novel' (Alden 1995, 382), expands on many of the thematic and literary-linguistic issues raised in his earlier works, including the Variations on the Theme of an African Dictatorship trilogy (made up of *Sweet and Sour Milk* [1979/1992], *Sardines* [1981/1992] and *Close Sesame* [1983/1992]). *Maps* further undermines the concept of Somali-ness as a homogeneous national entity, and, by extension, attacks the myth of the affinity between language and nation, and thus critiques the idea of Somali exceptionalism. In the same vein, *Links* interrogates issues of Somali identity in the wake of the collapse of the Somali nation-state. It is also informed by the botched American intervention in Somalia in 1992. *Links* appears to be linked to Farah's dividing his time between South Africa and the United States. Together, the three texts under discussion – though not a complete study of Farah's oeuvre – situate his literary contribution to the Anglophone African literary-linguistic tradition, embracing as they do a kind of mixed grill of contemporary international English, mostly a blend of British and American English, but other forms of literary Englishes as well.

Farah's literary-linguistic project

Farah's complex linguistic and cultural background prompted Derek Wright to observe that he is 'one of Africa's most multilingual and multicultural writers', whose 'highly eclectic body of fiction draws freely upon many cultural and religious sources and upon readings in many of the world's literatures' (Wright 1994, 98). This eclectic inclination has also attracted condemnation in some scholarly circles. In particular, the 'Britishisms' and 'Americanisms' Farah liberally includes in his novels have earned him a scathing attack from Said S Samatar (2000), a fellow Somali, as un-Somali. *Secrets*, the third in Farah's *Sun Trilogy*, for which he won the prestigious Neustadt International Prize for Literature in 1998, is set against the backdrop of Somalia's devastating civil strife. This novel recounts the family saga of a Somali clan from different narrative perspectives, condemning the killing done in the name of mythical ancestors. Samatar (2000, 138) contends that *Secrets* contains 'serious [socio-linguistic] errors' pertaining to English idioms that are supposed to reflect Somali utterances and experiences, since these 'sit rather awkwardly with Somali life and lore' and with 'Somali literary temper and tastes'. He cites fragments of dialogue from the novel's opening pages:

'Now *why on earth* did we not think of that?'

'I *gather that* Sholoongo was delivered [...].'

'I *cannot vouch for its truth* [...].'

'I named you Kalaman because *it is a cul-de-sac of a name*.'

'We are *damned if we do, and damned if we don't*.' (Samatar's added emphasis)

Samatar finds these linguistic expressions 'fiercely foreign to Somali speech mannerisms', and calls Farah's placing of these idioms in the mouth of a Somali 'positively a literary abomination'. He argues that Farah 'packs in, higgledy-piggledy, the accents, idioms, even mannerisms, of the British Isles' so that characters in the novel 'sound rather like a party of British dandies out on a picnic in the Bounds Green suburb of London' (Samatar 2000, 138). Moreover, he finds the presence of Americanisms such as 'daredevilry' and 'groupie' and Hebrew-English 'shibboleths' unpalatable to the representation of the Somali experience, claiming that Americanisms and Britishisms amount to 'the outrage of the reader appreciative of the violence done to the Somali style of speaking' (Samatar 2000, 138). Yet what if, following Anderson's concept of the imagined community, there is no essential Somali-ness but only a set of repeated images, cultural practices and rites that constitute a shared sense of national affiliation?

Generally, Anglophone African writers present speech acts to appear as though they were spoken in an indigenous tongue. Some do so in standard English without any nuances of the indigenous feeder language; others make sure that the mother tongue is inscribed on the English used through transliteration, 'literal translation' (Onwuemene 1999) in the case of African writers generally or what Bernth Lindfors (1969/1997) calls 'vernacular style', the simulation of indigenous idiom in English, for example in the case of Achebe – as illustrated in Chapter 2 – or cultural translation in the case of Gordimer – as evidenced in Chapter 3. Farah's *From a Crooked Rib* transliterates through a process that Miller (1990) in *Theories of Africans* calls 'anthropological rhetoric', defined as the 'devices by which cultures are represented to each other – through modes of address to a reader who is presumed to be alien to the culture in the text', with the goal of providing the reader with 'necessary cultural information' (Miller 1990, 6). Farah abandons any such pretence in his later novels, which collapse these linguistic boundaries. Sometimes it is even hard to distinguish between words spoken in Somali and those spoken in English within the dialogue of the narrative. Speech-simplification devices, missing in his first novel, start appearing in the speech of native Somali characters in *Maps*, and become even more frequent in *Links*. For example, Askar in *Maps* says, 'My father had a job to do, did he?'; Misra, his surrogate mother, replies: '*That's* correct' *(Maps* 77; emphasis added). Both characters are speaking Somali. Characters in his fiction may speak Somali; in some cases, speech simplifications appear, but not consistently within the same novel or even for the same characters. Are such devices un-Somali? Certainly, there is no cardinal rule – theoretical or practical – spelling out how one can represent local speech in indigenous languages in English literary productions.

In literary discourse the base language – in this case, English – tends to limit the extent to which one can distort or deform the literary language without alienating the reader or end up creating a new language altogether. Overall, there is no correspondence between the original in the supposed vernacular and the transliterated version in the former colonial language. As Day Wylie (1991, 40) puts it:

> Problems in foreign-language expression arise precisely because the relationship between word and object, and between inner sensibility and verbal projection, is not absolute. The word is not the thing; the word, once detached from its historical and material context, necessarily abandons an unspoken residue of association and cultural meaning […].

The success of African writers in reproducing with fidelity or, in some form, the speech from their own language into English varies from writer to writer, and depends on that writer's aptitude, creativity and literary-linguistic choices. But there is no guarantee that what has been produced will be perceived as closer to, or further from, any indigenous original.

Intricacies of re-imagining the nation in a former colonial language

From a Crooked Rib presents the story of Ebla, an almost illiterate nomadic woman, running away from a planned forced marriage. It is set in the context of the run-up to Somalia's independence. The novel shares some aspects with first-generation, Anglophone, modern African writers such as Achebe, although Farah generally refrains from Africanising the English language of his novels. Indeed, Farah admits that he cannot give a strong flavour of another language in English as Achebe does because, he says, his 'writing is metaphor and leitmotiv-based', a quality 'which is also Islamic, because Islam is a very symbol-conscious culture' (*From a Crooked Rib* 1970/2003, 51). Farah concedes that Achebe's 'conscious effort' allows his proverb-based writing to 'bring to the fore some of the things' that he himself cannot make readers see, yet Farah also remains 'conscious of [...] being Somali', with the result that '[his] novels are basically Somali' (Farah 1970/2003, 50). Although Farah does not accept the label of proverb-based writer he particularly reserves for Achebe, he does employ proverbs in his fiction, albeit neither to the same degree nor with the same effect as Achebe. In the fictional nomadic society of *From a Crooked Rib*, 'the old men talked poetry and told proverbs' (Farah 1970/2003, 14). When presenting Somali proverbs such as 'To travel is to learn' (Farah 1970/2003, 116) or 'Console a miser to save his liver' (Farah 1970/2003, 73), Farah translates them into English – as Achebe does in his books – so that some Somali proverbs end up resembling English adages, including the one Ebla's brother uses: 'Birds fly with their own type of birds' (Farah 1970/2003, 139). He refers to Somalis living in the city as 'all of the same type here: misfits, filthy and mean' (Farah 1970/2003/139), but the proverb sounds a lot like the English aphorism, 'Birds of a feather flock together'. Farah's epigraph invokes a Somali proverb, a blend of Islamic and Somali cultural beliefs: 'God created woman from a crooked rib; and anyone who trieth to straighten it, breaketh it' (Farah 1970/2003, 1). The English is an archaic but authoritative language found in the King James version of the Bible. Farah uses this proverb ironically. In many cases, he uses such proverbs to draw attention to and criticise conventional beliefs and practices that he sees as harmful to society – in this case, the widely-accepted male chauvinism that disadvantages women.

Like many other African writers, Farah intercalates – that is, embeds – Somali words such as 'Jes' and 'Fal', and Somali greetings such as 'Nabad' to retain the Somali flavour in the novel:

> It was the dwelling of a certain Jes (a unit of several families living together) [...]. Ebla was a member of this Jes. (Farah 1970/2003, 7)

Or,

> '*Nabad*', Ebla heard a man's voice from behind. She had just placed the grass in front of the calf...
>
> He repeated '*Nabad*', which means 'peace be unto you'. (Farah 1970/2003, 41)

This procedure is not consistent: elsewhere, the reader is trusted to derive meaning from context. The following ordinary dialogue represents a non-naturalistic variant on the technique:

> '*Nadgalio* – goodbye,' said the widow, rushing through the door.
> '*Nabadino* – goodbye to you too,' replied Ebla. (Farah 1970/2003, 58)

Neither character speaks English. The English equivalent presented (without parentheses) constitutes an authorial intervention that has nothing to do with Somali speech but serves as a bridge for non-Somali Anglophone readers to make the writing comprehensible and acceptable.

From a Crooked Rib questions whether a shared language also means a shared discourse. Ebla encounters Somali language difficulties when she leaves the linguistic insularity of her rustic nomadic life for the cosmopolitan city. She wonders what 'this 'Qura' and 'Qado' mean' as 'Breakfast' remains 'a town-word and also a town-meal' beyond the comprehension of Ebla, who comes from where people only eat two meals, 'the first of the day at noon-time' (Farah, 1970/2003, 40). Urban Somali discourse turns Ebla into a stranger in her own language, as the following exchange illustrates:

> 'The bastards,' the widow exclaimed.
>
> 'Who?'
>
> 'The Police.'
>
> 'But who are they?'
>
> '[…] In town like Belet Wene, we have the police.'
>
> 'Is it the name of the tribe?
>
> 'Maybe in a way.'
>
> 'I have never heard the name of this tribe. Under which main sect do they come?'
>
> 'Did you hear about Government?'
>
> 'No. Another tribe?'
>
> 'No. No. No. In towns, we don't talk in terms of tribes. We talk in terms of societies. You see, in this town, there are many different tribes who live together.' (Farah 1970/2003, 66)

The passage proposes 'societies' rather than 'tribes' as a way of understanding the polyglot and multicultural nature of urban space, an assumption of cohesion undermined by inter-clan fighting in Farah's later novels. The police, government and 'office' are institutions that came with colonialism and thrive mostly in urban centres.

Cultural identification beyond linguistic expression

Sharing the same language does not necessarily mean sharing a discourse, and writing in that language requires an act of interpretation and even translation to bridge linguistic gaps. The dialects and social registers representing different social groups within the same ethnic groups, marking off urbanites from rural dwellers, create linguistic gaps, which the standard version of the language seeks to bridge. Thus, when Tiffo, Ebla's other suitor, flirts with her by extolling her beauty and asking her where she came from in 'a mixture of many dialects spoken in what is known as the Somali Republic', Ebla cannot follow because she is 'not familiar with these Southern dialects', and as result he is forced to use 'the common Somali' (Farah 1970/2003, 128).

Local superstitions underscore context-specific discourse in *From a Crooked Rib* (Farah 1970/2003). These include quivering ears (indicating that 'someone was talking about her somewhere far away', 52), twitching palms ('Someone will give me some money', 53), cutting nails and throwing them in the room (which 'brings famine', 122), or being photographed (which 'shortened one's life', 150), and the belief that if a recently adulterous woman sees the wound of a circumcised girl, the wound will not heal. Also, the nomads in *From a Crooked Rib* use a unique way of measuring distances: 'he will come home after 180 milking-instances', the narrator explains at one point: to these nomads, a 'day has two milking-instances, one in the morning and one in the evening' (Farah 1970/2003, 116). By paying attention to the traditions and beliefs of the people embedded in such Anglophone novels, we may also appreciate the diverse ways in which Anglophone writers try to localise their literatures as they variously deploy the English language.

Localisation is another way of expressing the particular pertaining to Somali society. Farah's novels make strong use of local anecdotes. Commenting on Farah's *Close Sesame*, Raymond Ntalindwa (1999, 191) points to the 'internal mechanism of the anecdote', as when the anecdote of King Wiil-Waal is used to educate young characters in the story (and the reader) about the importance of learning from the past. The character of Deeriye in *Close Sesame* serves as a symbolic link between the past and the present and uses that role to educate young Somali men and women about both. However, Farah's treatment of myth is telling.

The legend of Sayyed Mohammed and his beloved horse Hhin Fineen is used in *From a Crooked Rib* to question long-established but dehumanising Somali cultural beliefs. From the legend of Arrawello, the 'wisest Somali female to have ever lived', Ebla gets advice: 'Ye women, say "No"' and 'Be obstinate, and let no man shake your feminine resolve' (Farah 1970/2003 155). Ebla uses this legend to question whether 'she wasn't wiser than the men who were apparently superior to her' (Farah 1970/2003 155). Even early in his career, Farah resists romanticising these myths and legends. They have their place and role in African societies, but problems arise when African societies use them merely to reclaim and glorify the past.

Chapter 5

National mosaic

Maps (Farah 1986/1989) is a more intricate novel than *From a Crooked Rib*. Narrated in three conflicting voices, *Maps* subverts the foundations of Somali-ness. Askar, the protagonist, seeks 'a unique Somali identity', yet his birth in the Ogaden, a disputed territory between Somalia and Ethiopia, separates him from mainstream Somalia, and his adoption by Misra, an Ethiopian Oromo (one of the minority ethnic groups in Ethiopia) woman, as well as the absence of his parents further undermine his claim to 'true' Somali identity.

Historically, the creation of Somalia had an 'irredentist' aim, with 'the ambition of unifying all the Somali nations into one nation state' (Møller 2009, 3). The Somali were spread out through Somalia proper, the Ogaden in Ethiopia, Djibouti, and northern Kenya. Under colonial rule, Britain took control of the northern part (present-day Somaliland) as well as of all of Kenya, including the portion largely populated by Somali-speaking peoples. France established a colony in what is now Djibouti, and Italy took control of areas along the eastern coast of Somalia (excluding Somaliland). Ethiopia (then Abyssinia) also took control of the Ogaden province and its Somali majority, an area since renamed the Somali Region of Ethiopia. Thus, Askar faces 'inherent contradictions' in his identity since Misra is not 'his mother, and the country wasn't hers' and 'she was teaching [him] his people's lore and wisdom, and occasionally some Amharic' (Farah 1986/1989, 134). Farah presents a disputed national space. Michelle Lynn Brown (2010) argues that Askar's 'nationalist desire to return the Ogaden to the Somali motherland invalidates Misra's interethnic, transnational claim to be his mother', and yet his bid 'to privilege nation over mother metaphorically wounds him and is destructive to Misra until he recognises that the Somali cosmology of nation as clan is a cultural identification rather than a biological imperative' (Brown 2010, 126). Askar's surname, 'Cali-Xamari', connects him to Xamar, 'the local name for Somalia's capital Mogadiscio [the Italian spelling]', meaning 'the pearl of the Indian Ocean' (Farah 1986/1989, 138). One finds in this multicultural city Arabic, Amharic and Somali, spoken side by side. This multicultural identity prompts Askar's uncle Hilaal to implore Cusmaan, Askar's teacher, to avoid 'ethnocentric[ity]' (Farah 1986/1989, 212). The 'voice of the master of the mingis [spirit extraction or exorcism] ceremony singing, right in the heart of Mogadiscio, [is] in a language definitely not Somali', just as leaders of such ceremonies chant in Boran, 'the language the spirits understand' (Farah 1986/1989, 213).

This complication of the question of Somali language connects to the question of a unique Somali identity. Hilaal defines a Somali as 'a man, woman or child whose mother tongue is Somali', dismissing 'features which have nothing to do with a Somali's Somaliness' since one 'might meet with foreseeable difficulty in telling an Eritrean, an Ethiopian or a northern Sudanese apart from a Somali, unless one were to consider the cultural difference' (Farah 1986/1989, 174). One recollects Renan's words that a shared race does not necessarily make a nation. Yet Farah's references to a polyglot landscape undermine the concept of Somali cultural and linguistic homogeneity and expose Uncle Hilaal's misconceptions about Somali identity. He initially sees Somalis as 'a homogeneous people […] culturally' who 'speak the same language wherever they may be found', as opposed to other nationals such as Ethiopians, Sudanese, Eritreans, Nigerians, or Senegalese (Farah 1986/1989, 174) who lack a common linguistic and cultural identity. Although the Somalis' colonial experience spread them out in Somalia Italiana, British Somaliland, French Somaliland, the Northern Frontier District and a larger Ogaden, Hilaal views the main Somali nation as the nucleus of Somali identity. He insists that 'The Somali in the Ogaden, the Somali in Kenya both, because they lack what makes the self strong and whole, are unpersons' (Farah 1986/1989, 175). His later realisation of the limitation of language as a unifying factor is symbolised by his burning of his research papers on the issue. *Maps* displaces myths of national identity and of language as national emblems. Ngaboh-Smart (2001, 91) notes that 'Language, especially how language frustrates cultural insularity, is fundamental to Farah's criticism of Askar's nationalist ambition'. As Wright points out, Cusmaan's tutor, 'when […] not speaking Swahili', the East and Central African lingua franca, 'use[s] a bastardized, ungrammatical form of Somali' (Wright 1992/1993, 182).

Farah suggests that 'to speak a language is to take on the world, a culture' (Farah 1986/1989, 32); that every language exists alongside other languages. Language also 'transgresses all kinds of boundaries – social, gender, generational, identity, and geography – to show the idea of nation as having a "shifting and unstable significance"' (Yewah 2001, 45). Askar attempts to 'redraw [his] map of the Horn of Africa', in which the Ogaden 'always [remains] an integral part of Somalia', but his attempt proves futile since he falls into the same trap as the European colonial powers (Farah 1986/1989, 227). In fact, he realises 'that he had been moving in the wrong direction all along' (Farah 1986/1989, 159). The eventual collapse of Somalia as nation suggests that a unitary language does not necessarily guarantee nationhood.

European conquest and the imposition of foreign languages are frequent focal points in postcolonial analysis. *Maps* widens our understanding of cultural imperialism. As Hilaal explains, the Arabs also imposed 'on our African language their alien thought' (Farah 1986/1989, 173), just as the Europeans and Ethiopians did. Instead, the novel appears to support the confluence of cultures and traditions, as Hilaal urges his wife Salaado to 'Just teach [Askar] reading and writing'. Salaado chooses tales from *Khalila wa Dimna* in Somali, which she reads with her voice 'confident as a trickster's' – an allusion to the African folktale figure. Hilaal, on the other hand, reads him 'his favourite text', Al-Macarri's *Letter of a Horse and a Mule*, which is written in English. This immersion into literate culture in Somali and English together does not alienate Askar from an oral culture, however, since he cannot 'help comparing them to Misra'. He can thus 'adore them all three' (Farah 1986/1989, 146).

Language of violence and nationalistic discourse

In many ways, *Links* (Farah 2004) appears to build on the literary and linguistic elements of Farah's earlier works. One striking feature is the language of violence that features so prominently in this novel. In Farah's earlier novels, this language of violence is invariably inscribed on the bodies of the novel's subjects. It is also evident in Farah's fascination with female genital mutilation (FGM) in his writing. In this novel, Farah poses questions pertaining to common linguistic and cultural identity as a national unifier – similar questions to those that Askar in *Maps* grapples with as he struggles to envisage the Ogaden within the larger Somali nation on the basis of a shared language and culture. In *Links*, that larger Somali nation has collapsed in conflict that had 'generated a Somali diaspora of unprecedented scale' (Cassanelli 2001, 6). Exile does not necessarily alienate one from one's background so long as one engages, as Farah does, with that nation. Like Dante's *Inferno*, *Links* is cast as a rereading of national tragedy. Farah introduces each section with an epigraph from Dante, and Jeebleh, an émigré to the US and the novel's central character, did his dissertation in Italy on the *Inferno*, recasting the epic into a poetic idiom comprehensible to the Somali. The novel thus prominently references acts of cross-cultural translation. Yet this novel, the first part of a trilogy, attacks the notion that the Somali diaspora looks towards peace and reconstruction.

Links ought to be read against the backdrop of the 1992 American intervention in Somalia that informs the story and the splintering of the nation, hence raising questions about the country's exceptionalism:

> In those long-gone days, the people of this country were at peace with themselves, comfortable in themselves, happy with who they were. As one of the most ancient cities in Africa south of the Sahara, Mogadiscio [sic] had known centuries of attrition: one army leaving death and destruction in its wake, to be replaced by another and yet another, all equally destructive: the Arabs arrived and got some purchase on the peninsula, and after they pushed their commerce and along with it the Islamic faith, they were replaced by the Italians, then the Russians, and more recently the Americans, nervous, trigger-happy, shooting before they were shot at. The city became awash with guns, and the presence of the gun-crazy Americans escalated the conflict to greater heights. (Farah 2004, 14–15)

The Americans thus join a list of foreigners whose intervention and influence on the Somali culture and landscape are seen and felt. However, rather than sensationalising the violence, Farah uses the conflict as a fulcrum around which the Somali question is revisited through the dialogue and language of the novel. As Inezui Mzali (2010, 85) notes:

> Farah's *Links* counters the sensationalist media representation of Somalia by constantly deferring the direct experience of violence [...]. *Links* contributes an alternative anti-sensationalist representation of the events [...], a representation in which the direct spectacle of violence is often mediated and deferred rather than exposed. This approach benefits contextualization through various perspectives that broaden rather than limit the scope of interpretation.

The novel explores how language is integral to the process of understanding a failed nation. For example, it proves problematic to translate into English the Somali expression 'Dagaalka sokeeye' for the dehumanising civil war. Jeebleh translates the term as 'killing an intimate' or 'warring against an intimate' (Farah 2004, 137–38). But he fails to come up with an expression that does not include the aspect of kinship, hence exposing the brutality inherent in Somali strife. His American identity is correspondingly difficult.

The distrust the Somali have for the Americans and the Americans' effect on them predates the 1992 intervention (Lofland 2002, 1–12). As Jeebleh explains: 'The coinage of amerikaan to mean "weird", I should point out, precedes the Somali people's recent encounter with the Americans in the shape of the Marines and rangers who shot the daylights out of them', adding, 'maybe it came about as a result of the Hollywood movies we've seen' (Farah 2004, 262). As a naturalised American from Somalia, Jeebleh thus complicates the issue of national identity. Jeebleh represents the Somali diaspora from North Africa. As Farah notes, 'More and more Somalis, especially from North America, are going back to Mogadishu to help the reconstruction. And some are beginning to listen' (Appiah and Farah 2004, 58). Jeebleh returns home 'to learn and to listen' and 'assess the extent of [his] culpability as a Somali', 'reemphasize [his] Somaliness', and to receive 'a needed boost to [his] identity' (Farah 2004, 32), since he was 'fed up being asked by the Americans whether [he] belonged to this and that clan' (Farah 2004, 36). Even so, the trouble with the American intervention alluded to in this novel is that 'the Americans didn't listen to the Somalis' (Appiah and Farah 2004, 58). As a Somali, Jeebleh is expected to take sides in the clan warfare; as an American, he is supposed to be above it. He wonders whether one can 'continue to love a land one does not recognize anymore', which in itself remains a paradox because he has 'never asked himself whether he loved America' and is primarily 'engaged with America' through his love for his wife and children (Farah 2004, 42).

Chapter 5

The language of war in this 'inferno' makes the common language of Somali impotent as a unifying power. As Bile, recently released from prison during the civil strife, explains, 'In Somalia the civil war then was language [...], only I didn't speak the new language' (Farah 2004, 19). To the Somali question 'Yaad tahay?' ('Who are you?'), the normal response 'was no longer valid', as now the answer universally referred to the identity of one's 'clan family, your blood identity!' (Farah 2004, 19).

National identity has vanished, and there is no pretence that the Somali tongue can unify disparate groups. In consequence, Bile is forced to learn 'the correct responses in the flourish of the tongue', which he, 'in the idiom, the new argot' and as 'a good mimic', is able to speak 'in the correct Somali accent, nodding when my questioner mentioned the right acronym' (Farah 2004, 19). He utters 'the acronym of the period', the 'initial letters of the clan-based militia that ran the Tyrant out of the city' with his 'head down, as if embarrassed to have done so' (Farah 2004, 19).

Only then do the militia let him proceed. Here the Somali language is supplanted by clan languages that mark the destabilising clan-based fiefdoms. The idea of Somalia as a multilingual space emerges from the ruins of war and signals its future. For example, Jeebleh receives a thick parcel in which he finds a mobile phone with a manual in Arabic (indicating it might have been imported from Abu Dhabi, from where 'most Mogadiscians got their high-tech stuff'). It contains a note in Italian that advises him of the numbers entered into the phone's memory (Farah 2004, 125). The receptionist gives him an envelope containing a one-page message in Somali, 'written on a lined paper torn out of a child's exercise book' with six thumbprint signatures of clan elders and 'three printed names, difficult to decipher' at the bottom (Farah 2004, 125). Jeebleh further notes that the grounds of the nearby hotel were marked off from the street by a large sign handwritten in Somali (the national language), Arabic (a religious language), English (the dominant colonial language) and Italian (a former colonial language), warning against bearing firearms on to the premises (Farah 2004, 37). And when he fills in hotel forms, 'the words for date and place of birth, sex, marital status, and permanent address were in Italian' (Farah 2004, 40). The coexistence of these languages offers a peaceable, pluralistic alternative to the chaos associated with clan warfare of a people who share the same national language.

When Jeebleh tries to find a solution to 'pronoun obsession', he turns to Seamus, a polyglot from Northern Ireland, and asks him which pronoun he finds 'appropriate when you refer to the people of Belfast? Not in terms of being Catholic or Protestant, but just people?' But Seamus is not so 'conscious of the pronouns' as Jeebleh, who uses 'we' when referring to Somalis in general and 'they' when referring to clan politics and those who promote it (Farah 2004, 219). Seamus explains that enemies 'matter to those who create them' when one 'think[s] of them as "they" and therefore create[s] them' (Farah 2004, 219). This differentiation of 'them' from 'us' within a nation of people who speak the same language mocks the nationalism that had hitherto held the Somalis together. Conversely, the relationships between Bile and Jeebleh – two friends from different clans – and the two of them with Seamus, an Irishman who shared an apartment with them in Italy, suggest the way forward for Somalia. Farah imagines Somalia not as a homogeneous nation, but as a trans-national, polyglot and multicultural space, the putative national language of Somali notwithstanding. The trio describe their friendship as 'a country – spacious, giving, and generous'. They held 'no secrets from one another, and lived out of one another's pockets, sharing all' (Farah 2004, 57).

The character of Seamus also broadens and helps to undermine the myth that common language and national ancestry can link people together. The interreligious home of Seamus' family does not save the family from sectarian violence, as their Belfast apartment is blown up when a grenade is thrown through an open window from a passing car. Seamus and his mother survive because they happen to be out. This 'massacre' happens despite Seamus' 'inclusive' upbringing, 'in which sectarian differences were never privileged' by his 'Protestant mother and a Catholic father' (Farah 2004, 181). Moreover, Seamus travels on a British passport and he is asked by Jeebleh whether his 'loyalty lies with Britain or Ireland' (Farah 2004, 188), a deliberate parallel to Jeebleh, who travels on both American and Somali passports. Seamus had lived in England during his teens, and had then gone to Cambridge, where he had taken his first degree before spending time in Italy, France and Egypt. His dual citizenship raises questions of loyalty, but Seamus explains that his 'loyalties do not lie with the Union Jack' but remain 'an all-inclusive Irish loyalty, with a good measure of cosmopolitanism. The idea of having allegiance to a country is foreign to me' (Farah 2004, 189). Seamus appears to reflect Farah's view in this respect, for Farah's cosmopolitan stance helps him look at Somalia with detachment, and to use English rather than Somali to imagine its problems and let the world know about them.

For Farah, cosmopolitanism requires fostering the particular, including Somali tradition. The place named 'The Refuge', which brings together splintered groups of Somalis, for example, makes eating together into an antidote to the paralysing and divisive clan politics. As Bile explains, 'We have resorted to the traditional method of eating together daily from the same mayida […] in belief that we create camaraderie and we'll all trust one another' (Farah 2004, 157). Their 'experiment bears out' as 'anyone meaning to do harm to a fellow sharer of the mayida will not dare look him, or anyone else, in the eye'; as a result, 'many people prefer staying away […] when there is bad blood', for when they 'share the mayida, there can be no bad blood' (Farah 2004, 158). This space thus privileges common traditions over clanship.

The novel, too, creates a space that transcends clan, ethnic and linguistic divisions, as symbolised by Raasta, a Somali 'special child', and Makka, a child with multiple identities. Raasta is 'seen as a symbol of peace' (Farah 2004, 304). At a few days old, she attracted hundreds of people 'whenever there was fighting' and found sanctuary in 'the house with the big compound' (Farah 2004, 53). This 'special child' (fashioned along the lines of Saleem Sinai and a thousand and one other special or gifted children born between midnight and 1a.m. at India's independence in Salman Rushdie's *Midnight's Children*) allows those near her to feel 'protected' because of the magical powers she is believed to have been born with. Raasta's birth also breaks social taboos – an allusion to clan politics – as Bile, her uncle, violates the 'traditional medical code of conduct' to help his younger sister give birth: 'Never mind the medical or traditional code, which [he] disregarded,' the experience 'gave [him] great joy to deliver a lovely dreadlocked [hence her nickname] miracle baby into the world'. She is named Rajo, 'Hope', in the belief that she represents every Somali's hope.

Makka, who has Down's syndrome, is 'half Somali, half European, the European half unspecified' (Farah 2004, 161). This girl's multiple identities connect the colonial heritage (the past) with the postcolonial (the present) to question the Somalis' obsession with clan warfare, which renders them oblivious to the nation's varied historical, linguistic and cultural experiences. Makka is presented as fond of 'repeating a stock phrase, "Aniga, anigro ah!"' (Farah 2004, 162), a Somali phrase meaning 'I myself am', as though to reinforce her elusive identity. Raasta and Makka are 'like Siamese twins, neither [of whom] makes a move without the other being there': 'Where Raasta intimates care, Makka communicates boundless, generous love'. Makka seems 'held together within the framework of a narrative not yet known to us, that she's an untold story' and her 'every word points to so many unasked questions needing answers' (Farah 2004, 161). The difference between Makka and Raasta centres on memory. Makka, the girl of a moment, is 'innocence, pure and simple' and is in 'no one else's camp, only in her own'; she belongs to no clan, hence 'her absolute loyalty' to the cause of a multicultural co-existence – as opposed to Raasta, who has been 'taught […] what her clan family was, from the instant she opened her lungs with the cry of life' (Farah 2004, 163). Paired together, the two children help create a new language of the nation devoid of jingoism. The dialogue amongst these characters towards the conclusion of the novel features what Mzali calls 'linguistic deferrals' – refusal to provide definite and simplistic answers – 'which ultimately reflects the strategically evasive conclusion of the novel' (Farah 2004, 94).

Conclusion

On the whole, Farah's use of English to tell the story of Somalia and its peoples in his fiction helps to create 'particular solidarities' (Anderson 1991, 133) relating to Somalia, as Anderson suggests, but within a broad-based cosmopolitan environment.

This exploration of Farah's works demonstrates how cosmopolitanism can be deployed as the frame through which one can productively approach Farah's work in an increasingly globalised world. In fact, this exoteric view is very much in line with Farah's own largely cosmopolitan approach to his writing, in which he uses Somalia as the epicentre even as he writes from exile. Such cosmopolitanism extends Farah's writing beyond the confines of any one nation, and it does so in the service of a broadly humanistic agenda. In fact, Farah is engaged in what Yewah calls 'subversive activities of de-centring the nation' (Yewah 2001, 45), which reveals that a language can be used to imagine the nation for the benefit of humanity, but it does not necessarily make a nation unite. Indeed, just as Renan had envisioned in the nineteenth century before the Scramble for Africa, Farah's fictions show that a language may invite nations to unite, but it does not compel them to do so. Reading Farah's works from a cosmopolitan perspective sidesteps pro-nativist approaches that question the use of English in national narratives of traditionally non-English contexts. Moreover, Farah effectively interrogates issues of Somali exceptionalism in his English fiction before and after the fragmentation of Somalia as a unitary state. Farah has been contesting the question of Somali national homogeneity in practically all his fiction from the 1970s onwards, using the varied Somali conflicts as a fulcrum around which the Somali question is revisited through the dialogue and language of the novel. This becomes even more apparent when one examines Farah's works from a cosmopolitan perspective.

Note
1   This chapter is an adaptation of my article entitled 'English, Cosmopolitanism and the Myth of National Linguistic Homogeneity in Nuruddin Farah's Fiction', originally published in *Forum for Modern Language Studies*, 50(3), 256–274, 2014.

6

Anglophonism, the novel and the African literary-linguistic continuum

Introduction

The dynamism of the English language in its interaction with and representation of African discourses in the works of Achebe, Ngũgĩ, Gordimer and Farah accounts for diverse manifestations of English usage, as the preceding chapters have demonstrated. Even though what emerges in these fictions does not necessarily amount to new languages, the various manifestations of literary English in their writings attest to how English affects and is affected by the indigenous languages, cultures and discourses it encounters. This confluence has various implications for both the position of the English language in Africa and indeed in other traditionally non-English contexts where it is used as a literary language to foster pan-national, trans-national and cross-cultural literary discourse. It is indisputable that English has not only become established in Africa but has also influenced a literary-linguistic tradition in that language on the continent. This effect has far-reaching implications for the use of the language in the imagining of African nation-states, not only in traditionally Anglophone but also in Francophone and Lusophone Africa (i.e. through translation). In this final chapter, therefore, I begin by arguing for the recognition of English as an African language, contestable as that may appear for a variety of reasons, including those I have already outlined in the first chapter, and some of which I briefly revisit in this chapter to situate my argument. Then I interrogate the issue of the Anglophone African literary-linguistic continuum as informed by Derek Bickerton's (1973) conception of the Creole continuum before reaching some conclusions on the issue.

There is a need generally for a shift in attitude towards English in the study of Anglophone-African literatures. This shift is important to ensure a full understanding and interrogation of the effect of English in Africa and other traditionally non-English contexts and how it is affected by the languages and discourses it intermingles with without the additional baggage of the language being perpetually an alien tongue in a space and time where it serves functions of an established, if not an indigenous, language. In this regard, the English language cannot permanently have its home in 'Europe' when it has simultaneously established its 'home' on the African soil. In fact, despite evidence suggesting that English has found a 'home' in Africa, with political and institutional support to sustain its presence, the general trend has been to treat works published in English as African works of art, produced in a European language, which are, as Ngũgĩ and Wali would argue, in essence 'appendages' of the English (hence Afro-European) literary tradition, a label that fails to do justice to African letters produced in this language.

As a result, a writer such as Gordimer, whose works remain South African because her home is in Africa, insists that although her 'home is in Africa', her 'language home is European' (March and Gordimer 2011, n.p). Such a perception creates an unnecessary contradiction in Anglophone African literatures. Her statement implies that the African continent can embrace her identity as African, yet it cannot consider as African her first contact language with established roots on the continent and a literary tradition belonging to Africa. In fact, this tendency limits our exploration of the diverse trends that emerge in the varying application of English in African literary discourse. For more than a century, and longer in some cases, English has been the language of settlers who made Africa their home. Olive Schreiner's 1883 novel, *The Story of an African Farm*, even helped to establish an African literary tradition for white liberals in South Africa, which also includes ways through which they could use English to reflect their African situation. To complicate the situation, African descendants of freed African-American slaves in Liberia and to some extent Sierra Leone also use English as their first language.

Many of these 'Creole intellectuals', such as George Padmore and Alexander Crummell, African-American by birth and Liberian by adoption, with the latter regarded as the 'father of African nationalism' (Appiah 1990, 385), had had no pretext for using English as it was their first contact language. They had seen the language as their heritage, and both were pro-English language usage in African discourse, including for nationalistic purposes. In fact, some of the early fictional writings in English in West Africa cannot be extricated from the influences of these early Creole intellectuals. Here I have in mind the early development of Anglophone African writing. Joseph Ephraim Casely, for example, published *Ethiopia Unbound* in 1911, which had initially been treated as one of the earliest novels to be written by an African until the discovery of *Guanya Pau: The Story of an African Prince*, which had been published a decade earlier in 1891 by Joseph Jeffrey Walters. Both these writers had connections with education in Sierra Leone and Liberia, respectively, both of which had benefited from the relocation of Creole intellectuals from largely British controlled lands and the United States in the two West African countries. I am not mentioning this here as a digression, but to illustrate how reductive at times we have been by dismissing any writing in English as non-African or belonging to a tradition that is not necessarily indigenous African. Yet all the early writings by Africans in English had been informed and influenced by the African environment and experiences. With Ngũgĩ also admitting that even his native Gikuyu had 'traces of colonial violence' (Nicholls 2010, 195), one wonders what constitutes an indigenous African literary-linguistic tradition from a purist perspective, but this is not the subject of my argument.

On the other hand, the situation might be different for writers such as Achebe, Farah and Ngũgĩ, whose first language is not English. They had or still have an option of writing in an indigenous African language – an option that Ngũgĩ eventually chose to exercise in the latter part of his literary career – yet wrote or have been writing in English for reasons I have outlined in the first chapter and respective sections dedicated to their writings. In various ways, all these writers confirm and establish English as one of the major languages of African literary discourse beyond the esoteric discourse of ethnic and non-trans-national literary discourses. Although Ngũgĩ has argued otherwise, his works in translation remain relevant within and outside Africa in English and cannot be discussed outside the Anglophone African literary tradition, since they survive largely in English translation (rather than in the Gikuyu originals, as Gikandi [1991, 164] has contended elsewhere) and engage with the same literary tradition that Ngũgĩ seems to repudiate.

In the increasingly globalised world, the debate on the question of African literature is not as fierce as it used to be, even though the issue remains largely unresolved. Even so, English varyingly embodies many of the African discourses and continues to serve as the language through which many African writers express their thoughts about Africa, and through which the world learns about Africa. This is a line of enquiry this book has pursued, focusing primarily on how English affects and is affected by the indigenous languages, cultures and discourses it seeks to embody concretely in the various writings of African writers. In fact, African governments continue establishing support systems that foster the development of Anglophonism – or the use of English in traditionally non-English contexts – rather than diminish it, and, by doing so, they sustain the Anglophone African literary-linguistic continuum, which in this book has been defined as variations in the literary usage of English in African discourse, with the language serving as the base to which writers add variations inspired by indigenous languages, beliefs, cultures and, sometimes, nation-specific experiences. This definition is justifiable because the variations evident in the usage of English in traditionally non-native literary universes of discourse attest to what happens when a language operates in diverse sociocultural and linguistic situations.

Yet, the mixed signals sent through the use of English in African literary discourse extend to black Africans writing in that language as well. This ambivalent position of former colonial languages in Africa has created often embarrassing and seemingly intractable dilemmas regarding the ambivalent position of English and other former colonial languages. Mudimbe notes that written literary discourses in such languages, for example, 'do not constitute a hiatus in terms of African experience' , as this 'neo-African literature', 'a commodity' and a 'recent invention', should be classified 'for what it is as discourse' and what 'it could mean in the larger context of local and regional discourses', instead of as 'a mirror of something else': 'of Africa's political struggle, of processes of acculturation, or of human rights objectives' (Mudimbe 1994, 180). At least, this is how we generally tend to read African writers, which often raises questions – some necessary and some unnecessary – that prompted Mudimbe to allude to the state of ambivalence in which modern African literature finds itself: being both authentically African, and an appendage of the European literary tradition, be it the Anglophone, Francophone or Lusophone.

Against this backdrop, it is not surprising that we have seemingly endless debates surrounding the place of literatures written in former colonial languages (see, for example, Galafa 2017; Adeseke 2016; Ndede 2016; Browne 2012; Gikandi 2012; Ten, 2011). Notwithstanding these debates, African literatures in English thrive in their diversity. In this regard, Ngũgĩ's argument for the dismissal of African literatures in former colonial languages from the continent's canon applies only to a limited extent, since Anglophone African literatures remain an integral part of African literary discourses and rely on African languages and cultures for their literary expressiveness. The former colonial languages are thus 'fronts' for indigenous African languages and cultures they seek or attempt to embody and should not be treated as replacements of such languages (and their cultural identity). There are many tacit 'behind-the-scenes' literary-linguistic and cultural influences that cannot be ignored, even in the representation produced in African English, French, German, Portuguese and other former colonial languages. Here the focus is on English – the Anglophone literary tradition in Africa.

The African novel and the English 'home' in Africa

Inescapably, Africa remains a multilingual and multicultural space in which a chosen medium of expression must concretely embody African experiences (largely in languages associated with Africa, including English in various social circles) and negotiate through a multiplicity of discourses, languages and cultures in meaningful ways. In this regard, the varied engagements of Achebe, Ngũgĩ, Gordimer and Farah with the Anglophone tradition are differing manifestations of what I have called an Anglophone African literary-linguistic continuum. Their literary Englishes embody or seek to embody varyingly African literary forms and discourses. After all, Anglophone African literature constitutes a discourse that emerged at a particular point in the history of Africans (as Mudimbe, 1994, would argue), and has continued to develop and prosper in diverse ways, hence defying Wali's (1963) prophecy of doom. Achebe's rebuttal came two years later in 1965, in a lecture entitled 'The African writer and the English language', when he pointed out that the language helped to bring together 'small, scattered' polities and unified them under present and still problematic nation-states. In his lecture, Achebe focuses on the functional value of English and the unifying role it plays in national spaces arbitrarily created at the table of the Berlin Conference. Wali and Ngũgĩ, on the other hand, focus more on the politics of language in their attempt to promote the indigenous African languages and their functions on the continent, which in their own right have not been spared by linguistic and sociocultural influences engendered by the colonial encounter. In this final chapter, I do not seek to revisit the arguments of the so-called nativist camp – justifiable as they might be – but I attempt to acknowledge the reality that English as a language of communication in Africa survives with or without the language decolonisation 'agnostics' (a term Okonkwo [1999] has aptly used). What I admit here is that such divergent views – contestable as they can be at times – hint at the diversity of modern African literatures that need to be embraced in their multiplicity, the language debates aside.

If some of the pro-nativist adherents could have their way, they could even deny that English (in English-speaking or Anglophone Africa), and indeed the Anglophone tradition have had anything to do with the emergence of modern African literature as we know it today. Yet, sometimes it is better to acknowledge any foreign influences and their effect on an indigenised literary tradition. In this regard, we can take a leaf from China, which I had the privilege of recently visiting. The Chinese have made significant technological and communication advancement. I noticed how in the museum of the Communication University of China in Beijing they have documented the history and pioneers of the modern telephone, radio, TV and movies but then proudly document how the Chinese have cultivated their own niche in these areas. In the African case, Ngũgĩ would later denigrate his earlier works in English and dismiss them as part of the Afro-Saxon literary tradition and not true African novels because of the English language he used to produce these works, forgetting that there were good historical and even linguistic reasons why he started writing in English and not in Gikuyu. Moreover, the link between English and some early African writing cannot be obliterated. In fact, because of the highly politicised language of the African literature debate, an attempt is made to overlook the historical circumstances under which the modern written African literatures in Sub-Saharan Africa emerged, the African antecedents that Chinweizu and Madubuike (1983) remind us of notwithstanding.

On the whole, instead of a 'dead end' and the 'sterility' that Wali prophesised, many dynamic literary-linguistic developments have evolved in the multiplicity of African writings in the Anglophone tradition (and, indeed, as manifested in other traditions in the former colonial languages with a strong standing in Africa, such as French and Portuguese), as I have demonstrated in chapters 2 to 5. The diverse literary-linguistic aspects infused in the writings of the four writers examined in these chapters attest to the dynamic character of the encounter between English, other languages and other cultures, as well as discourses in Africa. In this regard, new ways of using English (the linguistic) coupled with new ways of writing poetry, plays and novels (the literary) have emerged in Africa (as, indeed, they have in other traditionally non-English contexts). Some of these aspects are attributable to individual authorial style, and others to social trends that have developed and been refined over the years as African writers learn from one another. Despite variations in the Anglophone literary-linguistic tradition of Africans, the English language has remained a constant factor as a language of Anglophone discourse. In literary terms, the language remains the main river to which a multitude of tributaries – some large and some small – add variants indicative of particularities linked with time and space of a given African locale. These particularities are buttressed by an individual author's background, ideological leanings, artistic prowess and even attitude towards the English language itself.

For many years, African writers have relied on standard English as a common means of literary expression for their creative endeavours. They variously experimented with literary and linguistic forms derived from both the oral literary tradition from indigenous languages and cultures that Irele (2001) asserts are the basis of African literature and the established Anglophone tradition generally. However, both 'Afrolect' (predominantly indigenous African influences) and 'Eurolect' (predominantly European influences that Bamiro [2000] talks about) are varyingly present in practically all African works of art in English.

What is not lost, regardless of the varied influences, is that Standard English appears to delimit the extent to which African writers can depart from communicable English. Moreover, it delimits the extent to which these authors can add diverse elements from different languages and cultures steeped in the African environment to this language in their literary expressions. After all, English, as a language of the 'world', is used largely for communication within individual Anglophone African nation-states, between and among African nation-states, and with the

Chapter 6

wider international community. In this regard, African writers – regardless of their linguistic affiliation – tap into indigenous languages and cultural beliefs to represent esoteric elements from one ethnic or social group in their respective quests for a broad exoteric audience to facilitate cross-cultural, intra-national and trans-national literary correspondence.

The similarities in the application of the English language we see in Ngũgĩ's earlier novels and Achebe's fictions, for example, have their roots in the African languages and cultures from which they draw. Indigenous African languages serve as feeder languages and cultures from which writers draw inspiration for their writing. This does not make the indigenous African languages and cultures inferior – far from it. Rather, they account for the variants in literary English emerging in particularised sociocultural and linguistic contexts, especially in a traditionally non-indigenous English space.

Moreover, fictional works tend to be based on historical events, events that inform and help define both the context in which the language is used and the way it is applied. For the new generation of writers, the context is the largely failed African nation-states that suffered a crisis of identity in the turbulent 1980s when many of these writers started writing. In this regard, there is more to African literatures than merely the question of which language writers on the continent choose for their writing. Indeed, there is more to African literatures in the colonial languages than the question of transliteration (a term adopted by the Kampala Conference to explain the writing process of an African writer writing in English in relation to the indigenous African language that inspires the thoughts and ideas) and intercalations (the inclusion in such literatures of words from indigenous languages). Consequently, the English they write remains an integral part of African literature, not otherwise (i.e. Euro-African literature, as Ngũgĩ points out in *Decolonising the Mind*). We also see continuity in the deployment of the former colonial languages and the engagement with African literary traditions and cultures.

As I have illustrated in this book, an Anglophone African literary-linguistic continuum is a realistic proposition worth further investigation. More studies in this area could assist in resolving some of the issues pertaining to the theory of the Anglophone novel in Africa. My discussion in this book has been limited to four established writers, but there is room to study emerging African writers to further illuminate this proposed Anglophone African literary-linguistic continuum. Rather than impede national imagining in Africa, the English language has facilitated the process in addition to establishing African literatures at home and abroad. African writers have been imagining their nations in this language primarily because the language makes it easy for them to do so.

However, as Ngũgĩ has pointed out, the primacy of English or of other former colonial languages in writing should not prevail at the expense of the development of writing in indigenous African languages, languages which serve as feeder languages to the Anglophone literary discourse. No one can dispute that. Nevertheless, one also cannot ignore the modern African literary tradition that has been thriving under Anglophonism. As Anglophone African literatures seem to be here to stay, there ought to be institutional support for the indigenous African languages so that Anglophone and indigenous African literatures can complement one another. Even though lack of resources in many African nations might hamper these efforts, this is an issue worth pursuing. Anglophonism benefits enormously from the input of indigenous African cultures, languages and discourses, some of the main defining and localising elements of African Anglophone literature in the African literary-linguistic continuum.

Bickerton's theory and the African literary-linguistic continuum

A 'continuum' is a 'continuous thing, quantity, or substance' or 'a continuous series of elements passing into each other' (Oxford English Dictionary 2010). In the 1970s, Bickerton used the term 'Creole continuum' to refer to the English-based Creole in Guyana, mainly because of a continuous range of variations, found in many Creole-speaking communities, between the forms used at the lowest social levels and those used at the highest. Similarly, in Africa and other traditionally non-English contexts there is a continuous range of English variations, found in many English-speaking nations, between the forms used in different social contexts and the standard variety. In this book I have focused on the range of varieties as they appear in the fictions of the four authors discussed, who are from diverse backgrounds and different parts of Africa. In this context, an Anglophone literary-linguistic continuum refers to the range of modulations the English language undergoes as writers attempt to use a 'foreign' language while trying to make the language relevant to their primary audience, fellow nationals, and wider international audiences. Before making further assumptions, it is perhaps wise to revisit what Bickerton further remarks on the nature of continuum:

> Language is then seen as a dynamic process *evolving through space and time*, 'leaky' grammars, variants that fit no system, conflicting native-speaker intuitions – all problems that vexed previous formulations are now seen as inevitable consequences of spatial or temporal segmentation of what is really a seamless whole. It follows that to speak of 'dialects' or even perhaps 'languages' may be misleading; these terms merely seek to freeze at an arbitrary moment, and to coalesce into an arbitrary whole, phenomena which in turn are ongoing and heterogeneous. (Bickerton 1973, 643; emphasis added)

The evolving of language through 'space' and 'time' here is significant. Africa is the space where the English language has found a home and is subject to various linguistic and cultural influences (i.e. it affects and is affected by the multiplicity of languages and cultures that it has encountered). It could not have survived on the continent all these years without being affected by the 'space' and all that it engenders and 'time' with all its implications. Bickerton's postulation above is on language per se, which can be applied to a broad spectrum of what has come to be known globally as 'New Englishes' – a term which has since the 1980s been applied to refer to non-native varieties of English spoken in the former colonies of England, chiefly in South Asia, Southeast Asia, West Africa and East Africa – as well as major varieties whose evolution is linked to settler English, in this case, in traditionally non-English contexts such as Africa.

This book has extended Bickerton's ideas to the study of the use of the English language in Anglophone African literature, since language is the basic building block of literature. Its variations in Africa present an opportunity for an intriguing study, which allows us to see convergences and divergences in the use of literary English in diverse Anglophone African writings. It particularly comes in handy in the absence of a trajectory that could facilitate a study of an African Anglophone literary tradition manifested by a multiplicity of variants in writings. In fact, in a discussion of Anglophone African literatures the English language is a common denominator amidst numerous variants of Anglophone literary expressions and diverse styles and linguistic manipulations.

This study of Achebe, Ngũgĩ, Gordimer and Farah has illustrated that within this Anglophone African tradition there are many varieties and multiplicities that ought to be studied for their convergences and divergences. After all, there is no single commonality in Achebe's combined use of the 'vernacular style', Standard English, African proverbs and Nigerian pidgin (a variant that he shares with Soyinka and other Nigerian writers) with Ngũgĩ's use of similar approaches. Or let alone Ngũgĩ's later shifts to more radical intercalations as well as the use of an indigenous language to engage with the Anglophone tradition. One can also add to the equation translations that reveal the intercourse that occurs between English and indigenous linguistic and literary forms in Ngũgĩ's work. Neither is there a single commonality with Gordimer, writing within white settler codes in an African context, and Farah, who defies some of the rules witnessed in the writings of Achebe and Ngũgĩ's earlier writings.

The insights from Bickerton are significant for an understanding of the relationships of various Anglophone literary projects reviewed in this book – Achebe's, Ngũgĩ's, Gordimer's, and Farah's. They help to establish order even in seemingly literary-linguistic chaos and extremes. I have placed the first two authors – Achebe and Ngũgĩ

– in that order in the discussion because they seem to be oppositional regarding the English language that they varyingly engage with. Gordimer follows, because of the racial and often contentious dimension that she brings to an African and postcolonial linguistic and literary space. Finally, I have considered Farah because of the complication that he introduces as the most famous son of a seemingly homogenous nation in culture and language, Somalia, who writes in English. Bickerton's theory refocuses our attention on how all these strands of English application enrich the understanding of African Anglophone literatures in their diversity to establish what constitutes an Anglophone African literary-linguistic continuum.

From Bickerton, we can infer the relationship between English, as a language, African literatures, those in translation from indigenous African languages or other former colonial languages such as French and Portuguese, and long-established African trans-national languages such as Arabic. Bickerton focused on the 'language continuum', which primarily deals with the relationship between basilects (socially stigmatised language varieties) and the acrolect (the prestigious variety) of a given speech community. A 'literary continuum', on the other hand, can refer to the continuity in a literary tradition. This study has focused on how the application of English in African literary discourse affects both the literary and – to a certain extent – the linguistic aspects of the works of art, hence the term 'literary-linguistic continuum' as it relates to African Anglophone discourse.

The continued use of what we can call Standard English as the base (acrolect) from which variants of Anglophone African literary expressions (basilects) spring suggests that this trend is likely to persist. It is likely to do so mainly because of the role of language in facilitating communication in multilingual, multi-ethnic and multicultural African societies in its function as either a national or official language, especially amongst educated African elites. With globalisation and English seemingly a de facto global language, there appears to be no end in sight to the continued use of English in an African space. The African linguistic situation – which allows the English language to enjoy an unprecedented prestigious status in relation to other languages, just like the acrolect-basilects linguistic relationship in a Creole community – also creates an environment for sustaining such a continuum. African writers who primarily write in English often subordinate indigenous languages and other cultural expressions to the primary base, English literary discourse. This reality appears to influence the extent to which African writers engage with the English language and its literary tradition. Inevitably, this situation leads to a plurality in the literary Anglophone tradition shaped by different socioeconomic, political, cultural and linguistic factors, but united by a common language, English. As a result, diverse manifestations of African literary discourse are linked together in a continuum by the English language and its literary tradition. More significantly, it appears there is also dialogue between varied Anglophone literary discourses in Africa and elsewhere because there are literary-linguistic rules governing such literary productions in English (which Bickerton hints at about the Creole continuum) that warrant further examination in Africa and other traditionally non-English contexts. These literary-linguistic rules are linked to the common language in use – in this case, English – that limits the extent to which a writer can manipulate the English language without necessarily creating a new language altogether that is inaccessible to those who understand the generally accepted Standard English.

Literary-linguistic continuum as a trajectory in modern African literatures

Specific implications pertinent to comprehending the complexities of African literatures in their multiplicity emerge from this book. As I have implied in the preceding section, the Anglophone African literary-linguistic continuum constitutes a trajectory through which we can examine how diverse linguistic, literary, cultural and religious expressions converge into a discourse that facilitates intra-, pan- and trans-national communication within and outside the continent. After all, a unitary theory has not been forthcoming so far on Anglophone African literatures mainly because of the diverse nature and multiplicity of works that fall in this category. The 'Anglophone African novel' stages a set of unresolved struggles over how to re-imagine African communities. In fact, this Anglophone African novel productively problematises a range of traditional genres from both the oral tradition of indigenous African languages and English literary tools. The indigenous and English genres meet and produce something of value so that use of the term 'literary-linguistic continuum' facilitates a grasp of the diverse works of fiction of Achebe, Ngũgĩ, Gordimer and Farah, primarily because of their shared linguistic heritage and usage in their fictions. This work has analysed the variations in their writings in relation to what they share with English as a language of literary discourse and what nation-specific and individual elements they add to that literary discourse. Furthermore, the writers discussed in this book attest to diversity in African literatures and how they deploy the English language in literary discourse. Their writings, primarily in former colonial languages, do not undermine their literature, and their works remain an integral part of African literary expression. A close analysis of these works helps to establish the nature of an Anglophone African literary-linguistic continuum.

Achebe, Ngũgĩ, Gordimer and Farah come from various parts of Africa and influence the African literary scene in a variety of ways. However, they are brought together through their varying use of English and how they engage with the Anglophone literary tradition. They reveal that Anglophonism is not uniform but consists of multiple diverse strata, since, as Ngũgĩ illustrates, one can engage with that tradition in both one's first language – if it is not English – and in the English language itself. Moreover, as Farah demonstrates, writing from a literary English point of view can actually work to one's advantage, especially when cut off from one's nation for so long. And, as Achebe has also demonstrated, English can accommodate oral African literary forms in English discourse. Furthermore, as Gordimer discovered, the English language has a home in Africa because the continent and its diverse ways of life have invigorated the language as it affects and is affected by indigenous languages, cultures and discourses. Despite disagreements on the position of Anglophone African literatures in the African canon, there is a sound basis for both the language and its literatures to be considered an integral part of African literary discourse. After all, English continues to influence the imaginings of many African Anglophone nation-states and is envisaged to continue doing so for years to come, and hence sustain continuity in what can be dubbed an Anglophone African continuum.

The diversity we witness in modern African Anglophone fictional representations stems from many factors, including what happens when two or more distinct cultures and languages meet, whether in conflict or in mutual confluence. In this regard, Gérard (1981) observes that as Western powers had settled in the Americas and Australasia by the end of the nineteenth century, and conquered parts of Asia and Africa, the impact of such hegemony on world literature could be far-reaching and was bound to be highly diversified, even when the same language was in use. It follows that any survey of this development should consider two parameters of equal importance: the cultural policy of the conquerors, and what Gérard (1981) calls 'the cultural substratum' of the conquered societies. Though the latter term appears to denigrate the value of indigenous cultures and languages in their intercourse with colonial culture and values, Gérard (1981) alludes to what emerges from that encounter, which is manifested in the writings of African writers.

For the cultural policy of the conquerors, the British system of indirect rule, for example, was a subtler form of control than the French centralism. This British approach did not seek to obliterate African languages and cultures but accommodated them alongside the English language and the Western culture it introduced. Consequently, this cultural policy determined the kind of literature that flourished in a given context, although in the greater context of Africa there are also some convergences and divergences, whether the language in use is English, French or Portuguese. This book has focused on the literary tradition of English-speaking or rather Anglophone Africa.

The variations in the Anglophone literary tradition that we witness in Africa should not come as a surprise because meaning in language depends on many sociological and historical factors. Thus, when we subject English to a different set of sociocultural and linguistic values, as in Africa, we begin to witness variations that we do not witness in traditionally native English settings. Hence, the confluence of English and indigenous African languages has led to conditions that allow for the development of new varieties and new meanings. For instance, Achebe's use in his novels of a multiplicity of standard and non-standard language varieties, including pidgin English, an offshoot of such an intersection, in depicting cultural and nation-specific speech communities, not only generates meaning in his novels but also situates his writings in realistic fictional local contexts, the Igbo and Nigerian universe. The same argument can variously be extended to Ngũgĩ, Gordimer and Farah.

Achebe's integration of traditional literary elements in his art orientates his fiction towards African rather than English aesthetics, even when he unapologetically uses English as the medium for his literary expression. His being dubbed a 'proverb-based' writer by Farah is an acknowledgement of his ability to use English while remaining rooted in the African landscape. Based on this distinction, Bamiro (2000) would classify Achebe's fiction as Afrolect rather than Eurolect. On the other hand, even the seemingly Eurolect influences in Gordimer's works are not immune to African contextual influences. Furthermore, Farah's modernist and post-modernist leanings are aesthetic and literary-linguistic approaches that he adopts to represent Somali. Yet, what appears to be 'Eurolect' influences in his works cannot be divorced from the 'Afrolect' influences, particularly with the way he contextualises the tragic story of Somalia. The hybrid nature of Anglophone African literatures accounts for both the Eurolect and Afrolect influences, both of which inevitably enrich these literatures.

In other words, variations within the Anglophone African novel – basically a hybrid of a European invention, the novel, and African oral traditions, orature – demonstrate that such reductive taxonomies are inadequate. For example, the literary works of Gordimer have a heavy dose of Eurolect influences, and yet she writes primarily from an African-centred consciousness even as she writes within white settler codes, and her works also contain some Afrolect features. She cannot represent South Africa and its multicultural, multiracial and multi-linguistic landscape without recourse to cultural translation. Though South Africa has been dubbed the 'Rainbow Nation' by Desmond Tutu (Tutu 2005, 47), a supposedly united nation, Gordimer's work is based on a South Africa comprising different languages and races, cultures and nations that inevitably requires such cultural translation. This cultural translation entails embodying linguistic and African cultural experiences either directly, as in Gordimer's later novels such as *July's People*, or indirectly, as in her earlier novels such as *The Lying Days*. Furthermore, many postcolonial African texts still have Afrolect influences despite lacking a significant presence of African oral traditions, mainly because of social heteroglossia – or the range of social dialects – in nation-specific contexts.

Here it is worth briefly recalling Bakhtin (1987, 263) and his conception of social heteroglossia, which affirms and accounts for the plurality of voices that we witness in Anglophone African writings. This capacity of the novel to represent the varied discourses and languages spoken in an African space allows it to facilitate the interaction of English and indigenous African languages, cultures and beliefs in literary discourse. These distinctive features, when nation-specific, also become useful indicators of a national literature. When applied to art coupled with the consciousness of the author, literary works emerge that are identifiable with certain locales because of the particularisms introduced in the use of English.

Generally, the introduction of English in many of the African linguistic communities has also helped to develop unique literary-linguistic features, mostly amongst the educated elite specific to particular national contexts. Hence, from Nigerian pidgin English as represented in Achebe's novels, we get a product of the intermingling of English and indigenous African languages since languages 'intersect with each other in many different ways' (Bakhtin 1987, 291). Such confluence of languages cannot be talked about without factoring in the languages involved, including English. In fact, this also raises another issue: Can we ignore that Nigerian Pidgin English is a product of the confluence of English and indigenous Nigerian languages? Of course, this rhetorical question reminds us that even when we want to look the other way, we cannot ignore the literary-linguistic influences evolving in an African space as a result of the intermingling of English and indigenous African languages and attendant cultures. Against this backdrop, the term Afrolect thus needs a broad-based scope to reflect the heteroglossic linguistic picture of African Anglophone literatures and the varied literary features they have adapted, adopted and absorbed in the discourse of the novel.

As Achebe has demonstrated in anglicised African discourse, we cannot anglicise without integrating local traditions, lore and cultural values available in the universe of particular local contexts, hence the diverse variants of literary and linguistic elements that have been introduced into the Anglophone text. Since the 'common' or the so-called Standard English remains the foil against which literary expressions are determined and the main conduit for the narrative frame of the creative effort, whatever aspects are introduced into the language do not necessarily represent a complete break – or departure – from the main African Anglophone literary-linguistic tradition, but rather a literary-linguistic continuum of some sort, with peculiar characteristics and divergences imposed by the local context. The continuity in English indicates that the usage of the language in colonial and postcolonial Africa transcends issues of abrogation and appropriation. Even when one dismisses the Anglophone African discourse as exclusionary and elitist, one has to realise that much more often than not, languages of power tend to be elitist. It is true of Ge'ez in Ethiopia and the language of the court in traditional Yoruba kingship, which has been captured effectively in Soyinka's (1975) character of Elesin Oba in *Death and the King's Horseman*. They are both elitist but in no way can they be classified as un-African, even among pro-nativist scholars.

In this context, Ngũgĩ, whose pro-nativist project has ruffled feathers in the debates on the language of African literature, offers a counterpoint for comparative purposes. I do not reinforce Ngũgĩ's ideas but sidestep the polarising linguistic debate to consider how both his English and Gikuyu texts are informed by and engage with the Anglophone tradition. For the latter case, this engagement becomes even more apparent in their English translations. I have therefore situated both sets of books in what I propose as the Anglophone African literary-linguistic continuum by examining how they deploy translingualism, and how the Gikuyu texts constitute a deeper form of engagement with the same Anglophone tradition Ngũgĩ appears to repudiate. The consciousness with which Ngũgĩ, as wordsmith, plays with words to represent his anti-colonial and anti-neocolonial agenda ensures that his written word captures the nuances of the local language and culture in both English and Gikuyu texts in translation.

Thus, an analysis of Ngũgĩ's English works and those in Gikuyu (now in English translation) reveals that the latter are in that language because of the author's reaction to the language debate and seeming incompatibility with his politics of engagement (Ngũgĩ, 1993). What remains undeniable is the continued dialogue between his works originally published in English and his later works in Gikuyu, whether in Gikuyu or in English translation. As I pointed out in Chapter 3, the traditional term 'translation' amounts to what Roman Jakobson (1959) calls 'interlingual translation', and defines as translation from one language to another. In Ngũgĩ's usage, both 'translation' and 'transliteration' are evident. In the Anglophone novels, it is the latter that could be considered primary and vice-versa for his novels originally written in Gikuyu. However, there is also a fusion of the two in his Gikuyu novels, as transliterated features are retained, even in translation.

In such an artistic orientation, African writers cannot bury their heads in the sand and pretend they write in English without having recourse to their indigenous languages, localised expressions and cultural values. After all, as pointed out in Chapter 3, African literary discourse falls generally into two types. The first type refers to traditional forms of translation and the second, as illustrated above, to transliteration (or what Gyasi [1999] calls 'creative translation'), which have come to define modern African writings generally. Gyasi's description applies readily to Ngũgĩ's writings both in English and in Gikuyu, since the author consciously engages with other linguistic landscapes in Gikuyu, knowing that his writing will also be translated into English. Such a creative process creates room for exposing the literary-linguistic variants that make the works produced in English Anglophone productions but with a difference related to the space and time in which they emerge. In other words, there is a complementarity to the relationship between the two projects of Ngũgĩ – one of transliteration and one of translation – that also demonstrates how the African Anglophone novel continues to grow in diversity and in the literary-linguistic features it exhibits.

As Chapter 3 demonstrates, there is generally a thin line between transliteration, which Ngũgĩ relies upon in his earlier works originally written in English, and translation, which his Gikuyu works undergo, hence placing them within Anglophone African literary discourse. The irony with Ngũgĩ's original Gikuyu works is that they survive largely in their English translation. The reasons are varied: political resistance by the regime in his country at the time the books were written, and because his works operate in an environment where English is more powerful than Gikuyu. This commonality is presumably what will ultimately determine the place of both his Anglophone African novels and his Gikuyu African novels (in translation) in the Anglophone African literary-linguistic continuum. It can also help us to understand the relationship between the two sets of texts. Ngũgĩ is engaged in the process of negotiating between and among languages through translingualism. In such circumstances, the African literary language is a product of many languages that attempt to find some commonality for the audience in English, whether directly in English after having undergone a process of transliteration or as translations or having benefited from both processes through translingualism.

Indeed, Ngũgĩ's first contact language and dominant culture remain central in both his Anglophone and Gikuyu fictions, with his rhetorical agenda shaping his literary output. The Anglophone and Gikuyu novels of Ngũgĩ are both products of the same African writer who cannot, as he puts it, 'invent [his] own history or a new world' and thus 'write[s] from [his] social perspective, from [his] class perspective' even 'in a marginalised language' (Rodrigues and Ngũgĩ 2004, 163). One could also add that neither can he create his own languages, Gikuyu or English. He works with both and ultimately the forms of his indigenous language are embodied in the English version. Thus, Ngũgĩ's Anglophone and Gikuyu novels (whether in translation or not) are not as far apart as we might be tempted sometimes to believe or as Ngũgĩ professes. Though he has misgivings about writing in English, Ngũgĩ nevertheless embraces it at the level of translation. Whereas in his earlier Anglophone novels, Ngũgĩ subordinates feeder languages such as Gikuyu and Kiswahili to English, in his Gikuyu fiction, he subordinates other languages, including English, to Gikuyu. Ultimately, Ngũgĩ's fiction in English and in Gikuyu (in translation) have convergences albeit with divergences. In fact, Ngũgĩ, even in his Gikuyu fiction, appears to be writing for a particular esoteric as well as a general exotic audience. Many of Ngũgĩ's critics, therefore, should focus more on what we learn about Ngũgĩ's contribution not only to translation studies, but also to our understanding of the relationship between so-called minor and major languages through his use of translingualism. It is Ngũgĩ's original works in English that inform, shape and ultimately indicate how he attempts to distance from and disengage with what he sees – rightly or wrongly – as Europhone forms. Yet his Gikuyu works, whether in that language or in translation, cannot be understood without recourse to the Anglophone tradition they seek to negate. After all, African novels tend to be 'situated in a particular time and space by means of the multilinguality of the texts' (Marais and Feinauer, 2017, 3), which hints at intertextuality and linguistic interaction that cannot be wiped off the slate through denial or simply claiming to use another language other than English.

More significantly, Ngũgĩ also reveals how dynamic and accommodative the Anglophone African tradition remains. In short, to grasp fully Ngũgĩ's complementary African Anglophone and Gikuyu novels, both in themselves and in translation, we must consider elements of translingualism variously at play in the novels in English, where transliteration dominates, and the Gikuyu versions in English, where translation and other forms of translingualism occur. Finally, both sets of texts reveal how they concretely embody diverse cultures in confluence in an African landscape. There is therefore much that we still have to learn about the processes of transliteration, translation and translingualism in general, particularly as they relate to literatures in minor languages as they are transliterated or translated in major languages. A fuller grasp of these processes can further shed light on how variants of English continue to emerge, alter and be reinforced in African Anglophone literary discourse.

This brings us to Gordimer, the subject of Chapter 4. As mentioned there, it is apparent that when transcribing trans-cultural discourse, Gordimer acts as a 'translator', whose primary duty, according to Bassnett (2002), is to produce a literary text in the target language that readers can comprehend while simultaneously retaining the nuances of the source. In this regard, English, as the target language, respects and accommodates the local languages and cultures in the space that Gordimer represents. Here it is also worth revisiting Steiner's (2010, 302) definition of 'translation' as an 'interlingual transfer' that facilitates transference 'across linguistic and cultural boundaries'. In South Africa, English is both a colonial and a South African language. Though serving as a colonial language, or even a language of apartheid, Gordimer used it to question and even subvert the racial stereotypes, hindrances and cultural separations engendered by racialised politics. In this regard, English comes out as having what Steiner (2010, 305) calls 'doubled-edged possibility of translation', which is also at the heart of the 'language debate' in African literature.

For Gordimer's fiction, this duality arises primarily because of her dual heritage, that is, colonial settler and African. Yet she is a product of the same African space that she wants to make sense of and represent to her readers. By criticising divisive racial politics, she refuses to be colonial as her mission is to bridge that gap, which is evident in her writing. Inevitably, the duality extends to the negotiation of textual meaning by readers of her novels. Moreover, the colonial legacy and the confluence of cultures it engendered made cultural translation an integral part of cross-cultural interaction, albeit in a lopsided manner favouring the centre, which has made English a major language of both speech and literary expression. In the context of Gordimer's apartheid novels, cultural communication under divisive colonial subjectivities tends to limit meaningful cross-cultural exchange. But this does not imply a total absence, since interaction continues amongst the varied social groups even as they occupy different worlds.

Cultural translation in the novels of Gordimer is inevitable because Gordimer operates in a space not only with South African English but whose English communicates with indigenous African languages. Moreover, apart from the white settler codes, her society has indigenous African cultures ever in contact with white African cultures, whether in an antagonistic manner or otherwise. As her fiction is a product of a South African multilingual and sociocultural context, it inevitably negotiates with the indigenous languages and cultures of the African landscape that are relevant to understanding how her characters deal with various issues and forces at play in their experiences. As in all other cases I have reviewed thus far, the issues of space and time also impinge on the kind of literary expressions Gordimer produces. South Africa remains a multicultural space, as manifests in her writings. Gordimer's novelisation also shows that beyond the issue of language, for example South African English, there were additional issues at play that inform and shape her writing. Consequently, she had to accommodate the dictates of the South African space by incorporating African languages, cultures and discourses in her novels. This exposed the extent to which the divide between 'them and us', fostered by the colour-bar, hindered the emergence of a situation in which whites could 'merge [...]with an indigenous culture' (Gordimer, 1980, 46). This reality, however, does not mean an absence of intermingling, or linguistic exclusivity. Her work exemplifies how she still seeks to embody the languages and cultures of the South African space on both sides of the divide.

Furthermore, her apartheid-era novels demonstrate how problematic cross-cultural communication can become when social entities remain insulated behind the privileges sanctioned by divisive laws and sustained by the language of power. They also demonstrate that cross-cultural interaction is more necessary than the artificial barriers created by the apartheid policies. In her apartheid-era fiction, Gordimer exposes the limited and convoluted cross-cultural exchange between black and white through her representation of African discourses, thus evoking the debilitating effects of the divisive apartheid policies on both blacks and whites. The reader is left with the task of negotiating between what is either directly or indirectly stated in the various discourses of the novel to grasp the seemingly paralysing effects of the divisive politics and policies that Gordimer so strongly attacked.

More significantly, Gordimer's Anglophone novels generally reveal that they cannot be separated from the African context (space) in which they have been produced, the African consciousness shaping her work, the combination of African cultures her works seek to embody, and the beliefs of the cultures she seeks to represent. One temptation is to examine the extent to which her fiction deviates from 'traditional' English literature. However, doing so would only limit such a study to looking at how South African her English is and overlook many other features that contribute to her works as being African rather than European. Moreover, the issue of cultural translation also implies that she is engaged in the act of building the cross-cultural interaction that the Anglophone tradition has come to represent in Africa and other traditionally non-English contexts. Overall, the writings of Gordimer and other white South Africans are bound by both space and time; they are not immune to the dictates of the varied linguistic and cultural surroundings prevailing in South Africa. As such, the variants evident in her work and, indeed, in those of other South African writers such as Alan Paton, Peter Abrahams, John Maxwell Coetzee and Dennis Brutus can be understood in terms of what they introduce into English literary discourse. As this book has focused only on one author, it cannot generalise; each individual author might introduce some variants in style influenced by sociocultural background, approach and even taste. What it can do is highlight what emerges in Gordimer's fiction in relation to the other authors in Africa examined in this book.

Finally, we revisit Farah and his work. Generally, Farah remains an enigma who defies the existing scholarship in relation to questions of linguistic play and/or syncretism in his work, particularly regarding language and national representation, as Chapter 5 has demonstrated. In other words, Farah complicates the two polar voices that for many years symbolised the major sides of the African literature/language debate: pro-nativism and pro-English. Rather than dwell on which camp Farah belongs to, his works force one to consider how he manipulates and deploys English in his fiction. The question thus is what still makes his works Somali despite writing in English when he could have done so in Somali, as his maiden and short-lived attempts in the early 1970s illustrate. His intervention in this regard has been sobering, as it illustrates not only how rich Anglophone African literatures are in their diversity but also the varying effect of the confluence of English and indigenous segments. Beyond the effect associated with time and space that relate to changes in the use of language in general, there have also been varying effects on individual authors depending on their sociocultural backgrounds and ideological leanings as well as their stand on the question of the language of African literature.

In fact, there has lately been a marked shift towards recognition of linguistic diversity as articulating the complex and multi-faceted features of Africa's identity. As such, there is call for accepting the use of indigenous African languages on the one hand, and the use of the adopted former colonial languages on the other, since they are complementary in the representation and articulation of African experiences. This has created a win-win situation, as the indigenous languages need no justification for their being used in literary circles on the African continent. Similarly, the former colonial languages, which have established a 'home' in Africa since the colonial period, continue to thrive in a sustainable manner and hence their effect, and how they are affected by the indigenous languages, cannot be ignored. Farah cannot be faulted for using English, as circumstances have created conditions under which he uses the language so eloquently to represent Somali while mainly living in exile. In this regard, his fiction is both a 'factor and product' (to quote Menang, 2001, n.p. once again) of his Somali identity. In addition, his doing so is also grounded in Somali lore as well as its belief system and culture, the myriad of influences he has been exposed to as a cosmopolitan person notwithstanding. As Farah has also been influenced by other cultures and languages, the study of his works demands the consideration of both external linguistic and cultural influences that his oeuvre reflects. Farah conflates some of the binaries associated with African writing, including what we have already seen as Bamiro's classification, into 'Afrolect' or 'Eurolect' literary influences in Anglophone discourses. In other words, it is not a case of either Afrolect or Eurolect, but a fusion of so many sociocultural and literary-linguistic influences that make the Anglophone African novel. After all, the strength of African literatures lies in their plurality and diversity. Farah, on his part, fuses both Eurolect and Afrolect literary influences, hence demonstrating how malleable and accommodating African writing in English can be. It is apparent that Farah's cosmopolitan position shapes and complicates his contribution to Anglophone African literary discourse, which in turn reveals the complexity and plurality of Anglophonisms not only in Africa but also in other non-native English-speaking contexts. It also reveals that when we can talk of an Anglophone African literary-linguistic continuum, it need not be seen as a linear effect and change, but one that has twists and turns in its path as it adopts, adapts and accommodates the varied influences imposed on it by the space and time of the places it has ventured into, thanks to colonialism.

Also, Farah's works demonstrate that the Anglophone African tradition transcends national boundaries and affiliations as it broadens – rather than limits – the scope of national and trans-national literatures. After all, Africa is not a country but a continent with an indisputable need for a trans-national language or languages to make communication possible. For years now, English, French and Portuguese have served this purpose, with languages such as Arabic, Kiswahili and Hausa joining the fray, albeit in a qualified manner. Nevertheless, for Anglophone Africa, English has been at the heart of fostering various cross-cultural discourses on the continent. Indirectly, Farah's works also undermine the importance attached to nativism in determining authentic African literatures, and extends Menang's (2001) more inclusive view of this theme. After all, in the broader picture, nativism remains largely limited to an esoteric literary audience (which explains why Ngũgĩ's works are largely read in their English translations) when an exoteric audience is also imperative to foster a pan-African spirit.

Apparently, what shapes and informs Farah is not only Somali language and culture but also English, both British and American, as well as a multiplicity of other languages and cultures – African, European and American – as his many travels and exposures merit. To expect a person with such a myriad of influences to produce what pro-nativist would call 'pure' Somali or so-called authentically African texts in an indigenous African language would amount to ignoring history, socioeconomic realities, and cultural intercourse and fusions in Africa. In any case, representations of African discourses, languages and beliefs in English, whether through transliteration or translation, constitute reproductions mediated by authorial creativity and invention and all the attendant influences that the author has been exposed to within and outside his traditional social context. One can also factor in the colonial and postcolonial baggage. After all, Anglophone literary reproductions in Africa (and indeed elsewhere in traditionally non-English contexts) have depended on multiple factors such as linguistic, cultural and social influences based on geographical space (including exile) and historical time when the writing is being carried out with the attendant time-bound influences. The latter factors also allow us to distinguish, for example, the first generation and second generation African writers and the post-1960s writers, whom Abdourahman Waberi (1998) has called 'Les Enfants de la postcolonie' (children/writers born in the post-independence era).

Furthermore, sharing the same language does not necessarily mean sharing a discourse, and writing in that language requires an act of interpretation and even translation to bridge linguistic gaps. This is true of Farah as manifested by his representation of dialects and social registers in the same Somali space (for example, the capital of Mogadishu) to capture the domains of different social groups within the same ethnic communities, hence marking off urbanites from rural dwellers, and creating linguistic gaps which the standard version of the language seeks to bridge. Farah in *Maps*, for example, reminds the reader that 'the voice of the master of the *mingis* [spirit extraction or exorcism] ceremony singing, right in the heart of Mogadiscio, [is] in a language definitely not Somali', just as leaders of such ceremonies chant in Boran, 'the language the spirits understand' (Farah 1986/1989, 213). And this is supposed to be a nation that speaks one language, Somali, and is endowed with what on the surface appears to be one culture, Somali, shared by one people (now seemingly eternally fragmented), the Somali. In other words, rather than seek to separate what is, indeed, African in Anglophone literary production, it is more constructive to examine what it reveals about the African languages, cultures and beliefs the English language seeks to embody, because such close scrutiny helps to reveal what constitutes Anglophone African literatures and sheds light on this literary-linguistic continuum.

Conclusion

Taken together, the four African authors discussed in this book constitute co-ordinates used to examine what they reveal about African writing and the Anglophone African literary-linguistic continuum. In no way can they constitute the complete picture of the Anglophone African literary corpus. What they do reveal, however, is that when we pay close attention to what they represent about their African societies, and the way they integrate African languages, values, beliefs and cultures, we can discover what constitutes the Anglophone African literary-linguistic continuum. From the literary-linguistic substratum in traditionally non-English contexts, we find that African Anglophone writers continue not only improvising but also re-making the English language to represent the particular without necessarily creating a whole new language that is totally incomprehensible to the Anglophone world. In this regard, what we witness are variants that expose both convergences and divergences in the use of the English language while remaining as strands of the whole – the Anglophone African literary-linguistic tradition. Eventually, this continuum is the glue that binds together multiplicities of writings on the continent. The emergence of modern African writings, whether in indigenous or former colonial languages, particularly in Sub-Saharan Africa, cannot discount how the Anglophone tradition affected and was, in turn, affected by this confluence that continues manifesting varyingly in African literary productions. Certainly, there is more room to explore this Anglophone continuum, even outside the confines of African literatures, as this book has attempted to do.

Bibliography

Abrahams, R. D., and B. A. Babcock. 1977. "The literary use of proverbs." *Journal of American Folklore* 90 (358): 414–429. doi:10.2307/539608.

Achebe, C. 1958/1992. *Things Fall Apart*. New York: Every Man's Library/ Alfred A. Knopf.

Achebe, C. 1960/1994. *No Longer at Ease*. New York: Anchor.

Achebe, C. 1964/1969. *Arrow of God*. New York: Anchor.

Achebe, C. 1966/1989. *A Man of the People*. New York: Anchor.

Achebe, C. 1975. *Morning yet on Creation Day*. Garden City: Anchor P/Doubleday.

Achebe, C. 1987. *Anthills of the Savannah*. New York: Anchor.

Adam, I. 1984. "Nuruddin Farah and James Joyce: Some Issues of Intertextuality." *World Literature Written in English* 24 (1): 34–43. doi:10.1080/17449858408588868.

Adejunmobi, M. 1999. "Routes: Language and the Identity of African Literature." *Journal of Modern African Studies* 37 (4): 581–596. doi:10.1017/S0022278X99003146.

Adeseke, A. E. 2016. "African Literature (Drama) and Language Use." *Social Science Review* 2 (1):49–59. http://www.ssr-net.com/issues/Vol_2_No_1_June_2016/15.pdf

Afrique. 1962/1997. "Interview with Chinua Achebe." In *Conversations with Chinua Achebe*, edited by Bernth Lindfors, 7–10. Jackson, MS: University Press of Mississippi.

Ahmed, A. J. 1996. "Farah and the (Re)writing of Somali Historiography: Narrative as a Politically Symbolic Act." In *Daybreak is Near: Literature, Clans, and the Nation-State in Somalia*, 75–79. Lawrenceville, NJ: Red Sea Press.

Ahmed, A. J., ed. 1995. *The Invention of Somalia*. Lawrenceville, NJ: The Red Sea Press.

Alden, P. 1995. "Review of *The Novels of Nuruddin Farah*." *Modern Fiction Studies* 41 (2): 381–383. doi:10.1353/mfs.1995.0089.

Amoko, A. O. 2005. "The Resemblance of Colonial Mimicry: A Revisionary Reading of Ngũgĩ wa Thiongo's *The River Between.*" *Research in African Literatures* 36 (1): 34–50. doi:10.2979/RAL.2005.36.1.34.

Anderson, B. 1991. *Imagined Communities: Reflections on the Origin and Spread of Nationalism.* Revised edition. London: Verso.

Appiah, K. A. 1990. "Alexander Crummell and the Invention of Africa." *Massachusetts Review* 31 (3): 385–405.

Appiah, K. A. 2006. *Cosmopolitanism: Ethics in a World of Strangers.* New York, London: W. W. Norton.

Appiah, K. A., and N. Farah. 2004. "Nuruddin Farah." *Bomb* 87: 54–59.

Arnove, A. 1993. "Pierre Bourdieu, the Sociology of Intellectuals, and the Language of African Literature." *NOVEL: A Forum on Fiction*, 26 (3): 278–296. doi:10.2307/1345837.

Bakhtin, M. 1987. *The Dialogic Imagination,* Trans. Caryl Emerson and Michael Holquist. Austin, TX: University of Texas Press.

Bamiro, E. 2000. *The English Language and the Construction of Cultural and Social Identity in Zimbabwean and Trinbagonian Literatures.* Berkeley, CA: Peter Lang.

Bandia, P. 2008. *Translation as Reparation: Writing and Translation in Postcolonial Africa.* Manchester: St Jerome Publishing.

Bassnett, S. 2002. *Translation Studies.* London, New York: Routledge.

Batchelor, K. 2009. *Decolonizing Translation: Francophone African Novels in English Translation.* Manchester: St Jerome Publishing.

Batibo, H. 2005. *Language Decline and Death in Africa: Causes, Consequences, and Challenges.* Clevedon, Buffalo: Multilingual Matters.

Bazin, N. T. 1995. "An interview with Nadine Gordimer." *Contemporary Literature* 36 (4): 571–587. doi:10.2307/1208941.

Bhabha, H. 1993. *Location of Culture.* London: Routledge.

Bickerton, D. 1973. "The Nature of Creole Continuum." *Language* 49 (3): 640–669. doi:10.2307/412355.

Bjornson, R. 1991. *The African Quest for Freedom and Identity: Cameroonian Writing and National Experience.* Bloomington, IN: Indiana University Press.

Blommaert, J., ed. 1999. *The Language Ideological Debates.* Berlin, New York: Mouton de Gruyter. doi:10.1515/9783110808049.

Brennan, T. M. 1990. "The National Longing for Form." In *Nation and Narration: Post-Structuralism and the Culture of National Identity*, edited by Homi Bhabha, 44–70. London: Routledge.

Brink, A. 1984. "Writing against Big Brother: Notes on Apocalyptic Fiction in South Africa." *World Literature Today* 58 (2): 189–94. doi:10.2307/40139944.

Brink, A. 1998. "Languages of the Novel: A Lover's Reflections." *New England Review* 19 (3): 5–17.

Brown, M. L. 2010. "Bleeding for the Mother(Land): Rereading Testimonial Bodies in Nuruddin Farah's *Maps*." *Research in African Literatures* 41 (4): 125–143. doi:10.2979/ral.2010.41.4.125.

Browne, R. (2012). "Debating Relevance: African Literature in Politics and Education." *Postamble*, 7 (2): 1–6. http://www.postamble.org/wp-content/uploads/2016/09/RuthBrownefinal.pdf

Cary, J. (Original work published 1939) 1995. *Mister Johnson*. London: Everyman.

Cassanelli, L. 2001. "The Somali Studies International Association: A Brief History." *Bildhaan*, 1: 1–10. http://digitalcommons.macalester.edu/bildhaan/vol1/iss1/

Chapman, M. 2003. "African Literature, African Literatures: Cultural Practice or Art Practice?" *Research in African Literatures* 34 (1): 1–10. doi:10.2979/RAL.2003.34.1.1.

Chazan, N. 1988. "Patterns of State–Society Incorporation and Disengagement in Africa." In *The Precarious Balance: State and Society in Africa*, edited by Donald Rothchild and Naomi Chazan, 121–148. Boulder, CO: Westview.

Chege, M. 1997. "Africans of European descent." *Transition* 73 (73): 74–86. doi:10.2307/2935445.

Chinweizu, O. J., and I. Madubuike. 1983. *African Fiction and Poetry and their Critics*. vol. I. Toward the Decolonization of African Literature. Washington, DC: Howard University Press.

Clarke, B. 1998. "The African Writers Series: History, Development and Effect of the Series on African Cultures and Publishing." Paper presented at Oxford Brookes University, Oxford, UK, 28 May.

Clingman, S. 1981. "History from the Inside: The Novels of Nadine Gordimer." *Journal of Southern African Studies* 7 (2): 165–193. doi:10.1080/03057078108708025.

Clingman, S. 2009. *The Grammar of Identity: Transnational Fiction and the Nature*

Bibliography

of the Boundary. Oxford: Oxford University Press. doi:10.1093/acprof:oso/9780199278497.001.0001.

Cooke, J. 1985. *The Novels of Nadine Gordimer: Private Lives/Public Landscapes*. Baton Rouge, LA: Louisiana State University Press.

Coundouriotis, E. 2000. "Rethinking Cosmopolitanism in Nadine Gordimer's *The Conservationist*." *College Literature* 33 (3): 1–28.

Cozier, D. H., and R. M. Blench. 1992. *An Index of Nigerian Languages*. 2nd ed. Dallas, TX: Summer Institute of Linguistics.

Deleuze, G. and F. Guattari, 1986. *Kafka: Toward a Minority Literature*. Trans. Dana Polan. Minneapolis, IL: University of Minnesota Press.

Diamond, I., and L. Quinby. 1988. *Feminism and Foucault: Reflections on Resistance*. Boston, MA: Northeastern University Press.

During, S. 1990. "Postmodernism or Post-Colonialism Today." In *Postmodern Conditions*, edited by Andrew Milner, Philip Thompson, and Chris Worth, 113–131. New York: St. Martin's Press.

Egar, E. E. 2000. *The Rhetorical Implications of Chinua Achebe's* Things Fall Apart. Lanham, MD: University Press of America.

Erritouni, A. 2006. "Apartheid Inequality and Post-Apartheid Utopia in Nadine Gordimer's *July's People*." *Research in African Literatures* 37 (4): 68–84.

Farah, N. 1970/2003. *From a crooked rib*. London: Penguin.

Farah, N. 1979/1992. *Sweet and Sour Milk*. Saint Paul, MN: Gray Wolf Press.

Farah, N. 1981/1992. *Sardines*. Saint Paul, MN: Gray Wolf Press.

Farah, N. 1983/1992. *Close Sesame*. Saint Paul, MN: Gray Wolf Press.

Farah, N. 1986/1989. *Maps*. New York: Penguin.

Farah, N. 1993/1999. *Gifts*. New York: Penguin.

Farah, N. 1998a. *Secrets*. New York: Penguin.

Farah, N. 1998b. "Celebrating differences: The 1998 Neustadt lecture." Focus on Nuruddin Farah *World Literature Today* 72 (4): 709–712. doi:10.2307/40154256.

Farah, N. 2000. *Yesterday, Tomorrow: Voices from the Somali Diaspora*. London, New York: Cassell.

Farah, N. 2004. *Links*. New York: Riverhead Books.

Galafa, B. 2017. "The Work Must Be African, Not Just the Writer." *Bashabandhan Literary Review.* http://bhashabandhanliteraryreview.com/2017/04/15/the-work-must-be-african-not-just-the-writer/

Gellner, E. 1987. "Nationalism and Cohesion in Complex Societies." In *Culture, Identity and Politics*, 6–28. Cambridge: Cambridge University Press.

Gérard, A. 1981. *African Language Literatures: An Introduction to the Literary History of Sub-Saharan Africa.* London: Longman.

Gikandi, S. 1991. "The Epistemology of Translation: Ngũgĩ, Matigari, and the Politics of Language." *Research in African Literatures* 22 (4): 161–167.

Gikandi, S. 1997. "Resurrecting the Devil: Notes on Ngũgĩ's Theory of the Oral-Aural Novel." *Research in African Literatures* 28 (1): 134–140.

Gikandi, S. 2000. "Traveling Theory: Ngũgĩ's Return to English." *Research in African Literatures,* 31 (2): 194–209. doi:10.2979/RAL.2000.31.2.194.

Gikandi, S. 2001. *Ngũgĩ wa Thiong'o.* New York, NY: Cambridge University Press.

Gikandi, S. 2012. "African Literature and the Colonial Factor." In *African and Caribbean Literature.* vol. 1., edited by F. Abiola Irele and Simon Gikandi, 379–397. Cambridge: Cambridge University Press. doi:10.1017/CHOL9780521832755.021.

Gordimer, N. 1953/2002. *The Lying Days.* London: Bloomsbury.

Gordimer, N. 1959. "Where do whites fit in?" *Twentieth Century,* 165: 23–24.

Gordimer, N. 1960/1991. *Occasion for Loving.* New York: Penguin.

Gordimer, N. 1973. *The black interpreters: Notes on African Writing.* Johannesburg: Spro-Cas/Ravan.

Gordimer, N. 1974. *The Conservationist.* New York: Penguin.

Gordimer, N. 1976. "English-Language Literature and Politics." *Journal of Southern African Studies*, 2 (2): 131–150.

Gordimer, N. 1980. "From Apartheid to Afrocentrism." *English in Africa* 7 (1): 45–50.

Gordimer, N. 1981. *July's People.* New York: Penguin.

Gordimer, N. 1994. *None to Accompany Me.* New York: Farrar Straus and Giroux.

Gordimer, N. 2001. *The Pickup.* New York: Farrar Straus and Giroux.

Gyasi, K. A. 1999. "Writing as Translation: African Literature and the Challenges of Translation." *Research in African Literatures* 30 (2): 75–87. doi:10.2979/RAL.1999.30.2.75.

Hamilton-Jones, R. 1998. "The African Writers Series." Paper presented at Oxford Brookes University, Oxford, UK, May 28.

Harris, M. 1992. "The Cultural Clash: Joyce Cary and Chinua Achebe." In *Outsiders and Insiders: Perspectives of Third World Culture in British and Post-Colonial Fiction*, 79–109. New York: Peter Lang.

Harrow, K. W. 2001. "Introduction: Special Issue: "Nationalism." *Research in African Literatures* 32 (3): 33–44. doi:10.2979/RAL.2001.32.3.33.

Hauptman, R. 2005. "Gikuyu and Realistic Necessities." *World Literature Today* 79 (3/4): 5. doi:10.2307/40158913.

Hawley, J. C. 1992. "José María Arguedas, Ngũgĩ wa Thiong'o, and the Search for a Language of Justice." *Pacific Coast Philology* 27 (1/2): 69–76. doi:10.2307/1316713.

Head, D. 1994. *Nadine Gordimer* (Cambridge Studies in African and Caribbean Literature). Cambridge: Cambridge University Press. doi:10.1017/CBO9780511554391.

Heywood, C. 1983. *Nadine Gordimer*. Windsor: Profile Books.

Ibinga, S. S. 2010. "Post-Apartheid Literature Beyond Race." *This Century's Review*. http://history.thiscenturysreview.com/post_apartheid.html

Indangasi, H. 1997. "Ngugi's Ideal Reader and the Postcolonial Reality." *Yearbook of English Studies* 27:193–200. doi:10.2307/3509142.

Irele, F. Abiola. 2001. "Homage to Chinua Achebe." *Research in African Literatures* 32 (3): 1–2.

Jackson, H. T. 1991. "Orality, Orature, and Ngũgĩ wa Thiong'o." *Research in African Literatures* 22 (1): 5–15.

Jahn, J. 1968. *Neo-African Literature: A History of Black Writing*. New York: Grove Press.

Jakobson, R. 1959/2000. "On Linguistic Aspects of Translation." In *The Translation Studies Reader*, edited by L. Venuti, 113–118. London: Routledge. doi:10.4159/harvard.9780674731615.c18.

JanMohamed, Abdul R. 1985. "The Economy of Manichean Allegory: The function of Racial Difference in Colonialist Literature." *Critical Inquiry* 12 (1): 59–87. doi:10.1086/448321.

Julien, E. 2011. "From Orality to Writing to …" Paper presented at the Contemporary Debates Workshop: Literary and Cultural Studies, Makerere Institute of Social Research (MISR), Kampala, Uganda, June 6–7, 2011.

Jussawalla, F., and R. W. Dasenbrock. 1992. *Interviews with Writers of the Post-Colonial World*. Jackson, MS: University Press of Mississippi.

Kachru, B. B. 1992. *The Other Tongue: English Across Cultures*. Urbana, IL: University of Illinois Press.

Kasanga, L. A., and M. Kalume. 1996. "The Use of Indigenized Forms of English in Ngũgĩ's *Devil on the Cross*: A Linguistic and Sociolinguistic Analysis." *African Languages and Cultures* 9 (1): 43–69. doi:10.1080/09544169608717799.

Knipp, T. R. 1967. "Two Novels from Kenya: J. Ngũgĩ." *Books Abroad* 41 (4): 393–397. doi:10.2307/40121788.

Korang, K. L. 2011. "Making a Post-Eurocentric Humanity: Tragedy, Realism, and *Things Fall Apart*." *Research in African Literatures* 42 (2): 1–29. doi:10.2979/reseafrilite.42.2.1.

Lazarus, N. 1990. *Resistance in Postcolonial African Fiction*. New Haven: Yale University Press.

Lindfors, B. 1969/1997. "Interview with Chinua Achebe." In *Conversations with Chinua Achebe*, 27–34. Jackson, MS: University Press of Mississippi.

Lindfors, B. 1972. *"The Palm Oil with Which Achebe's Words Are Eaten."* African Literature Today, 1-4, 2–18. London: Heinemann.

Lofland, V. 2002. "Somalia: US Intervention and Operation Restore Hope." *Case Studies in Policy Making*, 56: 1–12. http://www.au.af.mil/au/awc/awcgate/navy/pmi/somalia1.pdf

Lomberg, A. 1976. "Withering into the Truth: The Romantic Realism of Nadine Gordimer." *English in Africa* 3 (1): 1–12.

Lovesey, O. 2000. *Ngũgĩ wa Thiong'o*. New York: Twayne.

Madumulla, J., E. Bertoncini, and J. Blommaert. 1999. "Politics, Ideology and Poetic Form: The Literary Debate in Tanzania." In *Language Ideological Debates*, edited by Jan Blommaert, 307–341. Berlin, New York: Mouton de Gruyter. doi:10.1515/9783110808049.307.

Mahood, M. M. 1965. *Joyce Cary's Africa*. Boston, MA: Houghton Mifflin.

Marais, J., and I. Feinauer. 2017. "Introduction." In *Translation Studies in Africa and*

Beyond: Reconsidering the Postcolony, edited by J. Marais and I. Feinauer, 1–6. Cambridge: Cambridge University Press.

Mazrui, A. 1975. "English and the Origins of African Nationalism." In *The Political Sociology of the English Language: An African Perspective*. The Hague: Mouton.

Mazrui, A. 1976. *A World Federation of Cultures: An African Perspective*. New York: The Free Press.

Mazrui, A. 1984. "Reviving African Culture." In *Nationalism and New States in Africa*. Nairobi: Heinemann.

Mazrui, A. 1986. *The Africans: A Triple Heritage*. London: BBC Publications.

Mazrui, A. 1993. "Language and the Quest for Liberation in Africa: The Legacy of Frantz Fanon." *Third World Quarterly* 14 (2): 351–363. doi:10.1080/01436599308420329.

Mazrui, A., and M. Tidy. 1984. *Nationalism and the New States in Africa from 1935 to the Present*. Nairobi: Heinemann.

Mbele, J. 1992. "Language in African Literature: An Aside to Ngũgĩ." *Research in African Literatures* 23 (1): 145–151.

McLaren, J. 1998. "Ngũgĩ wa Thiong'o's *Moving the Centre* and its Relevance to Afrocentricity." *Journal of Black Studies* 28 (3): 386–397. doi:10.1177/002193479802800307.

Menang, T. 2001."Which Language(s) for African Literature: A Reappraisal." *TRANS: Internet- Zeitschrift für Kulturwissenschaften*, 11 (December): n.p. http://www.inst.at/trans/11Nr/menang11.htm

Miller, C. 1990. *Theories of Africans*. Chicago, IL: University of Chicago.

Miller, C. 1993. "Nationalism as Resistance and Resistance to Nationalism in the Literature of Francophone Africa." *Yale French Studies* 82 (1): 62–100. doi:10.2307/2930212.

Møller, B. 2009."The Somali Conflict: The Role of External Actors." Danish Institute for International Studies (DIIS) Report 2009. http://subweb.diis.dk/graphics/Publications/Reports2009/DIIS_report_2009_03_Somali_conflict.pdf

Mudimbe, V. Y. 1994. *The Invention of Africa: Gnosis, Philosophy, and the Order of Knowledge*. Bloomington, IN: Indiana University Press.

Mwangi, E. 2004. "The Gendered Politics of Untranslated Language and Aporia in Ngũgĩ wa Thiong'o's *Petals of Blood*." *Research in African Literatures* 35 (4): 66–74. doi:10.2979/RAL.2004.35.4.66.

Mwaura, P. 1980. *Communication Policies in Kenya*. Paris: UNESCO.

Mzali, I. 2010. "Wars of Representation: Metonymy and Nuruddin Farah's *Links*." *College Literature* 37 (3): 84–105. doi:10.1353/lit.0.0124.

Ndede, L. A. 2016. "African Literature: Place, Language or Experience." *International Journal of Educational Investigations* 3 (3): 1–10. http://ijeionline.com

Ngaboh-Smart, F. 2000. "*Secrets* and a New Civic Consciousness." *Research in African Literatures* 31 (1): 129–136. doi:10.2979/RAL.2000.31.1.129.

Ngaboh-Smart, F. 2001. "Nationalism and the Aporia of National Identity in Farah's *Maps*." *Research in African Literatures* 32 (3): 86–102. doi:10.2979/RAL.2001.32.3.86.

Ngũgĩ wa Thiong'o and M. Jaggi. 1989. "*Matigari* as Myth and History: An Interview." *Third World Quarterly*, 11(4): 241–251.

Ngũgĩ, W. T. 1964/1987. *Weep Not, Child*. Oxford: Heinemann.

Ngũgĩ, W. T. 1965. *The River Between*. Oxford: Heinemann.

Ngũgĩ, W. T. 1967/1986. *A Grain of Wheat*. Oxford: Heinemann.

Ngũgĩ, W. T. 1977/1991. *Petals of Blood*. New York: Penguin Books.

Ngũgĩ, W. T. 1981/2006. *Detained: A Writer's Prison Diary*. Oxford: Heinemann.

Ngũgĩ, W. T. 1982/1987. *Devil on the Cross*. Oxford: Heinemann.

Ngũgĩ, W. T. 1985. "On Writing in Gikuyu." *Research in African Literatures* 16 (2): 151–156.

Ngũgĩ, W. T. 1986/1997. *Decolonising the Mind: The Politics of Language in African Literature*. Oxford: James Currey.

Ngũgĩ, W. T. 1987/1990. *Matigari*. Translated by Wangui wa Goro. Oxford: Heinemann.

Ngũgĩ, W. T. 1990. "Kiingeretha ruthiomi rwa thi yoote? Kaba Githwairi." "English: A language of the world?" *Yale Journal of Criticism* 4 (1): 283–293.

Ngũgĩ, W. T. 1993. *Moving the Centre: The Struggles for Cultural Freedoms*. Oxford: James Currey.

Ngũgĩ, W. T. 1997. *Writers in Politics: A Re-engagement with Issues of Literature and Society*. Oxford: Currey.

Ngũgĩ, W. T. 2000. "Borders and Bridges: Seeking Connections Between Things." In *The Pre-occupation of Postcolonial Studies*, edited by Fawzia Afzar-Khan and Kalpana Seshadri-Crooks, 119–125. Durham: Duke University Press.

Ngũgĩ, W. T. 2004. "Recovering the original." *World Literature Today* 78 (3/4): 13–15. doi:10.2307/40158475.

Ngũgĩ, W. T. 2006. *Wizard of the Crow*. New York: Pantheon Books.

Ngũgĩ, W. T., and M. G. Mugo. 1976/2004. *The Trial of Dedan Kimathi*. Long Grove, Illinois.: Waveland Press, Inc.

Ngũgĩ, W. T., and W. M. Ngũgĩ. 1982. *Ngaahika Ndeenda: Ithaako ria Ngerekano*. Nairobi: Heinemann Kenya.

Ngũgĩ, W. T., and W. M. Ngũgĩ. 1986. *I Will Marry When I Want*. Oxford: Heinemann.

Niang, S. 1989. "Linguistic Deviation in African Literature." *Dalhousie Review* 6 (8): 1–2, 111–136.

Nicholls, B. 2010. *Ngugi Wa Thiong'o, Gender, and the Ethics of Postcolonial Reading*. Burlington, VT: Ashgate.

Nkosi, L. 1966/1997. "Chinua Achebe." In *Conversations with Chinua Achebe*, edited by Bernth Lindfors, 3–6. Jackson, MS: University Press of Mississippi.

Ntalindwa, R. 1999. "Linkages of History in the Narrative of *Close Sesame*." Literature and History *Journal of African Cultural Studies* 12 (2): 187–202. doi:10.1080/13696819908717849.

Nwoga, D. I. 1964. "The Chi Offended." *Transition* 4 (15): 5.

Ogbaa, K. 1997. "Interview with Chinua Achebe." In *Conversations with Chinua Achebe*, edited by Bernth Lindfors. Jackson: University Press of Mississippi.

Okonkwo, C. 1999. *Decolonization Agonistics in Postcolonial Fiction*. New York: St Martin's Press. doi:10.1057/9780230375314.

Onwuemene, M. 1999. "Limits of Transliteration: Nigerian Writers' Endeavor toward a National Literary Language." *PMLA* 114 (5): 1055–66. doi:10.2307/463464.

Owusu, K. 1986. "A Political Choice: Interview with *Ngũgĩ wa Thiong'o*." *West Africa* 18 (8): 1734–1735.

Oxford English Dictionary – OED. 2010. Oxford: Oxford University Press. doi:10.1093/acref/978019971123.001.0001.

Pearsall, S. 2000. "'Where the Banalities Are Enacted': The Everyday in Gordimer's Novels." *Research in African Literatures* 31 (1): 95–118.

Postel, G. 2007. "The Diviner's Task: Confinement and Transformation through Myth and Ritual in Gordimer's *The Conservationist*." *Research in African*

Literatures 38 (4): 47–60. doi:10.2979/RAL.2007.38.4.47.

Pugliese, C. 1994. "The Organic Vernacular Intellectual in Kenya: Gakaara wa Wanjaũ." *Research in African Literatures* 25 (4): 177–187.

Pütz, M, ed. 1995. *Discrimination through Language in Africa? Perspectives on the Namibian Experience*. Berlin, New York: Mouton de Gruyter. doi:10.1515/9783110906677.

Rao, V. D. 1999. "A Conversation with Ngũgĩ wa Thiong'o." *Research in African Literatures* 30 (1): 162–168. doi:10.2979/RAL.1999.30.1.162.

Renan, E. 1996. "What is a Nation?" In *Becoming National: A Reader*, edited by Geoff Eley and Ronald Grigor Suny, 42–56. New York, Oxford: Oxford University Press.

Rich, P. 1984. "Apartheid and the Decline of the Civilization Idea: An Essay on Nadine Gordimer's *July's People* and J. M. Coetzee's *Waiting for the Barbarians*." *Research in African Literatures* 15 (3): 365–393.

Rodrigues, Â. L., and the Ngugi wa Thiongo. 2004. "Beyond Nativism: An Interview with Ngũgĩ wa Thiong'o." *Research in African Literatures* 35 (3): 161–167. doi:10.1353/ral.2004.0074.

Rowell, C. H. 1989/1997. "An interview with Chinua Achebe." In *Conversations with Chinua Achebe*, edited by Bernth Lindfors, 165–184. Jackson, MS: University Press of Mississippi.

Samatar, S. S. 2000. "Are there Secrets in 'Secrets'?" *Research in African Literatures* 31 (1): 137–143. doi:10.2979/RAL.2000.31.1.137.

Scott, P. 1990. "Gabriel Okara's *The Voice*: The Non-Ijo Reader and the Pragmatics of Translingualism." *Research in African Literatures* 21 (3): 75–88.

Searle, C. 1987/1997. "Achebe and the Bruised Heart of Africa." In *Conversations with Chinua Achebe*, edited by Bernth Lindfors, 155–164. Jackson, MS: University Press of Mississippi.

Shelton, A. J. 1964. "The Offended Chi in Achebe's Novels." *Transitions* 3 (13): 36–37. doi:10.2307/2934425.

Sicherman, C. 1989. *Ngũgĩ wa Thiong'o: A Bibliography of Primary and Secondary Sources 1957–1987*. New York: Hans Zell.

Snead, J. 1990. "European Pedigrees/African Contagions: Nationality, Narrative, and Communality in Tutuola, Achebe, and Reed." In *Nation and Narration*, edited by Homi Bhabha, 231–249. London, New York: Routledge.

Soyinka, Wole. 1975. *Death and the King's Horseman*. London: Eyre Methuen.

Soyinka, Wole. 1996. *The Open Sore of a Continent: A Personal Narrative of the Nigerian Crisis*. New York: Oxford University Press.

Steiner, T. 2010. "'Of Cracked Lenses: Cultural Translation, Opacity and the African Novel." *Social Dynamics.*" *Journal of African Studies* 36 (2): 302–314.

Sullivan, J. 2001. "The Question of a National Literature for Nigeria." *Research in African Literatures* 32 (3): 71–85. doi:10.2979/RAL.2001.32.3.71.

Talib, Ismael S. 2002. *The Language of Postcolonial Literatures*. London: Routledge. doi:10.4324/9780203470183.

Ten, K. 2011. "Vehicles for Story: Chinua Achebe and Ngũgĩ wa Thiong'o on Defining African Literature, Preserving Culture and Self." *Student Purse*, 3 (5). http://www.studentpurse.com/a?id=350

Thorpe, M. 1983. "The Motif of the Ancestor in *The Conservationist*." *Research in African Literatures* 14 (2): 184–192.

Tutu, D. M. 2005. *TheRainbow People of God: A Spiritual Journey from Apartheid to Freedom*. Cape Town: Doubleday.

Uchendu, V. 1965. *The Igbo of Southeast Nigeria*. New York: Rinehart and Winston.

Visser, N. 1997. "Postcoloniality of a Special Type: Theory and its Appropriations in South Africa." *Yearbook of English Studies* 27: 79–94. doi:10.2307/3509134.

Vivan, Itala. "Nuruddin Farah's Beautiful Mat and its Italian Plot. *World Literature Today* (Focus on Nuruddin Farah: The 1998 Neustadt Prize), 72 (4): 786–790.

Waberi, W. 1998. "Les Enfants de la Postcolonie: Esquisse d'une Nouvelle Génération D'écrivains Francophones d'Afrique Noire." *Notre Librairie* 135: 8–15.

Wali, O. 1963. "The Dead End of African Literature?" *Transitions* 10 (10): 13–16. doi:10.2307/2934441.

Weaver, J. 1997. "Native American Authors and Their Communities." *Wicazo Sa Review* 12 (1): 47–87. doi:10.2307/1409163.

Weedon, C. 1987. *Feminist Practice and Poststructuralist Theory*. Cambridge: Blackwell.

Wilkinson, J. 1987. "Interview with Chinua Achebe." In *Conversations with Chinua Achebe*, edited by Bernth Lindfors, 141–154. Jackson, MS: University Press of Mississippi.

Williams, K. 1991. "Decolonizing the Word: Language, Culture, and Self in the Works of Ngũgĩ wa Thiong'o and Gabriel Okara." *Research in African Literatures* 22 (4): 53–61.

Wright, D. 1992/1993. "Parenting the Nation: Some Observations on Nuruddin Farah's *Maps*. *College Literature* (Teaching Postcolonial and Commonwealth Literatures), 19/20 (3/1): 176–184.

Wright, D. 1994. *The Novels of Nuruddin Farah*. Bayreuth: Eckhard Breitinger, Bayreuth University.

Wylie, D. 1991. "Language Thieves: English-Language Strategies in Two Zimbabwean Novellas." *English in Africa* 18 (2): 39–62.

Yewah, E. 2001. "The Nation as a Contested Construct." *Research in African Literatures* 32 (3): 45–56. doi:10.2979/RAL.2001.32.3.45.

Index

A

Achebe, Chinua
    aesthetics in works of   28–31, 38–45
    on African literatures   17
    Anthills of the Savannah   25–27, 39, 40, 43
    Arrow of God   18, 29, 31–32, 34–35, 42–43
    audience of   37, 40, 45
    'Black Writer's Burden, The'   85
    duality of purpose   31–37
    on English language   7, 15, 23, 114
    Farah and   25, 98–99, 122
    first language of   112
    literary elements   4, 27–31, 118, 121–123
    Man of the People, A   18, 27, 40, 42–44
    Ngũgĩ wa Thiong'o and   4, 54, 118–119
    No Longer at Ease   18, 35, 37, 40, 43
    thematic orientation   29, 33, 38–39
    theory on language of African literature   25–27
    Things Fall Apart   18, 30–31, 35, 36–37, 42–43, 54
acrolect   2–3, 34, 119
Adam, Ian   92
Adejunmobi, M.   53
aesthetics in Achebe's works   28–31, 38–44
Africa, borders of   10, 33–34
African-Americans in Africa   8–9, 111–112
African literatures   1, 17–23, 47, 121–122
Africans, The   6
African Writers Series (AWS)   18, 37
Afrikaans language   21–22, 83
'Afrolect' influences   21, 28–29, 94, 115, 122, 129–131
'Afro-Saxons'   8, 114
Alden, P.   96
allegory   63, 64–65
American English   22–23, 96–98
American intervention in Somalia (1992)   104–105
Amnesty International   60
Amoko, A. O.   54–55
Anderson, Benedict   5–6, 11, 90
Anglophonism   5, 9, 13–14, 16, 52–53, 117, 120–121, 129–130
Anthills of the Savannah   25–27, 39, 40, 43
'anthropological rhetoric'   35, 56, 97–98
anti-slavery liberation rhetoric   9–10
apartheid   20, 69–72, 74–89, 126–128
Appiah, K. A.   92
Arabic language   13, 15, 91, 106
Arnove, A.   61–62
Arrow of God   18, 29, 31–32, 34–35, 42–43
Arusha Declaration (1967)   12
audience
    of Achebe's works   37, 40, 45
    of African writers   5
    of Farah's works   91–94
    of Ngũgĩ's works   48–49, 52–53, 56–57, 63, 65–67
AWS see African Writers Series

B

Bakhtin, Mikhail   4, 28–29, 70, 123
Bamiro, Edmund   21, 28, 68, 94, 122, 129
Bandia, P.   51
basilects   3, 119
Bassnett, Susan   71, 126
Batchelor, K.   51
Batibo, H.   12
Berlin Conference of 1884/5   10, 33–34
Bertoncini, E.   11
Bickerton, Derek   2, 3, 25, 43, 117–120
Bjornson, Richard   3
Blommaert, J.   11
'bolekaja' scholars   7
borders of Africa   10, 33–34
Brennan, Timothy   6, 15
Brink, André   69–70, 81

Index

British colonial rule 83, 102, 121
British English 22, 96–98
Brown, Michelle Lynn 102

C

Caaitani Mutharaba-ini (Devil on the Cross) 19, 50, 52, 60, 63–65
Callaway, Rev Henry 77
Cary, Joyce 32–33
Casely Hayford, Joseph Ephraim 18, 111–112
census, as colonial institution 6
Chapman, Michael 1, 17
Chazan, Naomi 93
Chege, Michael 83
chi 36
China 114
Chinweizu, O. J. 7, 115
Christian beliefs 55
Clarke, Becky 37
Clingman, Stephen 69–70, 81
Close Sesame 101
colonialism
    Achebe, Chinua 31–34
    Farah, Nuruddin 100, 129–130
    Gordimer, Nadine 72–74, 84–85, 126–127
    impact of 5–7, 10, 121
    Ngũgĩ wa Thiong'o 50, 53–57, 59, 61–62, 124
colonial languages 5–8, 10–13, 16, 33, 49, 98–100, 113, 126, 129
'colonial mimicry' 54–55
Conference of African Writers of English Expression (1962) 17, 30, 40, 47, 116
Conrad, Joseph 32, 54
Conservationist, The 69–71, 76–80
contextualisation 65, 105, 122
'continuum', definition of 117
controversy
    Farah's views 93
    Ngũgĩ's views 8, 45, 47, 48–49, 124
Cooke, John 72
cosmopolitanism 91–95, 107–109, 129–131
Coundouriotis, Eleni 79–80
'creative translation' 50, 124–125

'Creole continuum' 2–3, 9, 25, 111–112, 117
cross-cultural communication 15–16, 26–27, 33, 75, 78–91, 127–128
Crummell, Alexander 111
cultural diversity 93, 95, 100–101, 103, 106–108, 113–114, 127, 130
'cultural substratum' 2, 68, 121

D

Dante Alighieri 104
Death and the King's Horseman 124
Decolonising the Mind 15, 60, 62, 116
'de-contextualization' 38
Deleuze, G. 14
'de-situation' 38
Detained 60, 63
Devil on the Cross (Caaitani Mutharaba-ini) 19, 50, 52, 60, 63–65
dialects 101, 130–131
Dialogic Imagination, The 28
Dickens, Charles 54
diglossic situations 14, 41
discourse, definition of 69
diversity
    of African literatures 114, 119–120, 121
    cultural 93, 95, 100–101, 103, 106–108, 113–114, 127, 130
    linguistic 8–14, 17, 33, 53, 63, 81–84, 113–114, 129
During, Simon 73

E

education 7, 22–23
Egar, E. E. 37
ekwe 36
elitist languages 123–124
English language
    Achebe, Chinua 27–31, 33–37, 41–45, 121
    as African language 8–9, 14–15, 110–113
    colonialism 5–7
    Farah, Nuruddin 22–23, 90–96, 108–109, 121, 128–130
    Gordimer, Nadine 20–22, 78–79, 85–87, 88, 121

Index

Ngũgĩ wa Thiong'o 8, 10, 15–16, 51, 54–55, 78, 114, 116–117
Standard English 3, 30–31, 43–45, 115, 119–120, 123
  unifying role of 3, 10–14, 33–34, 90–91, 103, 106–109, 114
  variations in usage of 3–4, 28, 34–37, 41–45, 54, 110–116, 121–123, 131
  as vehicular language 14–16
Erritouni, A. 81, 87
ethics of translation 51
Ethiopia 95, 102, 124
Ethiopia Unbound 18, 111–112
ethnic languages 12–13, 14, 17, 27, 48
'Eurolect' influences 21, 28, 72–73, 94, 111, 115, 121–122, 129–131
European languages 5, 10–11
exile, Farah's life in 92, 94–95, 104

F

Farah, Nuruddin
  Achebe and 25, 98–99, 122
  audience of 91–94
  career of 95
  Close Sesame 101
  cosmopolitanism 91–95, 107–109, 129–131
  From a Crooked Rib 96, 97, 98–101
  cultural diversity 93, 95, 102–104, 106–108, 130
  cultural identification 100–101
  dialects, use of 101, 130–131
  education of 91
  English language 90–94, 96–98, 108–109, 112, 118, 120–121, 128–130
  in exile 92, 94–95, 104
  Links 96, 98, 104–108
  literary-linguistic project of 96–98
  Maps 91, 96, 98, 102–104, 130–131
  nationalism 90–91, 93–95, 104–109
  proverbs 98–99, 122
  Secrets 96–97
  social registers, use of 101, 130–131
  Somalia 22–23, 92–93, 99–100, 119, 122
  translation 92
  unifying role of language 90–91, 103–104, 106–107, 109
  urban vs rural space 100–101
  violence 104–108
  Yesterday, Tomorrow 95
female genital mutilation 55, 104
fiction, importance of 5–7
first literary language, English as 93
Foucault, Michel 69
French colonial rule 102, 121
French language 11, 13–14
From a Crooked Rib 96, 97, 98–101

G

Gakaara wa Wanjaũ 48
Gellner, Ernest 12, 90–91
Gérard, A. 2, 68, 121
Gikandi, S. 15, 23, 48, 53, 55–56, 61–64
Gikuyu language, Ngũgĩ's works in 19–20, 23, 45, 47–55, 58–66, 124–126
globalisation 5, 14
Gobard, Henri 14
Gordimer, Nadine
  African literature, works seen as 18, 68–69
  apartheid 20, 69–72, 74–89, 126–128
  Conservationist, The 69–71, 76–80
  cross-cultural communication 88–89, 127–128
  Eurolect influences 21, 28, 72–73, 111, 121–122
  House Gun, The 70
  July's People 20–21, 69–71, 78–88, 122
  Lying Days, The 18, 20, 68, 69–76, 79, 81, 122
  Pickup, The 20, 81
  racial issues 20–21, 68, 74–76, 119
  'them and us' 88, 127
  translation 71, 126
  'Where do Whites Fit in?' 20, 83
  white settlers in South Africa 68–69, 72, 74, 81–82, 84–85
governments, promotion of indigenous languages by 12–13, 112
Grain of Wheat, A 19, 52, 56–57

Grammar of Identity 81
Guanya Pau 18, 111–112
Guattari, F. 14
Guyana, English Creole used in see 'Creole continuum'
Gyasi, K. A. 50, 124–125

H

Harris, M. 32
Harrow, K. W. 57
Hauptman, R. 61
Hausa language 13, 33, 41
Hawley, J. C. 61
Head, Dominic 73, 76
hierarchy of language stature 12
historical events, fiction based on 116
House Gun, The 70

I

Ibinga, Stephane Serge 70
identity 74, 81, 105–108
idioms 30–31, 39–41, 65, 97
Igbo community 4, 18–19, 29
Igbo language 23, 33–39, 41
Imagined communities 5–6
Indagasi, H. 57
indigenous African languages
    African literatures 1, 16
    diversity in 8–12, 129
    English language and 3–4, 28, 34–37, 44–45, 54, 110–116, 121–123, 131
    Gordimer, Nadine 22, 76–84, 86–88, 127–128
    Ngũgĩ wa Thiong'o 47, 49–50, 55–56, 117
    oral tradition 23
    support for 12–13, 112, 117
Inferno 104
institutional support for indigenous African languages 117
intercalations 19, 34–35, 66, 77, 99–100, 116, 118
'interlingual transfer' 71
'interlingual translation' 50–51, 124–126
Irele, F. Abiola 30, 38, 54, 115

Italy 102
I Will Marry When I Want (Ngaahika Ndeenda) 52, 59–60

J

Jackson, H. T. 59
Jahn, Janheinz 7
Jakobson, Roman 50, 51, 124
JanMohamed, Abdul 74
Jones, Ruth-Hamilton 37
Joyce, James 92
Julien, Eileen 77
July's People 20–21, 69–71, 78–88, 122

K

Kachru, B. B. 41–42
Kalume, M. 65
Kasanga, L. A. 65
Kenya 19, 53
Kiswahili language 12–13, 15
Knipp, T. R. 54
Korang, K. L. 32
Krio language 9

L

Liberia 5, 8–10, 13, 111–112
Lindfors, Bernth 30, 36, 39, 97
linguistic diversity 8–14, 17, 33, 53, 63, 81–84, 113–114, 129
'linguistic-literary continuum', definition of 2
Links 96, 98, 104–108
'literary continuum', definition of 2, 119
literary elements in Achebe's works 18–19, 28–31, 122
'literary-linguistic continuum', definition of 119
'literary-linguistic', use of term 2
localisation 39–41, 101
Lomberg, Alan 72
Lovesey, O. 63
Lying Days, The 18, 20, 68, 69–76, 79, 81, 122

M

Madubuike, I. 7, 115
Madumulla, J. 11

Index

Mahood, Molly Maureen 32
Man of the People, A 18, 27, 40, 42–44
Maps 91, 96, 98, 102–104, 130–131
maps, as colonial institution 6
Mateene, Kahombo 11
Matigari 19, 61, 64
Matigari ma Njiruungi 48, 52, 64
Mazrui, Ali 6, 8–9, 13–14, 49
Mbele, J. 57
McLaren, J. 52–53, 61
Miller, Christopher 4–5, 56, 97
mines, lingua franca of 79
missionaries 7
Mister Johnson 32
modern African literatures 7, 17–23
Mpashi, Stephen A. 48
Mphahlele, Ezekiel 40, 47
Mudimbe, V. Y. 7–8, 113
Mugo, Micere Githae 60
Murogi wa Kagogo (Wizard of the Crow) 50, 52
museums, as colonial institution 6
Mutiiri 52
Mwangi, E. 58–59, 64
Mwaura, P. 49
My Life in the Bush of Ghosts 30
'mythical inter-textuality' 80
myths 101
Mzali, Inezui 105

N

nationalism 3–6, 9–13, 17, 22, 33, 62–63, 90–95, 102–109
nativism 130
neocolonialism 6–7, 63, 124
Neogy, Rajat 58
Neustadt International Prize for Literature 96
'New Englishes' 118
Ngaahika Ndeenda (I Will Marry When I Want) 52, 59–60
Ngaboh-Smart, Francis 93, 103
Ngũgĩ wa Mirii 52
    Ngũgĩ wa Thiong'o
        Achebe and 4, 54, 118–119
        on African literatures 111, 113
        audience of 48–49, 52–53, 56–57, 63, 65–67
        Caaitani Mutharaba-ini (Devil on the Cross) 19, 50, 52, 60, 63–65
        colonialism 6–7, 10, 49–50, 112
        controversy 8, 45, 47, 48–49, 124
        Decolonising the Mind 15, 60, 62, 116
        Detained 60, 63
        detained without trial 60
        on English language 8, 10, 15–16, 78, 114, 116–117
        English language works 17, 52–56, 112, 114
        in exile 52
        Gikuyu language works 19–20, 23, 45, 47–55, 58–66, 124–126
        Grain of Wheat, A 19, 52, 56–57
        Matigari 19, 61, 64
        Matigari ma Njiruungi 48, 52, 64
        Ngaahika Ndeenda (I Will Marry When I Want) 52, 59–60
        Petals of Blood 19, 52, 58–60
        River Between, The 19, 52, 53–54
        transition phase 56–61
        translation 47–52, 61–67, 112, 124–126
        translingualism 47–52, 66–67, 124–126
        Trial of Dedan Kimathi, The 60
        Weep Not, Child 19, 52, 54
        Wizard of the Crow (Murogi wa Kagogo) 50, 52
Niang, S. 59
Nigeria 17, 18–19, 29, 33, 43
Nigerian Pidgin English 4, 29, 33, 42–45, 122, 123
No Longer at Ease 18, 35, 37, 40, 43
novels 5–8, 19–20, 23, 28–29, 54, 62–63, 69, 113–117, 122
Ntalindwa, Raymond 101
Nwoga, Donatus Ibe 36

O

Onwuemene, M. 40
oral literary traditions 7–8, 19–21, 23, 36–38, 44, 52, 59–65, 120

'ornamentalism' 77
otherness 74, 84–85
   see also 'them and us'

P

Padmore, George 9, 111
Palm-Wine Drinkard, The 18, 30
Pan-Africanism 9
parables 65–66
Pearsall, Susan 70
Petals of Blood 19, 52, 58–60
Pickup, The 20, 81
pidgin languages see Nigerian Pidgin English; South African pidgin language
pluralism 17–23, 55, 106
polyglossic situations 41
Portuguese language 11, 14
postcolonial literatures 16
postcolonial theory 73–74
Postel, Gitte 77, 80
proverbs 25, 36–39, 44, 56, 98–99, 122
provincial languages 11, 13

R

racial issues 20–21, 68, 74–76
radio broadcasts 6
'Rainbow Nation' 122
readership see audience
Religious System of the Amazulu, The 77
Renan, Ernest 12, 90–91, 103
Rich, Paul 81–82
River Between, The 19, 52, 53–54
Rothman, Nathan 72
rural vs urban space 100–101

S

Samatar, Said S. 96–97
Schreiner, Olive 72, 111
Scott, P. 50
Secrets 96–97
'self-colonisation' 61
Shelton, Austin 36
Sierra Leone 5, 8–10, 13, 111–112

'simplistic technique' 54–55
Snead, James 31–32, 35
social heteroglossia 4, 28–29, 40–43, 70, 122–123
socialism 56–58
social registers 101, 130–131
Somalia 10, 22, 91, 96, 102–105, 109
Somali language 22, 92–93, 99–100
South Africa 8, 13, 17, 122, 126–127
South African pidgin language 79
Soyinka, Wole 124
Standard English 3, 26–27, 30–31, 43–45, 115, 119–120, 123
Steiner, Tina 71, 84, 126
stereotyping 38–44
Story of an African Farm, The 72, 111
Sudan 13
superstitions 101
syncretism 94, 128

T

Talib, Ismail 16
Tanzania 12–13
tetralinguistic model 14
'them and us' 87–88, 106–107, 127
   see also otherness
Theories of Africans 97
Things Fall Apart 18, 30–31, 35, 36–37, 42–43, 54
Thorpe, M. 80
Tidy, M. 13
Transitions 58
translation 36, 47–52, 56, 61–67, 71, 84, 92, 118, 124–126
translingualism 47–52, 66–67, 124–126
transliteration 40–43, 47, 50, 57, 66–67, 97–98, 116, 124–126
Trial of Dedan Kimathi, The 60
Tutu, Desmond 122
Tutuola, Amos 18, 30–31, 35

U

Uchendu, Victor 36
unifying role of language 10–14, 33–34, 90–91, 103, 106–109, 114

Index

University of Minnesota 95
unlearning process 72, 88
urban vs rural space 100–101
'us and them' *see* 'them and us'

V

vehicular language, English as 14–16
'vernacular style' 19, 39, 56
violence 104–108
Visser, Nicholas 73
Vivan, Itala 95

W

Waberi, Abdourahman 130
Wali, Obi 1, 8, 47, 57–58, 111, 114–115
Walters, Joseph Jeffrey 18, 111–112
Wangui wa Goro 64
Weaver, Jace 95
Weep Not, Child 19, 52, 54
'Where do Whites Fit in?' 20, 83
white settlers in South Africa 68–69, 72, 74, 81–82, 84–85
Williams, K. 63
Wizard of the Crow (Murogi wa Kagogo) 50, 52
Wright, Derek 96
Wylie, Day 98

Y

Yesterday, Tomorrow 95
Yewah, E. 109
Yoruba language 30, 33, 41

Z

Zambia 13, 34
Zimbabwe 8, 13
Zulu language 76–77, 84

www.ingramcontent.com/pod-product-compliance
Lightning Source LLC
Chambersburg PA
CBHW060456300426
44113CB00016B/2605